iCourse·教材

Critical Thinking and Critical Writing

思辨式英文写作

主 编 唐 磊 李 霞
副主编 时 雨
编 者 史逢阳 沈海波 张佳玥
　　　赵 翼 袁 芳

中国教育出版传媒集团
高等教育出版社·北京

图书在版编目（CIP）数据

思辨式英文写作 / 唐磊，李霞主编. -- 北京 ：高
等教育出版社，2023.3
ISBN 978-7-04-059833-9

Ⅰ. ①思… Ⅱ. ①唐… ②李… Ⅲ. ①英语 - 写作 -
自学参考资料 Ⅳ. ①H315

中国国家版本馆CIP数据核字(2023)第022671号

策划编辑	韦　玮	责任编辑	韦　玮	封面设计	王凌波	版式设计	孙　伟
责任校对	刘　瑾	责任印制	赵义民				

出版发行	高等教育出版社	咨询电话	400-810-0598	
社　　址	北京市西城区德外大街4号	网　　址	http://www.hep.edu.cn	
邮政编码	100120		http://www.hep.com.cn	
印　　刷	北京盛通印刷股份有限公司	网上订购	http://www.hepmall.com.cn	
			http://www.hepmall.com	
开　　本	850mm×1168mm　1/16		http://www.hepmall.cn	
印　　张	19.5	版　　次	2023年3月第1版	
字　　数	468千字	印　　次	2023年3月第1次印刷	
购书热线	010-58581118	定　　价	48.00元	

本书如有缺页、倒页、脱页等质量问题，请到所购图书销售部门联系调换
版权所有　侵权必究
物 料 号　59833-00

前　言

　　《思辨式英文写作》是国家级一流本科课程（线上一流课程）"思辨式英文写作"慕课的配套新形态教材。本教材面向我国具有英语写作教与学需求的高校师生和社会学习者，旨在系统地支持其开展英语写作混合式教学（学习）、课堂教学（学习）和自主学习。

　　本教材编写秉持以下理念：

　　第一，"激活思维"与"优化语言"双管齐下，从思想内容和语言形式两个维度提升英语写作能力。英语写作历来是我国学生英语学习中的"死穴"，其水平受思想内容和语言形式两个方面影响。语言形式教学一直受到大学英语教学的重视，但思想内容方面教学的匮乏使得学生文章言之无物，表现为作文观点不明确、立意浅显、缺乏说理等。因此，有效的英语写作教学应从思想内容和语言形式两方面着手。本教材正是遵循这一理念编写。教材充分借鉴了思辨思维（critical thinking）提升写作质量的相关研究成果，整体上将思辨思维的知识技能与英语语篇和语言的知识策略系统融合。通过思辨能力培养，激活学生的思维，提高其英语写作的内容质量；通过语篇和语言能力培养，优化学生的语言表达，提高其英语写作的形式质量，双管齐下，助力学生英语写作思想内容和语言形式的双维发展。

　　第二，将思政教育资源作为思辨与写作的话题载体，以"盐溶于水"的方式落实课程思政。英语写作是一种正式的书面交流方式，是讲好中国故事，传播中华民族文化和思想的重要工具。2020年教育部《高等学校课程思政建设指导纲要》也明确指出，高等教育应"深入挖掘各类课程和教学方式中蕴含的思想政治教育资源"。因此，在高校英语写作课程中开展课程思政十分必要。本教材为落实课程思政做了三方面工作：一、每章以中国传统思辨思想开篇，引入本章核心思辨知识点，以此唤起学生对中国传统文化的好奇心和认同感；二、章节内适时选取有关文化认同、科技强国、法治意识、道德修养等思政话题的文本作为例句、例文、习题、讨论等学习任务的素材，在潜移默化中增强学生文化自信，塑造其社会主义核心价值观；三、每章的综合读写任务（From reading to writing）选用富含思政话题的文章，并基于文章设计写作技巧分析、思辨讨论、文章写作三种学习任务，引导学生对中国文化、当代社会等话题进行正确认识、理性思考、主动表达，提高其用英语讲好中国故事的能力和意愿。

第三，践行 OBE 结果导向的教育理念，使学习目标、过程、结果、效果可见可控。OBE 教育理念是深化教学改革、建设一流专业和一流课程的先进理念。本教材以该理念为指导思想进行编写。首先，每章围绕一个英语写作关键问题，将其分解为具体的学习目标，作为本章学习路线图（Chapter roadmap），使学习目标可见。其次，全章所有教学内容均为实现这些学习目标而编排，使学习过程可见。再次，每章最后设有综合读写任务（From reading to writing），使学习结果可见。最后，每章安排详细对应本章学习目标的学习反思环节，学生对标反思，及时检测目标完成情况，使学习效果可见。

第四，对标"两性一度"标准，支持线上线下混合式教学。写作过程需要写作者运用分析、评价、反思等高阶认知能力，创新思想，精进表达。也正因如此，英语写作教学更需要落实高阶性、创新性、挑战度的"两性一度"教学标准，而混合式教学被研究证实是更适合发展学生高阶能力的教学模式。为此，本教材充分借鉴了国际上学习科学的前沿研究成果，重点为支持混合式教学而设计。首先，为支持学习者自主开展基础的知识性学习，教材将英语和思辨相关知识进行系统性的模块化设计，为每个知识点配备讲解视频。学习者还可加入教材配套的慕课学习，参与针对该知识点的在线练习、讨论、测验等活动，巩固理解。其次，针对每个知识点，教材设计了丰富的具有主动性、合作性、评价性、反思性等有效学习特征的学习任务，支持教师开展翻转课堂互动式教学，提高教学的高阶性和挑战度；再次，每章均设计适量的产出性学习任务，为学生应用所学、输出学习成果提供机会，从而提高教学的创新性。此外，每章最后设计了学习反思活动，支持学生进一步对所学内容进行意义建构，提高其元认知能力和学习的获得感。

本教材共分为两部分。第一部分聚焦文章写作，包括八章内容，以写作的一般过程为线索排序。每章通过对一个核心思辨知识点的教学，着力解决学生英语写作中的一个痛点问题。每章以中国传统文化之思辨精神导入，章内包括开篇漫画（Chapter opener）、本章路线图（Chapter roadmap）、学习目标（Learning outcomes）、核心知识输入（Core knowledge input）、典型示例分析（Model）、随堂练习（Practice）、综合读写任务（From reading to writing）、全章学习反思（Reflection）等多个学习模块。

第二部分为语言诊所（Language Clinics），聚焦英语语言能力。每节针对一个常见英语语言问题编写，通过本节学习目标（Learning outcomes）、核心知识输入（Core knowledge input）、典型示例分析（Model）、随堂练习（Practice）四个环节，提升学生英语书面表达的准确性。

本教材配套的参考答案可通过扫描答案页的二维码查看、下载。

在学习本教材的同时，学习者还可登录中国大学 MOOC（慕课）平台，加入"思辨式英文写作"课程开展学习（可通过扫描下方二维码进入）。学习者也可通过每章核心知识输入模块旁的提示，观看相应的教学视频和慕课课程章节。此外，也欢迎关注微信公众号"思辨与英语表达"，查看更多与教材相关的拓展性学习资源。

本教材的编写工作得到了高等教育出版社的大力支持，南开大学外籍教师 Michael Hooper 对教材语言的规范性与准确性进行了专业校对，南开大学的多名师生对教材的设计和内容提出了宝贵建议，南开日新国际学校张隽玮同学为本教材第一章 Model 1-3 制作了动画。在此一并致谢。

本教材是我们在大学英语写作教学中不断探索与实践的阶段性成果。教材中如有疏漏和其他不尽完善之处，恳请广大使用者提出宝贵意见和建议。

编者
2023 年 3 月

思辨式英文写作
国家级一流本科课程

CONTENTS

What is critical writing?

博学之，审问之，慎思之，明辨之，笃行之。

——《礼记·中庸》

A gentleman should study extensively, inquire prudently, think carefully, distinguish clearly, and practice earnestly.
——"The Doctrine of the Mean," *The Book of Rites*

Chapter opener

T: What are the common essay genres in English?

Ss: Description, narration, exposition, and argumentation.

S: Ma'am, what is a critical essay?

T: Er…

Chapter roadmap

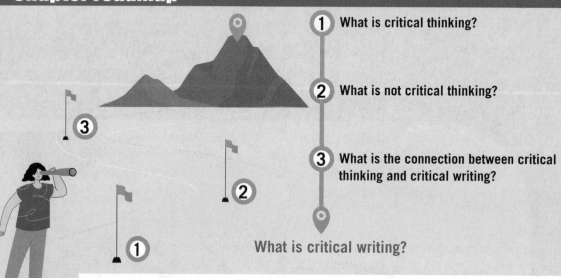

1. What is critical thinking?

2. What is not critical thinking?

3. What is the connection between critical thinking and critical writing?

What is critical writing?

Learning outcomes

At the end of this chapter, you will be able to
- use proper examples to explain what critical thinking is;
- correct three common misunderstandings about critical thinking;
- explain how critical thinking can benefit critical writing;
- identify the four characteristics of critical writing.

From reading to writing

Collect evidence of improvements in China's natural environment and analyze how a critical essay can be developed on this topic.

1. What is critical thinking?

Critical thinking has long been advocated by famous educators since the time of Confucius. The prerequisite of cultivating such thinking is then to form a clear conceptualization of it.

1.1 A consensus definition of critical thinking

Core knowledge input

 Micro-lecture **Critical Thinking: What and Why**
MOOC **Lesson 1**

Read the text about the conceptualization of critical thinking and consider the questions.

Critical Thinking: What and Why

None of us can escape life's risks and uncertainties. Uncertainties apply to potentially good things, too. For example, we might be uncertain when choosing a major, taking a part-time job, or making a new friend. Whatever the choice being contemplated or the problem being addressed, we need to employ purposeful, reflective judgement to maximize positive outcomes and to minimize undesirable ones. This means we need **critical thinking**. But what is critical thinking? To answer the question precisely, an international group of 46 recognized experts in critical thinking research collaborated. Here is what they agreed on.

Experts' consensus definition of critical thinking:
the process of forming a purposeful and self-regulatory judgment

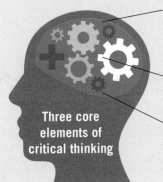

Three core
elements of
critical thinking

A straightforward purpose:
forming a well-reasoned and fair-minded judgment regarding what to believe or what to do

Adequate consideration of relevant factors:
the evidence, method, criteria, context, etc. on which the judgment is based

Intentional self-regulation:
monitoring our own thinking, spotting mistakes, and making needed corrections

Questions
1. When do we need critical thinking in life?
2. What is the experts' definition of critical thinking?
3. What are the three core elements of critical thinking?
4. Do you think critical thinking is a mysterious ability reserved for smart people? Why?

Chapter 1　What is critical writing?

Model 1-1

Positive examples of critical thinking

- A person attempts to interpret an angry friend's needs so as to offer support accordingly.
- A person running a small business is trying to anticipate the possible economic and human consequences of various ways to increase sales or reduce costs.
- A student confidently and correctly explains to his or her peers the methodology used to reach a particular conclusion, or why and how a certain methodology or standard of proof was applied.
- An applicant is preparing for a job interview, thinking about how to explain his or her particular skills and experiences in a way that will be relevant and of value to the prospective employer.
- Parents anticipate the costs of sending their young child to college, analyze the family's projected income, and budget projected household expenses in an effort to put aside some money for that child's future education.

Practice 1-1

Write down your understanding of critical thinking in three complete sentences.

1. _____

2. _____

3. _____

Practice 1-2

Can you think of more positive examples of critical thinking in your everyday life? List down at least two. Then share your answers with a partner.

1. _____

   _____

2. _____

_____

1.2 Cognitive skills of critical thinking

Core knowledge input

MOOC Lesson 1

Cognitive Skills of Critical Thinking

The 46 experts mentioned in the previous "Core knowledge input" also agreed that a well-cultivated critical thinker is proficient at many, if not all, of these skills.

Interpretation	to comprehend and express the meaning of a wide variety of experiences, situations, data, events, rules, procedures, etc. **Subskills:** categorizing, decoding significance, clarifying meaning
Analysis	to identify the relationships among statements, questions, concepts, descriptions, etc. **Subskills:** examining ideas, identifying arguments, identifying reasons and claims
Inference	to identify and secure elements needed to draw reasonable conclusions; to form conjectures and hypotheses **Subskills:** querying evidence, considering alternatives, drawing conclusions using inductive or deductive reasoning
Evaluation	to assess the credibility of statements; to assess the logical strength of the inferential relationships among statements **Subskills:** assessing credibility of claims, assessing quality of inductive or deductive arguments
Explanation	to present one's reasoning in the form of cogent arguments **Subskills:** stating results, justifying procedures, presenting arguments
Self-Regulation	to self-consciously monitor and correct one's cognitive activities **Subskills:** sell-monitoring, self-correcting

Practice 1-3

There are many familiar questions that invite us to use our cognitive skills of critical thinking. Often, our best critical thinking comes when we ask the right questions. Match the questions with the cognitive skills of critical thinking below.

1. Interpretation	A) What are the reasons? What are the pros and cons?
2. Analysis	B) What does it mean? What's happening?
3. Evaluation	C) How should I make my judgment and reasons clear to others? How can I be more convincing?
4. Inference	D) What does this evidence imply? Given what we have known so far, what conclusions can we draw?
5. Explanation	E) Did I miss any important evidence? Did I fail to consider every perspective on the question?
6. Self-regulation	F) Are the reasons credible? How meaningful are the pros and cons?

Model 1-2

Analysis of critical thinking skills

I'm gonna recommend that movie to my bestie!

The cognitive skills of critical thinking possibly involved in the judgment above may include

- **Interpretation:** e.g. understanding the story of the movie and the theme it reflects
- **Analysis:** e.g. identifying different development stages of the story in the movie or the cinematography techniques used
- **Evaluation:** e.g. evaluating whether the cinematography techniques are used effectively in expressing the theme
- **Inference:** e.g. deciding that her best friend should see the movie
- **Explanation:** e.g. persuading her best friend to see the movie
- **Self-regulation:** e.g. avoiding unfair judgment because of her bias toward the leading actor

Practice 1-4

Following Model 1-2, analyze the potential cognitive skills of critical thinking entailed in the following situations. Then share your answers with a partner.

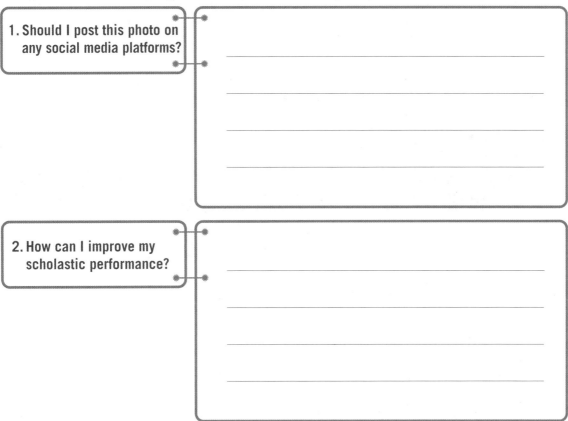

1. Should I post this photo on any social media platforms?

2. How can I improve my scholastic performance?

Practice 1-5

Did you practice any critical thinking today or yesterday? Think of a recent event in which you thought about a problem critically. Organize your story by following the questions below. Work in pairs and share your stories.

1. What was the problem you needed to solve in the event?

2. What questions did you consider before making a judgment or decision?

3. What was your judgment or decision?

4. Did you examine your own thinking process and correct mistakes if there were any?

5. What cognitive skills of critical thinking did you use? How did you use them?

2. What is not critical thinking?

To truly understand something, we must be acquainted with both its positive and negative sides. So, after learning what critical thinking is, our task in this section is to discover what critical thinking is not.

2.1 Critical thinking is not following your heart

Core knowledge input

 Micro-lecture Critical Thinking vs Non-Critical Thinking
MOOC Lesson 1

Critical Thinking vs Non-Critical Thinking

Misunderstanding:
"Since critical thinking means to make judgment, every time I make a judgment, I am engaged in critical thinking."

Correction: Not all judgments are products of critical thinking. There are times when our emotions prevail and the resulting judgments are driven by irrational thinking, such as feelings, hunches, and intuition. Critical thinkers should cautiously avoid emotional thinking. After all, thinking critically means we are skilled at tempering the irrational appeals of our hearts.

Practice 1-6

Critical thinking vs emotional thinking
In the video, Wang made a spur-of-the-moment trip. During the trip, he made a series of judgments. Did he think critically when making those judgments? Check or cross the box in front

of each evaluation question in the analysis table. **The first three have been done for you as examples.**

Judgments made by Wang	Was critical thinking involved?
1. To take the first bus coming	☒ With a clear purpose? ☒ Involving consideration of relevant factors? ☒ Involving self-regulation?
2. To get off at the last stop	☒ With a clear purpose? ☒ Involving consideration of relevant factors? ☒ Involving self-regulation?
3. To believe he was being derided	☐ With a clear purpose? ☐ Involving consideration of relevant factors? ☐ Involving self-regulation?
4. _____	☐ With a clear purpose? ☐ Involving consideration of relevant factors? ☐ Involving self-regulation?
5. _____	☐ With a clear purpose? ☐ Involving consideration of relevant factors? ☐ Involving self-regulation?

Practice 1-7

Decide whether the following cases are critical thinking or non-critical thinking. Check or cross the box in front of each sentence. Write down your reasons. Then share your answers with a partner.

1. ☐ I decided to order a takeaway because I didn't feel like going to the trouble of cooking.

   _____

   _____

2. ☐ I decided to enroll in the course *Modern Art* because my best friend recommended it.

   _____

   _____

Practice 1-8

Have you done anything inappropriately because of non-critical thinking? Recall such an experience and reflect on how you could have done it in a more sensible way with critical thinking. Share your story and reflection with a partner.

2.2 Critical thinking is not mistake-free

Core knowledge input

MOOC Lesson 1

Critical Thinking vs Wise Thinking

Misunderstanding:
"Since critical thinking means to make purposeful and self-regulatory judgments, when I think about a problem critically, I will produce a wise judgment."

Correction: Critical thinking cannot guarantee wise judgments. Rather, it is a rational way of thinking that aims to produce sound conclusions. So a critical thinker can never be too careful in the process of their thinking. Listen with an open mind to someone who is offering opinions with which you do not agree. Revisit a decision you made recently and consider whether it is still the right decision. See if any relevant new information has come to light. These critical thinking habits are what drive us toward wise judgments.

Critical thinking dose not guarantee wise judgments

Read the story about Mr. Li's choice of career and consider the questions.

Mr. Li graduated from an IT program of a top university in the 1990s. After graduation, he successfully joined Company D, a listed state-owned enterprise in City Y, which provided him with a considerable yearly salary. Two years later, however, Mr. Li quit his job and went back to school for a master's degree. Multiple factors contributed to his decision.

- The colleagues who joined the company together with him but also held a master's degree, earned a 30% higher yearly salary than him.
- The IT industry develops rapidly, so continuous learning is needed.
- If he stayed in his current position, there would be little room for his future development.
- He was single and didn't have any relatives in City Y, so there were no relational constraints on him resigning.
- He had enough savings to support himself for the next three years.

He did consider that by the time he graduated again, he would have to face competition with more graduates who would be much younger than him. But taking all the factors into account, he decided to give it a shot.

Was Mr. Li's resignation from Company D guided by critical thinking? Yes, however, when he received his master's degree three years later from another famous university, he only found employment at a small IT company and earned a lower salary than the one he had in the first year of his service in Company D.

Questions

1. Apparently, Mr. Li's resignation from the company turned out to be a poor decision. What factors do you think result in such a situation?
2. Could Mr. Li have foreseen those factors? Why or why not?

Practice 1-9 TXT

Read the beginning part of Ms. Shi's health examination experience in the text below. Think critically about the situation and make your own judgment about

what happened in the end: What could happen to Ms. Shi later? Would she catch a cold like her colleagues? Work in groups. Share your prediction and your reasoning. Then scan the QR code to see the complete story.

It was the annual health examination for employees of the company where Ms. Shi works. But she was faced with a dilemma: Should she take the health examination?

Reasons to take the examination:

- Regular health checks are very important for middle-aged women such as herself;
- She had been feeling tired and depressed in recent months;
- The company had paid everyone's examination fee.

Reasons to avoid the examination:

- More than ten colleagues who had taken the examination earlier caught a cold afterward;
- The health examination center is located a floor above the fever clinic in the hospital so that anyone who goes to the health examination center has to share the elevator with potentially ill patients;
- She has always been flu-sensitive.

Ms. Shi thought about it critically and decided to go and take the health examination.

2.3 Critical thinking is not negative

Core knowledge input

 Micro-lecture Critical Thinking vs Negative Thinking
MOOC Lesson 1

Critical Thinking vs Negative Thinking

Misunderstanding:
"Since critical thinking is critical, when I think critically I should criticize other people's ideas."

Correction: Strong critical thinking can be independent, it can lead us to diverge from the norm, and it can impel us to challenge cherished beliefs. But critical thinking is not about bashing what people believe just to show how clever we are. Critical thinking is skeptical without being cynical. We can thoughtfully and fair-mindedly reject an idea without ridiculing or embarrassing the person who proposed it. And we can also accept an idea from any source so long as the idea is well-supported with good reasons and solid evidence.

Practice 1-10

Here are two mistaken statements related to critical thinking. Briefly describe the mistake in each to a partner.

1. I'm always disagreeing with authority figures, so I must be a great critical thinker.

_____

_____

_____

2. I like many of the things that my school administration does, so I must be a weak critical thinker.

_____

_____

_____

Practice 1-11

Summarize your understanding of what critical thinking is and what it is not. Then share your answers with a partner.

Critical thinking is _____

_____.

Critical thinking is not _____

_____.

3. What is the connection between critical thinking and critical writing?

Have you wondered why you need to learn about critical thinking? What is the connection between critical thinking and critical writing? What exactly is a critical essay? These are the questions we will address in this section.

3.1 The chemistry between critical thinking and critical writing

Model 1-4

Critical thinking through a writing task

Imagine that you are writing on the topic "Will you recommend a younger cousin study the same major as yours? Why or why not?". You would possibly engage in the following critical thinking activities.

- ☑ To clarify what knowledge or skills are offered by the major
- ☑ To analyze what a student can gain from taking the major
- ☑ To evaluate the value of the gains for your cousin
- ☑ To consider alternative opinions about the major
- ☑ To make a judgment about whether your major is worth recommending
- ☑ To explain your answers to the questions in a written form
- ☑ To review your writing and improve it

Micro-lecture Critical Thinking and Critical Writing
MOOC Lesson 1

Critical Thinking and Critical Writing

After reading through the activities in Model 1-4, you have probably already realized that critical thinking plays an essential role in accomplishing such writing tasks. You think to make a judgment, which will be the central opinion you will justify in your essay. You consider relevant factors before making the judgment, which provides supporting details for the central opinion of the essay. You reflect on and adjust your thinking, which helps improve your essay.

In brief, when you explain in written language, after thinking about an issue critically, the judgment you make and the premises it is based on, you are doing **critical writing**. In this sense, you may consider critical writing as a written product of critical thinking. And the kind of essay you produce in this way is what we call a critical essay.

Practice 1-12

If you are going to write an essay on the topic "Why is cultural confidence essential to personal identity?", what critical thinking activities would you be engaged in? List at least three of them. Then share your answers with a partner.

1. _____

   _____

2. _____

   _____

3. _____

   _____

3.2 The shape of a critical essay

Core knowledge input

Micro-lecture Characteristics of a Critical Essay
MOOC Lesson 1

Characteristics of a Critical Essay

A critical essay is an essay in which the author expresses the result and process of their critical thinking on a certain topic. It has four innate characteristics.

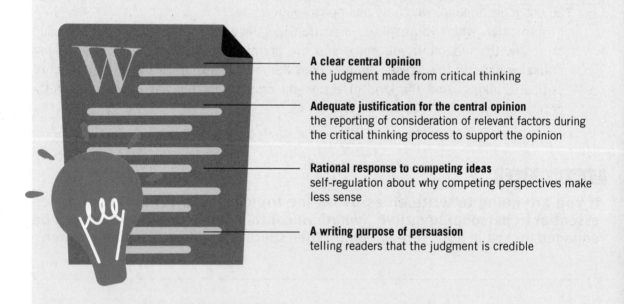

A clear central opinion
the judgment made from critical thinking

Adequate justification for the central opinion
the reporting of consideration of relevant factors during the critical thinking process to support the opinion

Rational response to competing ideas
self-regulation about why competing perspectives make less sense

A writing purpose of persuasion
telling readers that the judgment is credible

Critical essays by nature belong to the category of argumentation. They are, however, the most powerful and convincing argumentation in that they teem with the author's interpretation, analysis, evaluation of the evidence, and rational debates with competing perspectives on the subject topic.

Model 1-5

Analyzing characteristics of critical writing

Study the model critical essay and pay attention to the analysis of its critical writing characteristics.

Why Littering Is a Surprisingly Big Issue

a clear central opinion	❶ Compared with the glaringly obvious environmental issues we hear about every day, **littering often takes a backseat — but it's more pressing than we may think**.
1st line of justification [a competing idea] a rational response to the competing idea	❷ [If you were to toss, say, a banana peel out of your car while driving along the motorway, that would be a completely harmless action, due to the fact that it's part of a fruit — right?] <u>Actually, no. A banana peel can take up to two years to decompose, and with a third of motorists admitting to littering while driving, that's a whole lot of discarded banana peels, or much worse.</u> An orange peel and a cigarette butt have a similar biodegrading term to that of a banana, but tin and aluminum cans last up to 100 years; and plastic bottles last forever, as do glass bottles, Styrofoam cups, and plastic bags.
2nd line of justification [a competing idea] a rational response to the competing idea	❸ [Despite the fact that longer-lasting materials will serve to damage the environment and its animals for longer,] <u>we can't solely measure the severity of a certain type of rubbish by its lifetime.</u> For example, despite having a fairly short biodegrading span, more than 120 tons of cigarette-related litter is discarded in the U.K. every day. Similarly, our regular littering here and there has caused the U.K.'s rat population to increase by 60 million. This suddenly isn't so mysterious when you consider that since the 1960s our annual littering has increased by an astounding 500 percent.
3rd line of justification reason + evidence	❹ It's not a cheap habit either: U.K. taxpayers pay £500 million in order to keep our streets clean, and when you include our green spaces, that goes up to £1 billion. So, it's not surprising that if caught fly-tipping you could face a £20,000 fine or even jail time and, if you disposed of something hazardous, the court could give you five years to serve. Regardless of how severe these punishments might seem, however, among the reported cases only 2,000 were convicted out of 825,000, so we still have some way to go in making sure people abide by the rules.
conclusion: to persuade the reader to believe the central opinion	❺ To take back our beautiful countryside and cities **we need to do more than simply not leave rubbish where it ought not to be**. We need a pride makeover; we need to truly care more about the world around us.

Practice 1-13

Read the critical essay about young people's power in fighting against climate change. Then work in groups to identify its critical essay characteristics.

Why We Need Young People to Fight for the Climate

❶ We need young people to fight for the climate.

❷ If you underestimate the young activists of the world, you ignore a whole world of possible good. In 2019, more than 1.4 million young people around the globe took part in the School Strikes for Climate Action protests that were largely prompted by 17-year-old Swedish activist Greta Thunberg. The inspirational young Swede, while a media favorite, is far from the first or last young person to fight for a better environmental future — and with European summers set to increase by 4.7°C in 2050 (since 2000), it's no wonder.

❸ With the rise of social media in recent years, young people around the globe have easy access to startling information about how we're currently failing to look after the Earth. Websites provide accessible coverage on ecological matters that quickly garner millions of views, and links to new scientific information are easily shared between peers.

❹ Of course, just because young people are now readily armed with statistics such as these doesn't mean all adults will eagerly listen to them. Many write off young activists simply due to their age, but that doesn't mean a difference can't be made.

❺ In fact, there are some advantages to being a young activist. A study on participants aged 16 – 24 in the UN climate negotiations revealed that adults perceived younger activists as being more trustworthy due to the lack of financial incentives to be there. Young activists not only aren't smudged by agendas being forced on them, but also have an untainted view of what's going on, and, being free from politics, they often say what adults aren't willing to.

❻ So, it seems achieving a carbon-neutral world in the future might depend on young determined voices inspiring experienced adults who can make a difference. Preferably, young people wouldn't worry about the environment at all, but our civilization forced them into the conversation when their futures were put at stake, so their voices should be included in the solution.

Model 1-6

Critical essays vs non-critical essays

Narrative: to tell a story

A young man in jeans, Mr. Jones — "but you can call me Rob" — was far from the white-haired, buttoned-up old man I had half-expected. And rather than pulling us into pedantic arguments about obscure philosophical points, Rob engaged us on our level. To talk free will, we looked at our own choices. To talk ethics, we looked at dilemmas we had faced ourselves. By the end of class, I'd discovered that questions with no right answer can turn out to be the most interesting ones.

Critical: to justify an opinion

A young man in jeans, Mr. Jones — "but you can call me Rob" — was far from the white-haired, buttoned-up old man I had half-expected. And rather than pulling us into pedantic arguments about obscure philosophical points, Rob engaged us on our level. To talk free will, we looked at our own choices. To talk ethics, we looked at dilemmas we had faced ourselves. By the end of class, I'd discovered that questions with no right answer can turn out to be the most interesting ones. This experience demonstrates that competent teachers should be able to make a difficult subject accessible and appealing to students.

Descriptive: to give a detailed description

On Sunday afternoons I like to spend my time in the garden behind my house. The garden is narrow but long, a corridor of green extending from the back of the house, and I sit on a lawn chair at the far end to read and relax. I am in my small peaceful paradise: the shade of the tree, the feel of the grass on my feet, the gentle activity of the fish in the pond beside me.

Critical: to justify an opinion

Everyone needs some "nature time" once in a while because it relieves the social pressure we are faced with in modern society. On Sunday afternoons I like to spend my time in the garden behind my house. The garden is narrow but long, a corridor of green extending from the back of the house, and I sit on a lawn chair at the far end to read and relax. I am in my small peaceful paradise: the shade of the tree, the feel of the grass on my feet, the gentle activity of the fish in the pond beside me. All of this evokes in me a sense of tranquility and security which I aspire to but seldom have in social life.

Expository: to offer organized information

Carl Rogers' theory of a person-centered approach focuses on the freedom of the individual to determine what values should be used to measure successful personal outcomes or benefits, and is particularly relevant for social workers when wanting to take into account the diverse needs of the client group.

Critical: to justify an opinion

Carl Rogers' theory of a person-centered approach is particularly suitable for social workers wanting to work with a client group with diverse needs because it allows the client to determine what values should be used to measure successful outcomes, rather than those externally determined by, for example, the service state, or dominant culture in society.

Practice 1-14

Identify which of the following passages can be considered critical writing. Check the box in front of each passage if you think it is, or cross the box if you think it is not. Write down your reasons. Then share your answers with a partner.

☐ 1. In addition to competency-based questions, the candidates were asked to complete an in-tray exercise, which required them to allocate different priority levels to tasks, as an appropriate method to measure their likely performance in the actual job.

   Your reason: _____

   _____

☐ 2. Furthermore, there is adequate data that disproves the claim that Chinese workers are taking job opportunities at the expense of Africans' on the continent. In fact, the population of Chinese workers in Africa has been declining significantly for some years. Data available at the China Africa Research Initiative at the Johns Hopkins's School of Advanced International Studies reveals that from 2015 to 2019, the population of Chinese workers engaged in construction projects and others that are working in factories has fallen consecutively — from a peak of 263,659 in 2015 to 182,745 in 2019. This data casts doubt on claims that job opportunities for Africans are threatened by the employment of Chinese workers on the continent.

   Your reason: _____

   _____

☐ 3. The data shows that the incidence (new cases) of asthma rates in children under 15 years old increased rapidly from 1977, peaking in 1993, and then declining, though rates still remain significantly higher than pre-1976 levels.

   Your reason: _____

   _____

☐ 4. China proved to the world that it is possible to quickly and definitively reduce hunger and prevent malnutrition nationwide. China has managed to feed around one-fifth of the world's population with less than 9 percent of the world's arable land. This in itself is a major contribution to global food security. In just a few decades, China's experience in reducing hunger and applicable approaches offered much learning and know-how for other developing countries as a shining example. In the past five years, the WFP China Center of Excellence for Rural Transformation facilitated knowledge sharing with policymakers, technicians, and smallholder farmers in more than 80 developing countries through innovative methods such as webinars, study tours, field demonstrations, knowledge sharing platform, and online learning space.

Your reason: _____

_____

From reading to writing

■ Reading
Read the essay and finish the tasks.

Did Beijing Fail Air Pollution Battle Due to Sandstorms?

❶ In March, two sandstorms turned the skies in Beijing yellow and pushed the Air Quality Index (AQI) to 500, leaving the inhabitants of the Chinese capital gasping for fresh air under a canopy of dust. Venturing out of one's abode, one could feel the little particles of sand getting stuck between the fingers. The scene looked straight out of a doomsday movie.

❷ But does that mean Beijing's overall air quality has fallen? Let's see what the statistics show.

❸ Observing the weather conditions from over 35,000 kilometers above the ground, one can see that the cyclones and sandstorms were formed in Mongolia. The sandstorm was pushed by the cyclone all the way to north China during March 14 and 15.

❹ One may wonder if a decline in vegetation caused China's worst sandstorm in a decade. A close examination of China's vegetation map shows that from 2000 to

2020 the overall increase in forests and grasslands overpowers the decrease. In the Three-North region, from Heilongjiang to Xinjiang, this is even more evident. It's obvious that the green barriers have increased in size, but the cyclone was too powerful for the trees to hold back the storm.

❺ The main component of the sandstorms was PM10, which represents relatively large pollution particles. It includes dust from construction sites, landfills, and agriculture, along with wildfires, waste burning, and other industrial sources. But this pollutant and the smaller, more harmful PM2.5 have been decreasing. The steady decline of the AQI demonstrates improvement in Beijing's air quality. And the recent hike in PM10 caused by the sandstorms was an isolated event in the past five years. It did not offset the progress Beijing has made.

❻ But what about the rest of China? Have other areas also witnessed the dawn of victory in the battle against air pollution?

❼ Before we dive into the data, it is important to understand that China uses a complex set of six indicators — PM2.5, PM10, SO_2, NO_2, O_3, and CO — to measure AQI, which has been improving for a decade now.

❽ A map of PM2.5 concentration across 168 cities in China from 2019 to 2021 shows that while south China turned visibly green over the three years, northern and northwestern provinces of Shanxi and Shaanxi, as well as the Beijing-Tianjin-Hebei region, painted a much more beautiful picture. Moreover, NO_2 and SO_2 both declined from 2015 to 2021, but SO_2 reduction was the most significant. Amidst this overall positive trend, O_3's performance is alarming. From 2015 to 2021, as many as 49 of 74 cities reported rises in O_3. The increase is a good reminder that gaps still exist in China's fight against air pollution.

❾ Although the sandstorms this year do not overshadow the achievements China has made in improving its air quality, more needs to be done to maintain and expand the green zones, our source of fresh air and future hope.

Writing technique questions

Based on what you have learned in this chapter, consider the following questions. Then discuss with your group your answers and seek a consensus.

1. What is the author's central point of view?

2. How does the author justify the central view? What material does the author use? In which paragraphs of the essay can you find them?
3. What competing idea(s) does the author consider? How does the author respond to them? In which paragraph(s) can you find the response(s)?
4. What is the chief writing purpose of this essay?

Critical thinking questions
Consider the questions below and finish the tasks.
1. Has the air quality in your city or town been improving in recent years? What leads you to such a conclusion?
2. Share your answers to the questions above with your group. You may follow the format below.

> I think the air quality in [name of your city/town] has (not) been improving in recent years. I can offer [1/2/3] pieces of evidence to support my conclusion. First, ... Second, ...

3. Discuss with your group to make a list of possible materials that can be used as evidence of air quality improvement.
4. Present your list to the class.

Chapter 1 What is critical writing?

■ Writing

Complete the following piece of writing to tell why the essay "Did Beijing Fail Air Pollution Battle Due to Sandstorms?" counts as a critical one.

"Did Beijing Fail Air Pollution Battle Due to Sandstorms?" is a critical essay. It argues for the central opinion that _____

_____

by providing three lines of reasoning: 1. _____

_____

_____;

2. _____

_____;

3. _____

_____.

At the same time, it considers a competing idea that _____

_____, and refutes

it saying _____

_____.

So, the writing purpose is _____

_____.

REFLECTION

This chapter discussed some basic concepts about critical thinking and critical writing. Now it's time to review and reflect on what you have learned. Work in pairs and take turns to answer the following questions. Check them as you answer each one.

1) What is critical thinking?
- ☐ List three core elements of critical thinking.
- ☐ Give a positive example of critical thinking in your life.

2) What is not critical thinking?
- ☐ List three common misunderstandings about critical thinking.
- ☐ Correct the misunderstandings one by one.

3) What is the connection between critical thinking and critical writing?
- ☐ Explain how critical thinking benefits critical writing.

What is critical writing?
- ☐ List the four characteristics of a critical essay.
- ☐ Explain the differences between critical writing and narration / description / exposition / argumentation respectively.

How to develop arguments in a critical essay?

灯不拨不亮，理不辩不明。

——中国谚语

An oil lamp becomes brighter after being trimmed, while a truth becomes clearer after being argued.

—A Chinese proverb

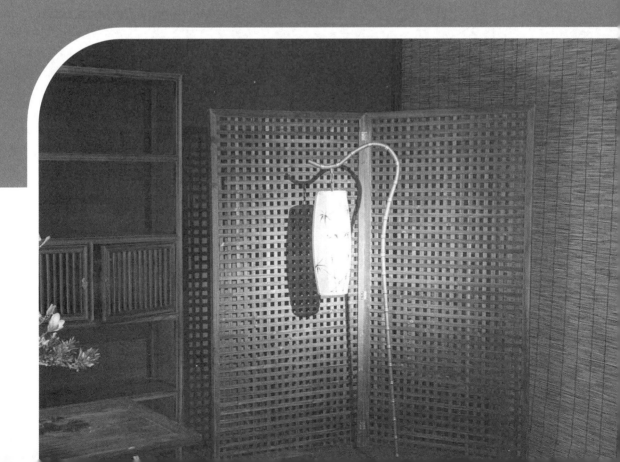

Chapter roadmap

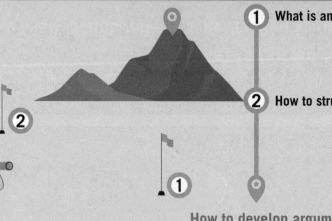

① What is an argument?

② How to structure a critical essay?

How to develop arguments in a critical essay?

Learning outcomes

At the end of this chapter, you will be able to

- understand what an argument is;
- explain the relation between arguments and critical essays;
- explain the functions of the three parts of an essay;
- compose an outline for a critical essay.

From reading to writing

Acknowledge the value of history and plan a critical essay on this topic.

1. What is an argument?

The Chinese proverb at the beginning of the Chapter tells us that arguments not only help us clarify and articulate our thoughts but also enable us to consider the ideas of others in a respectful and critical manner. Thus, in this section we will learn what an argument is and what an argument is not.

1.1 Concept of an argument

Core knowledge input

Micro-lecture Definition and Elements of an Argument
MOOC Lesson 2

Definition and Elements of an Argument

In everyday life, people often use "argument" to mean a quarrel between people. But in logic and critical thinking, an argument is NOT a quarrel, dispute, or disagreement. Formally, an **argument** is a series of statements that expresses a point of view on a subject and supports it with reasons and evidence.

An argument consists of two types of statements: a statement presenting the author's point of view, technically called the **thesis**; other statements as the **premises**, which include reasons and/or evidence that justify the thesis. So to judge if some statements make an argument, we can look for the three essential elements: the thesis, the premise, and the supporting relation between the former two.

thesis a statement that presents the author's point of view	← support	**premises** reasons and/or evidence that support the thesis

Chapter 2　How to develop arguments in a critical essay?

Model 2-1

Examples of arguments

Read the following two arguments and notice the analysis of the thesis, the premises, and how the premises support the thesis.

thesis [premises] supporting relations ①: having a better understanding of how languages are structured ②: improving people's understanding of their first language	**Bilingualism and multilingualism confer many benefits.** [① Speakers of more than one language have a better understanding of how languages are structured because they can compare across two different systems. People who speak only one language lack this essential point of reference. ② In many cases, a second language can help people to have a better understanding and appreciation of their first language.]
thesis [premises] supporting relations ①: regulating their breathing and sleeping ②: improved safety under their parents' supervision	**Newborn babies may benefit from sleeping with their mothers.** [① They could benefit from learning to regulate their breathing and sleeping, following the rhythm of their parent. ② Moreover, mothers who sleep next to their babies are better able to monitor their children for movement during the night. Consequently, it may be safer for newborn babies to sleep with their parents.]

1.2　Distinguishing arguments from non-arguments

Core knowledge input

MOOC Lesson 2

Non-Arguments

Disagreements, descriptions, explanations, and summaries are some other types of passages that can often be mistaken for arguments. But in fact, they are non-arguments. The following examples and analyses may facilitate your understanding.

Disagreement

Complementary therapies are an increasingly popular supplement to other forms of treatment. Those who use these therapies argue that treatments such as reflexology, homeopathy, and shiatsu complement the care provided by the medical profession. Indeed, some people claim that these therapies are more effective than traditional medicines. Anecdotal cases of miraculous cures abound and there are those who believe such methods can compete on equal terms with medical approaches. This just isn't persuasive.

The final sentence expresses disagreement with the idea that complementary therapies are the equivalent of medical treatments. But no reasons or evidence for this are given, so it's not an argument.

Description

The painting depicts several figures gathered around stacks of hay in the fields. These figures are dressed in farmer clothes. All of them are located in the shadows of the cottage. It is not possible to make out any individual features on their faces. By contrast, the figures of other villagers are located in the foreground of the painting, and their facial features are clear and distinguishable.

This passage is a description of a painting. There is no explicit point of view from the author. Descriptions only give an account of how something is done, or what something is like. Although descriptions sometimes provide a great amount of details, such details are not necessarily intended to persuade people into accepting a certain point of view.

Explanation

It was found that many drivers become drowsy when traveling, and drowsy driving for long hours was a major cause of accidents. Consequently, more places to stop were set up along the highways to allow drivers to take a break.

This example is an explanation of why more places to stop were set up along the highway. Explanations account for why or how something occurs, and they may include causes, leading to a final result, and signal words, such as *because* and *consequently*, which are similar to those used for arguments. However, they do not seek to persuade the reader to a point of view.

Summary

Csikszentmihalyi argues that there is unhappiness around because we do not focus enough on how we want the world to be. Thus, we act selfishly and focus on short-term gains, ignoring the longer-term consequences for other people. His answer is to live more in harmony with the wider world around us.

This passage summarizes Csikszentmihalyi's argument about unhappiness, but it's not an argument itself. Summaries are reduced versions of longer messages or texts, showing the key points and drawing attention to the most important aspects.

Practice 2-1

Work in pairs. Judge if the following passages are arguments. If yes, check the boxes in front and identify the premises and theses. If not, state what they are and why.

1. ☐ Twenties is a significant period in a person's life. We know that 80 percent of life's most defining moments take place by age 35. We know that the first 10 years of a career have an exponential impact on how much money you're going to earn. We know that more than half of Americans are married or are living with or dating their future partner by 30. We know that the brain caps off its second and last growth spurt in your 20s as it rewires itself for adulthood. We know that personality changes more during your 20s than at any other time in life, and we know that female fertility peaks at age 28. So your 20s are the time to educate yourself about your body and your options.

_____

_____

_____

2. ☐ The paper presented the difference between individual yawning and contagious yawning. It referred particularly to research by Professor Platek which suggests that only humans and great apes yawn sympathetically. Finally, the article indicates some social benefits of yawning, suggesting that contagious yawning might have helped groups to synchronize their behavior.

_____

3. ☐ There are reasons why the boy was two hours late for the lecture. First of all, a pot caught fire, causing a minor disaster in his kitchen. It took more than half an hour. Then, he couldn't find his apartment keys. That wasted another twenty minutes. Then, just as he closed the door behind him, the delivery guy arrived. Finally, of course, he had to re-open the door and place the parcels on the table.

4. ☐ The images of horses, bison, and red deer found in Creswell Crags, England, bear remarkable similarities to those found in Germany. It is unlikely that two separate cultures would have produced drawings of such similarity if there were not links between them. This suggests that there were greater cultural links between continental Europe and Britain during the Ice Age than was formerly believed.

5. ☐ Recently, Ice Age specialists were thrilled to find some cultural links between Ice Age peoples across Europe. On a return visit to Creswell Crags in England, they found images of horses, bisons, and red deers similar to those already found in Germany. There is controversy about other figures found on cave walls, which some researchers believe to be images of dancing humans, whereas others remain unconvinced.

2. How to structure a critical essay?

What is the connection between an argument and a critical essay? Why do we examine the concept of an argument before studying the structure of a critical essay? We will try to answer these questions in this section.

Core knowledge input

 Micro-lecture Argument and Essay Structure
MOOC Lesson 2

Argument and Essay Structure

Structure of a critical essay

Perhaps it is helpful to think of an essay in terms of a conversation or debate with a classmate. If we were to discuss an issue, there would be a beginning, middle, and end to the conversation. A critical essay also has three parts: the introduction, the body, and the conclusion.

- **The introduction:** one or more paragraphs that begin the essay and present the thesis, i.e. the central idea of the essay
- **The body:** paragraphs that support the essay thesis with details
- **The conclusion:** one or more paragraphs that wind up the essay by reemphasising the thesis

A common method for writing a critical essay, which is often applied by beginner writers, is the five-paragraph approach. It consists of one introduction paragraph, three evidentiary body paragraphs, and a conclusion paragraph. This is, however, by no means the only formula. Complex issues and detailed research call for essays that are more developed and extended.

Relationship between arguments and essay structure

We make arguments to present our opinions and justify them. This is the same with writing a critical essay (review Section 3, Chapter 1). A complete critical essay is then naturally an extended argument. Furthermore, each body paragraph can be an argument itself, since it supports the essay thesis. In this way, the overall argument of a critical essay may consist of several contributing arguments developed in the body paragraphs, and each body paragraph can then have its own thesis and premises.

A Critical Essay	An Argument
Introduction presenting the essay thesis that is to be supported by body paragraphs	**Thesis** presenting an opinion that is to be supported by premises
↓	↓
Body justifying the essay thesis with contributing arguments	**Premises** justifying the thesis with details
↓	↓
Conclusion restating the essay thesis	**Conclusion (optional)** restating the thesis

Model 2-2

Analysis of essay structure

Study the model critical essay and the analysis of its structure. Think about how arguments are formulated throughout the essay.

TV Can Be Good for You

Introduction	❶ Television wastes time, pollutes minds, destroys brain cells, and turns some viewers into murderers. Thus runs the prevailing talk about the medium supported by serious research as well as simple belief. But television has at least one strong virtue, too, which helps to explain its endurance as a cultural force. <u>In an era when people often have little time to speak with one another, television provides replacement voices that ease loneliness, spark healthful laughter, and even educate young children.</u>
thesis of the essay	

Chapter 2　How to develop arguments in a critical essay?

Body (Paras. 2–4)
1st contributing argument

[premises]

thesis of this paragraph

2nd contributing
argument

[premises]

thesis of this paragraph

3rd contributing
argument
thesis of this paragraph

[premises]

Conclusion (Paras. 5 & 6)
response to an opposing
argument

❷ [Most people who have lived alone understand the curse of silence, when the only sound is the buzz of unhappiness or anxiety inside one's own head. Although people of all ages who live alone can experience intense loneliness, the elderly are especially vulnerable to solitude. For example, they may suffer increased confusion or depression when left alone for long periods but then rebound when they have steady companionship. A study of elderly men and women in New Zealand found that television can actually serve as a companion by assuming "the role of social contact with the wider world, reducing feelings of isolation and loneliness" because it directs viewers' attention away from themselves.] Thus, television's replacement voices can provide comfort because they distract from a focus on being alone.

❸ The absence of real voices can be most damaging when it means a lack of laughter. Here, too, research shows that television can have a positive effect on health. [Laughter is one of the most powerful calming forces available to human beings, proven in many studies to reduce heart rate, lower blood pressure, and ease other stress-related ailments. A study reported in a health magazine found that laughter inspired by television and video is as healthful as the laughter generated by live comedy. Further, the effects of the comedy were so profound that merely anticipating watching a funny video improved mood, depression, and anger as much as two days beforehand.] Even for people with plenty of companionship television's replacement voices can have healthful effects by causing laughter.

❹ Television also provides information about the world. This service can be helpful to everyone but especially to children, whose natural curiosity can exhaust the knowledge and patience of their parents and caretakers. [While the TV may be babysitting children, it can also enrich them. For example, educational programs such as those on the Discovery Channel and the Disney Channel offer a steady stream of information at various cognitive levels. Even many cartoons, which are generally dismissed as mindless or worse, familiarize children with the material of literature, including strong characters enacting classic narratives.]

❺ The value of these replacement voices should not be oversold. For one thing, almost everyone agrees that too much TV does no one any good and may cause much harm. In addition, human beings require the give and take of actual interaction. They need to interact with actual speakers who respond directly to their needs. Replacement voices are not real voices and in the end, can do only limited good.

❻ But even limited good is something, especially for those who are lonely or neglected. Television is not an entirely positive force, but neither is it an entirely negative one. <u>Its voices stand by to provide company, laughter, and information whenever they're needed.</u>

Practice 2-2

Read the essay below. Outline its structure by completing the following diagram.

Ways Technology Can Make You Happier

❶ Technology has been a powerful force in our society, most recently with the rise of the Internet and the Information Revolution. This can make it harder to escape from work and increase our fear that we are being monitored without our consent. But that same technology can also be used to help us be happier and healthier.

❷ Modern technology can cut us off from others, but you can exploit this to find a happy vibe by using any of the excellent meditation apps. A pair of decent headphones and the right app can help you to escape from today's bustling world. Some apps provide structured and accessible meditation routines which can help you to develop your mindfulness over the long term, as well as provide refuge during a busy day. Meditation is not a new idea, of course, but technology makes it easier to access and use on a daily basis.

❸ You can use technology to help others. Perhaps the best way for you to use technology to find happiness is not to pursue happiness itself, but rather to help others. This may sound odd, but it is an idea based on sound science. Happiness is a practical emotion which has helped us to evolve by rewarding us when we have done something which increases our likelihood of our surviving or thriving. One of the key things humans do to thrive is helping each other. A website enables non-profit organizations to connect with people who have specific skills and want to volunteer. This model can enable you to do something valuable which results in you feeling happier. Everyone wins.

❹ You can even track your happiness with technology. One powerful strategy for approaching happiness is to train your brain to find happiness in things for which you are grateful. Technology can help with this. Whenever you learn something new you are literally building new connections between brain cells, and over time you can effectively reprogram it to think or feel differently. Each day, perhaps just before you go to bed, try making a list of the positive things which have happened to you that day. It can be a good idea you had, an interesting conversation, something you ate, or even good news about someone you care about. With an app you tap in the things that have enriched your life that day, and then you can access the list whenever you want. This helps to train your brain to record and recall positive experiences, which helps you to experience happiness more often and more easily.

❺ We live in a world that is often defined and limited by technology, but there are real ways in which that technology can really help us to be happier. Don't feel that you have to unplug completely to find real happiness.

Introduction (Para. 1)

Essay thesis: 1._____

Body (Para. 2._____ – Para. 3._____)

Contributing argument 1

Thesis: 4._____

Premises: 5._____

Contributing argument 2

Thesis: 6._____

Premises: 7._____

Contributing argument 3

Thesis: 8._____

Premises: 9._____

Conclusion (Para(s). 10._____)

How does the author reemphasize the thesis?

11._____

From reading to writing

■ Reading
Read the essay and finish the tasks.

Values of Studying History

❶ Some students allege that studying history is valuable only insofar as it is relevant to our daily lives. I find this allegation to be specious. It wrongly suggests that history is not otherwise instructive and that its relevance to our everyday lives is limited. On the contrary, studying history provides inspiration, innumerable life lessons, and useful values, all of which help us decide how to live our lives.

❷ To begin with, learning about the great human achievements of the past provides inspiration. For example, a student inspired by the courage and tenacity of history's great explorers might decide as a result to pursue a career in archeology, oceanography, or astronomy. This decision can, in turn, profoundly affect that student's everyday life in school and beyond. Even for students not inclined to pursue these sorts of careers, studying historical examples of courage in the face of adversity can provide motivation to face their own personal fears in life. In short, learning about the grand accomplishments of the past can help us get through the everyday business of living, whatever that business might be, by emboldening us and lifting our spirits.

❸ Studying human history can also help us understand and appreciate the morals, values, and ideals of past cultures. A heightened awareness of cultural evolution, in turn, helps us formulate informed and reflective values and ideals for ourselves. Based on these values and ideals, students can determine their authentic life path as well as how they should allot their time and interact with others on a day-to-day basis.

❹ Finally, it might be tempting to imply from the allegation that studying history has little relevance even for the mundane chores that occupy so much of our time each day, and therefore is of little value. However, from history we learn not to take everyday activities and things for granted. By understanding the history of money and banking we can transform an otherwise routine trip to the bank into an enlightened experience, or a visit to the grocery store into an homage to the many inventors, scientists, engineers, and entrepreneurs of the past who have made such convenience possible today. In short, appreciating history can serve to elevate our everyday chores to richer, more interesting, and more enjoyable experiences.

❺ In sum, we need to recognize that in all our activities and decisions — from our grandest to our most rote — history can inspire, inform, guide, and nurture. To study history is to gain the capacity to be more human, and I would be hard-pressed to imagine a worthier end.

Writing technique questions

Based on what you have learned in this chapter, consider the following questions. Then discuss with your group your answers and seek a consensus.

1. Which paragraph is the introduction? Which paragraphs are the body? Which paragraph is the conclusion?

2. What is the overall argument of the essay, i.e. what is the essay thesis and what are the premises?

3. In the body paragraphs, how many contributing arguments has the author formulated? List the thesis and premises in each of the contributing argument.

4. In which paragraph does the author respond to an opposing view? What is the opposing view? What premises are used to refute it?

5. How does the author reemphasize the essay thesis in the conclusion?

Critical thinking questions

Consider the questions below and finish the tasks.

1. How has learning history or historical knowledge benefited your study or life? Can you think of a personal experience or story to illustrate your point?

2. Share your answers to the questions above with your group. You may follow the format below.

One of the positive impacts of learning history on me is that [a statement of the benefit]. I realized this benefit when I [your experience or story].

3. Discuss with your group to categorize the benefits you have shared. Present your categorization and the corresponding stories in a tree diagram. You are suggested to show the stories in sketches. (Scan the QR code for a sample tree diagram. Note that you do not have to put the benefits into three categories. The number of categories should be based on your discussion.)

sample

4. Share your diagram and stories with another group.

■ Writing

Based on your answers to the critical thinking questions, outline a critical essay on the topic "Wisdom from History" by filling out the outline template below.

Introduction

Thesis: History imparts wisdom to us in that it [the categories of benefits you have worked out in the critical thinking questions]
_____

Body

Contributing argument 1

Thesis: [your first category of benefits]
_____

Premises: [your stories in this category]
_____

Contributing argument 2

Thesis: [your second category of benefits]
_____

Premises: [your stories in this category]
_____

Contributing argument 3

Thesis: [your third category of benefits]
_____

Premises: [your stories in this category]
_____

Conclusion

_____
_____

REFLECTION

This chapter discussed some basic concepts about arguments and essay structure. Now it's time to review and reflect on what you have learned. Work in pairs and take turns to answer the following questions. Check them as you answer each one.

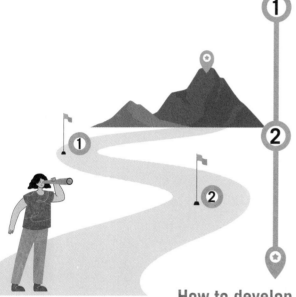

1 What is an argument?
☐ Draw a simple diagram to show the components of an argument.
☐ Explain the differences between arguments and other types of passages.

2 How to structure a critical essay?
☐ Identify the three parts and their basic functions in a critical essay.
☐ Explain the relationship between arguments and essay structure.

How to develop arguments in a critical essay?
☐ Compose an essay outline template.

How to open and close an essay?

善始善终。

——《庄子·大宗师》

Do well from start to finish.
——"The Great Supreme," *Zhuang Zi*

Chapter opener

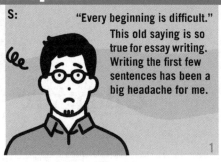

S: "Every beginning is difficult." This old saying is so true for essay writing. Writing the first few sentences has been a big headache for me.

T: Yes, but it pays to write a good introduction because you never get a second chance to make a first impression.

S: What about the end of an essay?

T: It's also very important!

Chapter roadmap

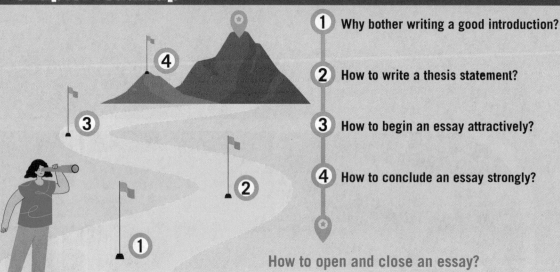

1. Why bother writing a good introduction?
2. How to write a thesis statement?
3. How to begin an essay attractively?
4. How to conclude an essay strongly?

How to open and close an essay?

Learning outcomes

At the end of this chapter, you will be able to

- use a variety of ways to create strong essay leads;
- use a variety of ways to close an essay;
- develop a valid thesis statement;
- produce effective essay introductions and conclusions.

From reading to writing

Analyze the causes of China's advances in science and technology and write the introduction and conclusion for a critical essay on this topic.

1. Why bother writing a good introduction?

As the Chinese saying goes, "do well from start to finish." The introduction and the conclusion are very important parts of an essay. Let's explore the writing of an essay introduction first.

1.1 Functions and components of an essay introduction

Core knowledge input

 Micro-lecture What Is an Essay Introduction
MOOC Lesson 3

What Is an Essay Introduction?

An introduction, the opening paragraph(s) of an essay, will provide readers with initial impressions of the argument, the writing style, and the overall quality of the writing. A vague, disorganized, or boring introduction will likely create a negative impression, while a clear, concise, and engaging introduction prompts readers to think highly of the author and the essay.

A good introduction normally fulfills the following functions:

- It captures the reader's attention and encourages them to read further on;
- It presents the essay thesis — usually in a sentence called the thesis statement;
- It demonstrates an overview of the arguments developed in the body paragraphs.

Consequently, we can usually find three essential components in an essay introduction: a **lead** to engage readers, a **thesis statement** to present the central point of the essay, and a **roadmap** to navigate readers through the following body paragraphs (though it is sometimes optional).

Chapter 3 How to open and close an essay?

Model 3-1

Examples of good essay introductions

Read the examples of good introductions and notice the analysis.

lead: personalized questions to engage readers	Has your school allowed students to use the Internet at any time? Or has your school been restricting students' access to the Internet? The role of the use of the Internet in learning is hotly debated. For many teachers who did not grow up with this technology, its effects seem alarming and potentially harmful. This concern, while understandable, is misguided. **The negatives**
thesis statement [roadmap]	**of Internet use are outweighed by its critical benefits for students and educators** — [as a uniquely comprehensive and accessible information source; a means of exposure to and engagement with different perspectives; and a highly flexible learning environment].
lead: suspenseful narration to engage readers	Her heart raced so fast that she was sure she was going to have a heart attack. She sped up. She was anxious to get home. One could even see the sweat dripping down her face. In an attempt to take a shortcut, she jaywalked across a wide street, zigzagging her way through it. She almost got hit by a truck, but she didn't care. She was not concerned. She was just a few meters from her place. She had only one goal in mind. She needed it so bad — to plug her phone in and get back to social media. She existed now. She was online again. Lisa won't admit it, but she
thesis statement [roadmap]	is addicted to social media. **Social media giants need to stop pretending they are changing the world into a better place but come forward to admit that they are deliberately selling a product that is, in fact, [addictive and harmful for us].**

Practice 3-1

Read the following passages. 1) Underline the leads. 2) Highlight the thesis statements. 3) Bracket the roadmaps if there is one.

1. Cloning, also referred to as asexual reproduction, is the process of creating genetically modified copies of biological matter such as cells and tissues. It is perceived as the most tremendous medical breakthrough in the contemporary age. So far, cloning has been successfully implemented and practiced on human beings, animals, and plants. However, it has presented insurmountable concerns, both ethical and biological, especially with regard to human beings.

2. If you suffer from shyness, you are not alone, for shyness is a universal phenomenon and social scientists are learning more about its causes. In fact, shyness in an individual can result from both biological and environmental factors.

3. Around the globe, policymakers are leveraging technological innovation to transform the transport sector, progressively shifting away from fossil fuel consumption to clean energy to achieve sustainable mobility. China is a trailblazer in this field, commendably serving as the major driver of the world's sustainable transport transition and also sharing technical expertise and innovation with the rest of the world.

4. In Britain, parents are now choosing to educate their children at home. This is often because some children find it difficult to fit into the school system because they are especially gifted or have problems of some kind. However, despite the various arguments that have been put forward for home tutoring, I would argue that it is better for a child to be educated at school.

1.2 Things that may spoil an essay introduction

Core knowledge input

MOOC Lesson 3

Don'ts for Writing an Essay Introduction
Don't skip the thesis statement.

Don't assume that readers will automatically understand the position or the central idea from the context of the essay. It is very likely for them to be confused about the central idea of the essay or to spend extra efforts extracting the message. Whatever the topic is, a thesis statement, the sentence telling the major opinion of the author, is a must.

Don't repeat the thesis.

Although a thesis statement is very important, it is not necessary to repeat it over and over again, not even in different wording. The risk in doing so is that each paraphrase will have a slightly different connotation, and this may cause confusion regarding the main point of the essay. Therefore, state the central idea only once in the introduction.

Don't include any incomplete supporting argument.

Normally, an essay introduction shall not include supporting details. For one thing, the limited space in introduction cannot guarantee a thorough support, and a hasty argument will leave a negative impression on readers. For another, the supportive ideas may have to be repeated in the body paragraphs, and this repetitive work makes the writing dull.

Model 3-2

Examples of bad essay introductions

Read the examples of bad introductions and notice the analysis.

skipping the thesis statement: What is the author's opinion on the topic?	Social networking websites are considered by many to have adversely influenced both individuals and communities. However, others believe that their effect has been mostly beneficial to individuals and society. It is undeniable that the influence of social networking websites has been a hotly-debated issue.
repeating the thesis: Different supporting details are needed to justify the two claims.	Social networking websites are considered by many to have adversely influenced both individual people and communities. However, I believe that the effect of those sites has been mostly beneficial to individuals and society. In other words, the advantages of social networking websites outweigh the disadvantages, and all people can gain what they want from online socializing.
including random supporting details that should be put in the body paragraphs	While I agree that sites such as Weibo have changed the way we communicate, I believe that the effect of those sites has been mostly beneficial to individuals and society. For example, we can communicate with family and friends more conveniently, or we have better platforms to express ourselves.

Practice 3-2

Underline the problematic parts of the following introductions by students and identify the problems.

1. During the pandemic, many students had to switch to online learning. After that, many people wondered whether online teaching would replace traditional classroom teaching. In my opinion, it will never happen. I think students will still learn in the classroom with the help of the Internet, but online teaching cannot replace traditional classes.

   Problem: _____

2. MOOCs will not replace traditional classroom teaching. Compared with traditional classroom teaching, MOOCs do have some benefits, such as the replay function that allows students to watch lectures many times. However, traditional classroom teaching also has many benefits that cannot be gained from MOOCs. For example, face-to-face interaction between the teacher and students enables teachers to adjust their instruction flexibly to meet students' learning needs.

   Problem: _____

3. Nowadays thousands of Chinese students regard a college education as their only choice to improve themselves and get a high-paid job. In order to polish their résumé and get a degree, students are very keen on taking the College Entrance Examination and many even choose to retake the exam in order to be admitted to their dream school. But surprisingly, statistics show that job hunting has become increasingly hard for college graduates in recent years, which worries the public a lot. Since a college education requires a good amount of energy and money, people begin to doubt whether a college education is worth it.

   Problem: _____

4. Now we are all receiving a college education. Why do we need to receive a college education? Is a college education worth it? My opinion is that it is worth it. Although we can also learn knowledge and develop our skills in society, going to college is a more efficient way to accomplish this mission. Let's consider some of the benefits a college education brings. The fact is that the majority of jobs require a college education, and

graduates earn more than non-graduates.

Problem: _____

2. How to write a thesis statement?

In Chapter 2, we learned that a thesis is the central opinion of the whole essay. But how can we effectively present the thesis in a critical essay? The answer is to write a good thesis statement.

2.1 Thesis and thesis statement

Core knowledge input

  Micro-lecture Understanding the Concept of Thesis and Thesis Statement
MOOC Lesson 3

Understanding the Concept of Thesis and Thesis Statement
What makes a thesis?

In a critical essay, there could be a major thesis, which is the point of view of the essay, and several sub-theses, which are the major points of view of the supporting arguments in the body paragraphs. In either case, they must be arguable or debatable, something that people could reasonably have differing opinions on. For example, both "The council's anti-pollution efforts should focus on privately owned cars." and "The council's anti-pollution efforts should not only focus on privately owned cars." are valid theses because there is room for others to disagree with either of them.

However, if the thesis is something that is generally agreed upon or accepted as a fact, then there is no point of developing an essay to justify it. The statement "Pollution is bad for the environment." is not debatable because people already have a consensus on this; they simply disagree on the impact pollution has or the scope of the problem. Neither is "I don't like painting." a thesis, since it is merely a statement of the author's personal preference. No one would argue and say "No, you like painting."

What makes a thesis statement?

A thesis statement is normally a one-sentence encapsulation of the essay's central idea, which will be defended in the body paragraphs. It is important to provide the thesis statement early in the essay — in most cases at the end of the introduction in order to orient readers toward the rest of the essay. In this sense, a thesis statement does the following jobs:

- It states the topic of the essay.
- It declares the author's position on the topic.
- It may provide a roadmap.

Model 3-3

Components of a good thesis statement

Read the examples of good thesis statements and notice the analysis of their components.

topic: prevention of juvenile crime the author's position [roadmap]	Juveniles can <u>be diverted from crime</u> by [active learning programs, full-time sports, and intervention by mentors and role models].
topic: strip-mining industry management the author's position [roadmap]	Strip-mining <u>should be tightly controlled in this region</u> to [reduce its pollution of water resources, its destruction of the land, and its devastating effects on people's life].

Practice 3-3

Decide if the following statements can be considered thesis statements. If yes, check the boxes in front. If not, give your reasons.

1. ☐ The earth goes around the sun.

2. ☐ A college education is well worth the expense.

_____

3. ☐ I won't sign up for the course of *French 101*.

_____

4. ☐ Obesity is unhealthy.

_____

5. ☐ It's unnecessary for people to intentionally develop their study skills.

_____

Practice 3-4

Read the following essay introductions. For each one, underline the thesis statement, bracket the roadmap if there is any, and then complete the analysis below.

1. Nearly 70% of American adults are overweight; over a third are obese. Grocery shops contain aisle after aisle of salty crisps, sugary drinks, and processed snacks. Cues to eat unhealthily abound. But if this is your archetypal American diet, you are looking in the wrong places. America has healthy cuisines — if you know where to look.

   The topic: _____

   The author's position: _____

2. It is said that we can know someone by the company he keeps. Similarly, I would say that we can know someone by the hobbies he pursues. Hobbies are quite important for those who deal with a lot of pressure at work and in life.

   The topic: _____

   The author's position: _____

3. We live in a society where celebrities are worshiped. Social media nowadays is full of headlines regarding the actions, feelings, faults, and successes of music and film celebrities. And workout schedules and dietary programs are released under the promise

that results will bear a resemblance to certain admired celebrities. We want to look like them, eat like them, exercise like them, and talk like them. We want to be them. Why? Because we need someone to look up to.

The topic: _____

The author's position: _____

2.2 Avoiding ineffective thesis statements

Model 3-4

Examples of ineffective thesis statements
Read the following ineffective thesis statements and notice the analyses of their problems.

I want to share some thoughts about the prevention of juvenile crimes.
This sentence is an announcement of the essay's topic. The author's position is not shown.

According to the study, ninety percent of kids who break the law during adolescence don't become adult criminals.
It is a statement of fact, reporting a finding from a scientific study. Rather, a thesis statement should be arguable or debatable.

Since strip-mining does harm not only to the environment but also to human beings, should we take any measures to control it?
This statement is a question. Normally, a thesis statement cannot be a question because it does not present the author's position. Instead, a thesis statement would be an answer to a question, not a question itself.

Diseases have shaped human history.
What kind of diseases? Which aspect of history? The statement is too broad to be

adequately addressed in an essay. The author can either narrow down this topic or develop it into a book.

College brings much independence.

This statement is too narrow. We probably need only a paragraph not an essay to justify it. The author can expand the topic by talking about the benefits of college study for an individual.

The National Theater is an interesting structure.

This statement is too subjective. It is difficult to define interesting, and the sentence does not give readers any clues about where the essay is going. A thesis statement should be sharply focused. Avoid general, hard-to-define words such as interesting, good, or negative. Instead, try to use specific language (Read Language Clinic 2 for more).

Core knowledge input

MOOC Lesson 3

Checklist of Thesis Statement Writing

☑ **It clearly suggests an essay's direction, emphasis, and scope.**

A thesis statement should not make promises that the essay will not fulfill. It should suggest how ideas are related and where the emphasis will lie.

☑ **It is arguable or debatable.**

A thesis statement shall present a viewpoint that can be questioned or challenged by other people.

☑ **It is neither too broad nor too narrow.**

The thesis determines the scope of an essay. If a thesis is too broad, the essay will be superficial; if a thesis is too narrow, the essay will have nowhere to go.

☑ **It is concise.**

Because the thesis statement's purpose is to make the major point of view clear, the sentence itself should be clear and concise, giving only the most relevant information.

☑ **It is specific and strong, not vague or weak.**

Make sure the thesis statement contains specific language. It should not create ambiguity.

Practice 3-5

Evaluate the following thesis statements against the checklist above. Check the ones that you think meet the above standards; cross the boxes in front of the ones that do not. Then explain your decisions to a partner.

☐ 1. Bike-sharing brings convenient transport to the public.

☐ 2. People should shoulder the responsibility of caring for their elderly parents.

☐ 3. Obesity can cause heart disease.

☐ 4. The Great Wall should be the first stop on the itinerary of any visitor to Beijing.

☐ 5. The sharing economy is a significant kind of economy.

☐ 6. College education provides people opportunities to learn more professional knowledge.

☐ 7. Social media is influential.

☐ 8. Mapping the human genome has many implications.

2.3 Developing a thesis statement

Core knowledge input

MOOC Lesson 3

Steps of Writing a Good Thesis Statement

Step 1

> Decide on a proper topic (neither too broad nor too narrow).
> The special problems that parents face raising children today.

↓

Step 2

> State clearly your position on the topic.
> My essay will show that raising children today is much more difficult than it was when my parents raised me.

↓

Step 3

> Ask yourself questions on the checklist on page 56.
> Answer: It's arguable, but "when my parent raised me" is a bit narrow.

↓

Step 4

> Revise the thesis statement if necessary.
> Being a parent today is much more difficult than it was a generation ago.

↓

Step 5

> Provide a roadmap if necessary.
> Being a parent today is much more difficult than it was a generation ago in that the demands on them from both the society and the family have greatly increased.

Practice 3-6

Revise the following thesis statements into good ones.

1. Bike-sharing brings convenient transport to the public.

   _____

   _____

2. The sharing economy is a significant kind of economy.

   _____

   _____

3. Social media is influential.

   _____

   _____

4. Since strip-mining does harm not only to the environment but also to human beings, should we take any measures to control it?

   _____

   _____

5. Environmental protection is important.

   _____

   _____

Practice 3-7

Write two thesis statements for each of the topics below. Then work in pairs to evaluate them for each other using the checklist on page 56. Revise them when necessary.

1. Building a community with a shared future for mankind

   1) _____

   2) _____

2. Development of ecological civilization

   1) _____

2) _____

3. Improving cultural confidence

1) _____

2) _____

3. How to begin an essay attractively?

In an essay introduction, we often need to create a lead to engage the reader. How should we create the lead? How can we make it attractive?

Core knowledge input

Micro-lecture Good and Bad Techniques for Essay Leads
MOOC Lesson 3

Good and Bad Techniques for Essay Leads

Good essay leads

The secret of getting readers interested is to make an intriguing **lead** in the essay introduction. So, what is a lead? It is a sentence or a group of sentences that indicate the essay's topic and draw readers' attention. A good lead sparks readers' curiosity, making them wonder what happens next. A good essay lead also makes an introduction stand out, which raises our chance of getting a high grade on an essay. The following table shows 8 effective ways to create good essay leads.

An intriguing question	A strong/unique statement	Impressive facts or statistics	A short story or anecdote
• Ask a question related to the topic. • Make the question the one where readers need to read the essay to get the answer.	• Make an assertive claim about your topic. • A claim conflicting with commonly-held ideas works even better.	• Give impressive facts about the essay topic. • Make sure the facts are accurate and reliable.	• Begin with a short story or anecdote related to the topic. • The story can be personal or someone else's.

A vivid description	A powerful quotation	A striking metaphor or simile	An effective counterargument
• Give a vivid description of a scene to draw readers into our writing. • Make the description tie into the essay.	• Begin with a powerful and memorable quotation. • Quote the words exactly. • Avoid clichés.	• Use a metaphor or simile to compare the topic to something seemingly unrelated. • Entice readers into discovering the connection by reading on.	• Present a common idea that the essay disagrees with. • Refute that idea to arouse readers' curiosity.

Bad essay leads

The opposite of an attractive lead is a boring lead — some bore-you-to-tears opening lines that drive readers away. At best, readers may be patient enough to read on. More often it provides little more than an excuse to stop reading. Thus, avoid the four types of boring leads below.

✗ Clichés

While starting our essays with a quote can be a simple and effective way to attract readers, we also need to be careful about the quotation we use. Don't quote words that are so commonly used that they become boring. Some bad examples are listed below.

Every coin has two sides.

To be or not to be.

It goes without saying that …

✗ Overly general statements

How many times have you started an essay with "With the development of science and technology, …" or "Man has always wondered…"? The risks in opening an essay with such grand statements lie in at least two aspects. First, overly general statements are often empty and thus provide weak connection to the topic. Second, if we don't follow such a big statement with something equally grand in the rest of the essay, the introduction then sound pompous.

✕ Plain announcements

Plain announcements are mechanical introduction to the contents of our essays. They are normally considered hasty. Below is such an example.

In this essay, after giving the subject a lot of thought, I am going to write about …

✕ Comments on the writing assignment itself

Although some essays are written to fulfill course or exam tasks, it is generally not acceptable to begin with statements like the one below.

On looking at the topic of this assignment, my first thought was …

Model 3-5

Examples of good essay leads

1. **Intriguing question lead**

   What is the difference between successful college students and unsuccessful college students? (Topic: succeeding in college)

2. **Strong/unique statement lead**

   McDonald's is bad for your kids. I do not mean the flat patties and the white-flour buns; I refer to the jobs teenagers undertake, mass-producing these choice items. (Topic: harms of part-time jobs to teens)

3. **Impressive facts or statistics lead**

   Almost 75% of all UFO reports turn out to be a weather balloon, meteors, or the reflection from clouds and ice. (Topic: existence of UFOs)

4. **Story or anecdote lead**

   I got off the train and pulled my luggage behind me. A cab pulled up to the curb, and the driver got out. He lifted my luggage and said, "Miss, I'm just going to put your stuff in the boot." I didn't know what he meant until I saw him open the car's trunk. Then I realized the boot means car trunk. I got in the cab, wondering how many other words would be different in England. (Topic:

differences between British and American English)

5. Description lead

Her heart raced so fast that she was sure she was going to have a heart attack. She sped up. She was anxious to get home. One could even see the sweat dripping down her face. In an attempt to take a shortcut, she jaywalked across a wide street, zigzagging her way through it. She almost got hit by a truck, but she didn't care. She was not concerned. She was just a few meters from her place. She had only one goal in mind. She needed it so bad — to plug her phone in and get back to social media. (Topic: social media addiction)

6. Quotation lead

Nelson Mandela said, "Education is the most powerful weapon you can use to change the world." (Topic: significance of education)

7. Metaphor or simile lead

A business blog is a magnet pulling clients to a company. (Topic: effects of business blogging)

8. Counterargument lead

The dynamics of the digital book market resembled the dynamics before the holiday buying surge. That was one of the key findings in "Book Publishing Digital Transition Report in 2011." Many begin to expect an upwards shift in the number of people only reading digital books and a decline in book buyers intending to stick solely to print. In fact, despite the jump in both the number of digital readers and book buyers with devices, the percentage of book readers who said they only read digital books remained below 1%, while the percentage of readers who said they will only read print books stayed at 40%. 33% of book buyers said they read both print and digital books. (Topic: future of print books)

Practice 3-8

Work in pairs. Compare the following pairs of essay leads. Discuss which one is more appealing and explain why.

1. A. I once hosted a group of American college students visiting China. After I introduced the history and experience of China's poverty alleviation, the usual Q&A session took place. What impressed me the most was the question they asked: "Your government has allocated so much fiscal budget to help the poor who are usually the lazy people at the bottom, do your taxpayers agree with their money being spent this way?" Recently, some colleagues from other departments also asked me whether the conditional cash transfer in the poverty alleviation policy to some extent contributed to the inertia of some lazy people. Both of these two questions reflect a social issue — the phenomenon of welfare dependence. Is China's poverty alleviation creating welfare dependence? Does it support the lazybones? The answer is clearly "no."

   B. Recently a heated debate on welfare dependence goes viral. Many people begin to question whether China's poverty alleviation is creating welfare dependence. My answer to this question is "No."

2. A. With the development of science and technology, people from different parts of the world are getting closer and closer. The phenomenon of globalization is more and more obvious. On one hand, globalization has boosted the global economy. On the other hand, it has also caused some problems. One of them is the loss of cultural identities.

   B. Although essentially an economic phenomenon, globalization could only be envisaged in the context of wider interaction between different cultures, and it is this aspect of globalization, its cultural over-spill, as it were, that many see as a greater threat than its purely economic aspect. Voices came to be raised against the globalization process, which comes from the fear that such a process might erode national cultures and individual identities. The specific cultural identities are at risk of being altogether lost or, at best, greatly diluted, in the context of globalization.

Choose two thesis statements from those you wrote in Practice 3-7. Write two complete essay introductions for each of them. Use the techniques discussed in the "Core knowledge input" on page 60 to create strong leads.

Tips

Work in pairs to evaluate your introductions for each other by considering the following prompt questions.
1. Is the lead attractive?
2. Is there a qualified thesis statement?
3. Is there a roadmap?

Essay 1

Thesis statement: _____

Introduction 1: _____

_____

_____

Introduction 2: _____

_____

_____

Essay 2

Thesis statement: _____

Introduction 1: _____

_____

_____

Introduction 2: _____

_____

_____

4. How to conclude an essay strongly?

Similar to introductions, conclusions play a special role in an essay. A strong conclusion will remind readers of the essay thesis as well as provide a sense of closure to the essay.

Core knowledge input

Micro-lecture Approaches to Strong Conclusions
MOOC Lesson 3

Approaches to Strong Conclusions

Conclusions can be difficult to write, but it's worth the time investment. While the introduction leads readers from their own lives into the argument of the essay, the conclusion transports readers back to their lives by inspiring them to see why the argument in the essay matters to them.

Ideally, a strong conclusion can reemphasize the major thesis, demonstrate its significance, and provide an inspiration for readers. The approaches below are often used by professional writers.

- Restate the thesis (and summarize the contributing arguments) in fresh language.
- Predict positive or negative effects of attending or not attending to the problem.
- Recommend a course of action or offer solutions to the issue.
- Return to an anecdote, example, or quotation introduced in the introduction, but add further insight that derives from the argument of the essay.

Model 3-6

Examples of strong conclusions

Study the examples of strong conclusions and notice the analysis of the strategies used.

1. Restating the thesis (and summarizing the contributing arguments) in fresh language

   In sum, we need to recognize that in all our activities and decisions — from our grandest to our most rote — history can inspire, inform, guide, and nurture. To study history is to gain the capacity to be more human, and I would be hard-pressed to imagine a worthier end. (Revisit the reading task on page 39 for the full text.)

2. Predicting positive or negative effects of attending or not attending to the problem

   Connectivity increases with every day that passes, yet somehow our social contact is more broken nowadays than ever before. It makes me wonder, as with smoking, will there be social media tables in restaurants in the future? Will social media consumption in large doses cause some sort of social cancer? Only time will tell how the future landscape will shape up, yet one day social media might have to include mandatory warnings like the ones present on cigarette packages today. (Go to Model 8-6 for the full text.)

3. Recommending a course of action or offering solutions to the issue

   Thus, parents should look at teen employment not as automatically educational. Youngsters must learn to balance the quest for income with the need to keep growing and pursue other endeavors that do not pay off instantly — above all education.

   Go back to school. (Go to Model 3-7 for the full text.)

4. Returning to an anecdote, example, or quotation introduced in the introduction

   Walker X is but a manifestation of China's soaring technological advancements. Innovation is the primary driver for development. In the past decade, with great prominence given to innovation, science and technology in China are surging ahead at a speed never seen before and getting integrated into people's lives to an unprecedented degree. Hence, the methods of production, people's lifestyles, and the ways economy functions are undergoing profound changes. In the future, science and technology innovations will enable China to usher in more benefits to its own people and others across the world. (Go to the reading task on page 73 for the full text.)

Core knowledge input

MOOC Lesson 3

Things That Might Spoil a Conclusion

Introducing a new idea or subtopic

A conclusion is where the essay should close by echoing the thesis statement. It is never a place to bring up a new debatable idea. A new idea in the conclusion will pathetically turn the essay into merely a prelude and indicate a need to start a new essay with that idea as the thesis statement.

Repeating the thesis statement

Repeating the thesis statement or mildly rephrasing it in the conclusion is by no means a wrong choice. But it does make the conclusion dry as well as expose the author's poor lexical resource.

Including supporting details

Normally the body paragraphs are where reasons and evidence should be provided to justify the thesis thoroughly. Concluding an essay with such details is not ideal.

Scan the QR codes to read three student essays. Identify the conclusions and explain their problems. Then share your answers with a partner.

1. Problem: _____

_____

_____

2. Problem: _____

_____

_____

3. Problem: _____

_____

_____

Model 3-7

Introduction and conclusion in a critical essay

Read the following model critical essay and notice the analysis of its introduction and conclusion.

Working at McDonald's

thesis statement lead: challenging a commonly accepted idea [roadmap]	❶ <u>McDonald's is bad for your kids.</u> I do not mean the flat patties and the white-flour buns; I refer to the jobs teenagers undertake, mass-producing these choice items. At first, such jobs may seem right for bringing up self-reliant, work-ethic-driven, productive youngsters. [But in fact, these jobs undermine school attendance and involvement, impart few skills that will be useful in later life, and simultaneously skew the values of teen-agers — especially their ideas about the worth of a dollar.]

❷ First, the McDonald's kind of job is highly uneducational in several ways. Far from providing opportunities for entrepreneurship or self-discipline, self-supervision, and self-scheduling, most teen jobs these days are highly structured — what social scientists call "highly routinised."

❸ True, you still have to have the gumption to get yourself over to the hamburger stand, but once you don the prescribed uniform, your task is spelled out in minute detail. The franchise prescribes the shape of the coffee cups; the weight, size, shape, and color of the patties; and the texture of the napkins (if any). Fresh coffee is to be made every eight minutes. And so on. There is no room for initiative, creativity, or even elementary rearrangements.

❹ There are very few studies on the matter. One of the few is a study by Ivan Charper and Bryan Shore Fraser. The study relies mainly on what teenagers write in response to the questionnaires rather than actual observations of fast-food jobs. The authors argue that the employees develop many skills such as how to operate a food-preparation machine and a cash register. However, little attention is paid to how long it takes to acquire such a skill, or what its significance is.

❺ What does it matter if you spend 20 minutes learning to use a cash register, and then — "operate" it? What "skill" have you acquired? A study by A. V. Harrell and P. W. Wirtz found that, among those students who worked at least 25 hours per week while in school, their unemployment rate four years later was half of that of seniors who did not work. This is an impressive statistic. It must be seen though, together with the finding that many, who begin as part-time employees in fast-food chains drop out of high school and are gobbled up in the world of low-skill jobs.

❻ Some say that while these jobs are rather unsuited for college-bound, white, middle-class youngsters, they are "ideal" for lower-class, "non-academic," minority youngsters. Indeed, minorities are "over-represented" in these jobs (21 percent of fast-food employees). While it is true that these places provide income, work, and even some training to such youngsters, they also tend to perpetuate their disadvantaged status. They provide no career ladders, few marketable skills, and undermine school attendance and involvement.

❼ The hours are often long. Among those 14 to 17, a third of fast-food employees (including some school dropouts) labor more than 30 hours per week, according to the Charper-Fraser study. Only 20 percent work 15 hours or less. The rest: between 15 and 30 hours. In affluent Montgomery County, MD, where child labor would not seem to be a widespread economic necessity, 24 percent of the seniors at one high school worked as much as five to seven days a week; 27 percent, three to five. There is just no way such amounts of work will not interfere with school work, especially homework. In an informal survey published in the most recent yearbook of the high school, 58 percent of seniors acknowledge that their jobs interfere with their school work.

❽ Another concern — the pay — is oddly the part of the teen work-world that is most difficult to evaluate. In the old days, apprentices learning a trade from a master contributed most, if not all, of their income to their parents' household. Today, the teen pay may be low by adult standards, but it is often, especially in the middle class, spent largely or wholly by the teens. That is, the youngsters live free at home ("After all, they are high school kids.") and are left with very substantial sums of money. And large amounts of the money seem to flow to pay for an early introduction into the most trite aspects of American consumerism: flimsy punk clothes, trinkets, and whatever else is the last fast-moving teen craze.

❾ One may say that this is only fair and square; they are being good American consumers and spend their money on what turns them on. At least, a cynic might add, these funds do not go into illicit drugs and booze. On the other hand, an educator might bemoan that these young, yet unformed individuals, so early in life driven to buy objects of no intrinsic educational, cultural or social merit, learn so quickly the dubious merit of keeping up with the Joneses in ever-changing fads, promoted by mass merchandising.

❿ Many teens find the instant reward of money, and the youth status symbols it buys, much more alluring than credits in calculus courses, European history, or foreign languages. No wonder quite a few would rather skip school — and certainly homework — and instead work longer at a Burger King. Thus, most teen work these days is not providing early lessons in the work ethic; it fosters escape from school and responsibilities, quick gratification, and a shortcut to the consumeristic aspects of adult life.

conclusion: proposing a course of action to an issue	⓫ Thus, parents should look at teen employment not as automatically educational. Youngsters must learn to balance the quest for income with the needs to keep growing and pursue other endeavors that do not pay off instantly — above all education. ⓬ Go back to school.

Practice 3-11

Read a student's essay about whether computers will replace teachers in education. Write a strong conclusion for the essay. Apply what you have learned in this section.

❶ Computers, as the most powerful tool in the information age, are widely applied in people's work, study, and daily life. A growing number of people think optimistically that computers will replace teachers in the classroom and play the leading role in study. As far as I am concerned, it will not take the place of teachers now — or ever.

❷ One of the main reasons is that computers work according to prescribed programs. They cannot work creatively. Suppose a new problem arises in study, computers will be at a loss and unable to respond to the questions put forward by students. Although there is good news about the international chess games between computers and human beings, computers will surpass humans because they are a product of human intelligence.

❸ Another reason is that computers cannot communicate emotions. Communication plays an important role not only in building personal relations, but also in understanding each other clearly. Study is not a mere process of acquiring knowledge. It is, more importantly, an indispensable sector for people to communicate with each other and build interpersonal relations. Without emotions, everybody would become a cold creature and make the world unbearable.

❹ Last but not least, computers cannot take the place of teachers to organize teaching activities and keep good order in the classroom. A good organizer can activate the atmosphere of study, triggering students' interest in studying. In addition, study can only proceed in the circumstance of good order. Otherwise, the classroom will become meaningless.

Conclusion: _____

_____

_____

_____

From reading to writing

■ Reading

Read the essay and finish the tasks.

What Drives China's High-Quality Development

❶ I'm a 5-year-old that is 1.3 meters tall and weighs 63 kilograms. I'm light-hearted. I like jogging and doing Tai Chi, and I am particularly good at Chinese chess, calligraphy, and drawing. I've worked in many roles such as an event host, a dancer, a docent, etc.

❷ Sounds like a prodigy, right? Well, no. This is the self-introduction of a robot. In 2021, Walker X, a robot that can run, play Chinese chess, and interact with people, debuted at the 4th World Artificial Intelligence Conference and immediately became the center of attention. While a robot that can mimic basic human movements needs to be powered by at least 20 to 30 servo motors, Walker X is equipped with 41 high-performance Chinese-made servos that allow it to perform more complex tasks such as playing Chinese chess, calligraphy, and drawing.

❸ Science and technology innovations are always at the foundation of China's development and the growth of its national strength.

❹ The "Two Bombs and One Satellite" project, the BeiDou Navigation Satellite System, and Lunar Exploration Program have all translated to the country's hard power; hybrid rice, the development of new drugs, and the high-speed rail network have helped to raise people's living standards; and domestically manufactured mobile phones, the 5G network, and breakthroughs in areas such as quantum information have shown to the world China's creativity and research and development capabilities.

❺ Since the 18th CPC National Congress, the central government has promoted science and technology innovations and introduced relevant policies at a scale never witnessed before, which is an important reason behind the country's robust science and technology advancements for the past decade. A case in point is the success of the city of Lianyungang in Jiangsu Province. Over these years, the city achieved many firsts, both globally and domestically. The world's longest wind turbine blade and first set of 8.8-meter intelligent mining scraper conveyors were manufactured in Lianyungang, and the city was also where China's first independently developed 10,000-ton carbon fiber production line was installed and more than 20 new drugs were developed. Thanks to favorable policies, 449 high- and new-technology companies had been established in Lianyungang by 2021, 10 times the number in 2012.

❻ The advent of products such as Walker X represents an accelerated integration of emerging technologies into people's life in China. The scaling of the 5G network and the widespread use of smartphones have driven everyday life online, making mobile payments, mobile car-hailing, and mobile information submission indispensable for almost everyone. Progresses in this regard have made China stand out above other countries and emerge as the most powerful engine for high-quality national development.

❼ According to statistics from the Ministry of Industry and Information Technology, during the ten years between 2012 and 2021, the size of China's digital economy increased from 11 to 45 trillion yuan and its share in national GDP rose from 21.6 percent to 39.8 percent. In spite of external factors, the recent years have seen digital technology uninterruptedly transforming traditional industries, as well as facilitating innovations. As online shopping flourishes, new business models such as live commerce, online education, remote medical consultations, and remote work are mushrooming. Additionally, digitalization picks up pace in all social sectors and traditional industries are increasingly digitalized, networkized, and intelligentized.

❽ Walker X is but a manifestation of China's soaring technological advancements. Innovation is the primary driver for development. In the past decade, with great prominence given to innovation, science and technology in China are surging ahead at a speed never seen before and getting integrated into people's lives to an unprecedented degree. Hence, the methods of production, people's lifestyles, and the ways economy functions are undergoing profound changes. In the future, science and technology innovations will enable China to usher in more benefits to its own people and others across the world.

Writing technique questions

Based on what you have learned in this chapter, consider the following questions. Then discuss your answers with your group and seek a consensus.

1. What technique is used to create a lead in this essay?
2. What is the thesis statement? Does it present the author's point of view? Does it indicate the overview of the supporting arguments?
3. How does the author close the essay in the conclusion?

Critical thinking questions

Consider the questions below and finish the tasks.

1. According to Para. 5 of the essay, favorable policies is a factor driving China's fast advancement in science and technology. Can you identify another factor contributing to the advancement? What experience, events, statistics, testimonies, etc. help you reach such a judgment?
2. Share your answers to the questions above with your group.
3. Discuss with your group to decide on the most important factor among all the ones you have thought of. Then formatting your ideas in the following way.

We think the most significant factor contributing to China's fast development of science and technology is [your group decision]. There are two/three reasons for us to think so. First, ... Second, ...

The other factors we have considered include [the other factors mentioned by your group members]. But we believe they are not as significant as [your group decision]. For example, [explain why one of the other factors from your group is less significant].

4. Present your ideas to the class.

■ Writing

Imagine you are writing an essay whose title is "What Drives China's Science and Technology Advancement?". Based on your answers to the critical thinking questions, write an introduction paragraph and a conclusion paragraph for the essay.

Introduction

_____

_____

_____

_____

_____

_____

Conclusion

_____

_____

_____

_____

_____

REFLECTION

This chapter discussed writing essay introductions and conclusions. Now it's time to review and reflect on what you have learned. Work in pairs and take turns to answer the following questions. Check them as you answer each one.

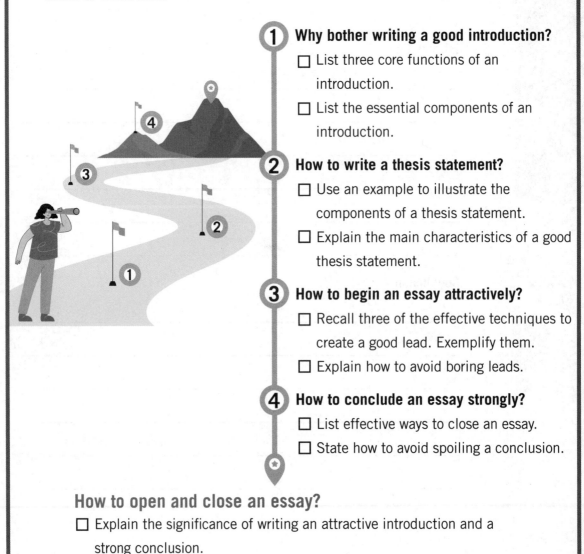

1 **Why bother writing a good introduction?**
- ☐ List three core functions of an introduction.
- ☐ List the essential components of an introduction.

2 **How to write a thesis statement?**
- ☐ Use an example to illustrate the components of a thesis statement.
- ☐ Explain the main characteristics of a good thesis statement.

3 **How to begin an essay attractively?**
- ☐ Recall three of the effective techniques to create a good lead. Exemplify them.
- ☐ Explain how to avoid boring leads.

4 **How to conclude an essay strongly?**
- ☐ List effective ways to close an essay.
- ☐ State how to avoid spoiling a conclusion.

How to open and close an essay?
- ☐ Explain the significance of writing an attractive introduction and a strong conclusion.
- ☐ Summarize the characteristics of good introductions and conclusions.

How to write a body paragraph?

事莫明于有效，论莫定于有证。

——《论衡·薄葬篇》

Things manifest themselves by efficacy; claims are ascertained by evidence.

——"Thrifty Funeral," *Balanced Inquiries*

Chapter opener

T:
You see, here in this body paragraph, you need to **build your argument.** Don't just repeat your opinion in different ways.

1

S:
But how do I build an argument?

2

T:
You'd better learn to reason.

3

S:
Reason —

4

Chapter roadmap

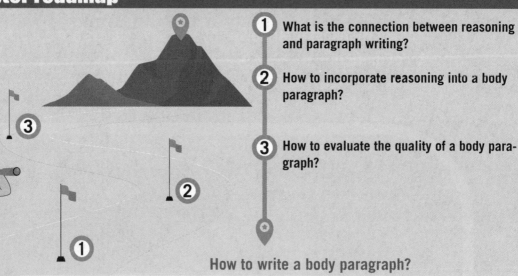

1. What is the connection between reasoning and paragraph writing?

2. How to incorporate reasoning into a body paragraph?

3. How to evaluate the quality of a body paragraph?

How to write a body paragraph?

Learning outcomes

At the end of this chapter, you will be able to

- understand what reasoning is and how it facilitates body paragraph writing;
- identify the three parts of a body paragraph;
- evaluate the quality of a body paragraph from four aspects;
- write a body paragraph with effective reasoning.

From reading to writing

Recognize the benefits of innovative development and compose a body paragraph for a critical essay on this topic.

1. What is the connection between reasoning and paragraph writing?

In Chapter 2, we learned that a body paragraph is a contributing argument for the essay thesis. This implies that building a paragraph is not restating its main idea in different words, but justifying that idea with proper reasoning.

Core knowledge input

Micro-lecture Reasoning and Paragraph Writing
MOOC Lesson 4

Reasoning and Paragraph Writing

What is reasoning?

Imagine doing a simple calculation like 6+3=9 or 6÷3=2. With two numbers and then an operation rule, we can draw a result. **Reasoning** follows a similar pattern. On the left of the equation are premises. The premises would go through a logic operation and then produce an inference — the thesis.

This process of leading the reader through the premises toward the desired thesis is called reasoning.

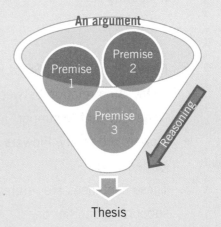

What does reasoning mean to paragraph writing?

On the one hand, a body paragraph as a whole is one of the lines of reasoning in an essay because it provides premises that can lead to the essay thesis. On the other hand, as each body paragraph is an argument itself, thus developing a paragraph means using details to justify the thesis of the paragraph, which is also the reasoning process. In either case, knowing what reasoning is and how to reason is critical for writing good body paragraphs.

Chapter 4   How to write a body paragraph?

Model 4-1

Examples of reasoning and non-reasoning

Reasoning Examples

- Every time I use a joke in my presentation, I would get applause at the end of the presentation. Therefore, a joke can help with a good audience response.

- Clare always smiles upon seeing him. Therefore, if Clare sees him today, she will smile.

- Here is a gentleman of a medical type, but with the air of a military man. Clearly an army doctor, then. He has just come from the tropics, for his face is dark, and that is not the natural tint of his skin, for his wrists are fair. He has undergone hardship and sickness, as his haggard face says clearly. His left arm has been injured. He holds it in a stiff and unnatural manner. Where in the tropics could an English army doctor have seen much hardship and got his arm wounded? Clearly in country A.

Non-Reasoning Examples

- Flowers smell good. Grass is green. Colors are good.
  There is no relation between these sentences. None can be regarded as a thesis. None is meant to support another.

- Flowers are pretty. Flowers make people feel good. There are many flowers in this garden.
  These sentences are related by the same topic, but none can be seen as logically supporting another one.

- Young people should learn independence. Young people should learn to rely on themselves. Young people shouldn't always turn to their parents for help. They shouldn't use their parents' money.
  These sentences repeat the same thesis in different ways, and no premise can be found among them.

Work in pairs. Check the paragraphs that contain reasoning, bracket the theses, and underline the premises. Cross the box in front of each non-reasoning paragraph and explain why.

1. ☐ Students should be given more recess time. In fact, studies have shown that students who enjoy a recess of more than 45 minutes consistently score better on tests immediately following the recess period. Clinical analysis further suggests that physical exercise during recess greatly improves the ability to focus on academic materials.

2. ☐ Imagine that you are a student. After 40 minutes study, you are given a recess that allows only a few words with your neighboring classmate. If you have to use the washroom, those few words become impossible. Stepping out of the classroom and stretching your limbs is unimaginable. After your very short relief from the previous class, the next class begins.

3. ☐ My mum is a very kind person. She is always willing to help others. One day, a beggar came to our house and asked for some food. Besides giving him some bread and butter, she also offered him some clean clothes and cash. What's more, she later asked around and tried to find him a job. My mum is always very gentle. Whenever she speaks, her voice is calm and gentle. Even with people who are being a little unreasonable, she can still talk in a very gentle and polite way.

4. ☐ We should try our best to protect the environment. If we do so, our world will become better and better. If we don't, however, we will suffer. So it is very urgent to try what we can to protect humanity's home.

2. How to incorporate reasoning into a body paragraph?

Since writing a body paragraph entails reasoning, we will go further in this section to see exactly how to incorporate reasoning into body paragraphs.

2.1 Understanding the structure of a body paragraph

Core knowledge input

MOOC Lesson 4

Three Fundamental Elements of a Body Paragraph

A body paragraph normally consists of three parts: a topic sentence, supporting sentences, and a concluding sentence. The first two are indispensable, and the last one is optional.

A topic sentence

A topic sentence states the central idea of a paragraph. Since a body paragraph is also a contributing argument in an essay, the topic sentence is then the argument thesis. Therefore, most of the strategies of writing a thesis statement discussed in Section 2.1, Chapter 3 apply also to the writing of a topic sentence. The only difference is that a topic sentence of a body paragraph is narrower and more focused than the thesis statement of an essay.

A topic sentence is usually the very first sentence of a paragraph. Though sometimes, skilled writers can also place it in the middle or end, for beginner writers the first sentence is always a better choice: This arrangement not only helps readers immediately grasp the main idea of the paragraph, but also prevents writers from getting distracted.

Supporting sentences

These sentences provide premises to justify the topic sentence. They demonstrate the reasoning process in the paragraph. More about writing supporting sentences will be discussed in the next "Core knowledge input."

A concluding sentence

A concluding sentence rephrases the central idea. It is not a required part of a body paragraph, but a clever repetition of the central idea can leave an impression. The concluding sentence can also serve as a kind reminder of the main idea, especially when the paragraph is a long argument.

Note that in some cases, when a body paragraph is a long argument, it may be divided into two or more consecutive paragraphs.

Model 4-2

Examples of body paragraphs

Read the following body paragraphs and notice the analysis of their structures.

topic sentence [supporting sentences] concluding sentence	**Native people create legends to explain unusual phenomena in their environment.** [A legend from the Hawaiian island of Kauai explains how the naupaka flower, a flower that grows on beaches there, got its unusual shape. The flower looks like half a small daisy — there are petals on one side only. The legend says that the marriage of two young lovers on the island was opposed by both sets of parents. The parents found the couple together on a beach one day, and to prevent them from being together, one of the families moved to the mountains, separating the young couples forever. As a result, the naupaka flower separated into two halves; one half moved to the mountains, and the other half stayed near the beach.] <u>This story is a good example of a legend invented by native people to interpret the world around them.</u>
topic sentence [supporting sentences] concluding sentence	**Synonyms, words that have the same basic meaning, do not always have the same emotional meaning.** [For example, the words *stingy* and *frugal* both mean "careful with money." However, calling someone stingy is an insult, but calling someone frugal is a compliment. Similarly, a person wants to be slender but not skinny, aggressive but not pushy.] <u>Therefore, you should be careful in choosing words because many so-called synonyms are not really synonyms at all.</u>

Practice 4-2

Read the following body paragraphs. Analyze each one by highlighting the topic sentence, bracketing the supporting sentences, and underlining the concluding sentence if there is any. Then discuss your answers with a partner.

1. Students who learn how to write well will earn better grades in most classes. This is true because most instructors assign a variety of written assignments, and depending on the class, these written assignments often encompass a large percentage of a student's final grade. For instance, all college students seeking a degree will be required to take a composition class. In this class alone, students will write five different essays. Furthermore, other classes, such as history, psychology, nursing, etc., also require students to write multiple essays. According to John Doe, a professor of English at Aims Community College, the average undergraduate student will write twenty-five different

essays while seeking a bachelor's degree. This number increases dramatically for students who go on to seek a graduate degree. Because all students, regardless of major, will be required to compose a large number of essays, it is important that they learn how to write well.

2. The negative effect of advertisements is that they mislead audiences. More often than not, sales talk in advertisements is equivocal. They invite the audience to imagine their own favorable fantasy, which is seldom true in reality. For example, a soft drink advertisement may claim that it is "cheaper than the leading brand but with the same quality." Potential buyers are tricked to think that this drink is less expensive than the most famous brand and the quality is still guaranteed. Actually, "leading" is a vague description that is open to interpretation.

3. Today, privacy has become a commodity that can be bought and sold. While many would view privacy as a constitutional right or even a fundamental human right, our age of big data has reduced privacy to dollar figure. There have been efforts — both serious and silly — to quantify the value of privacy. Browser add-ons (插件) such as Privacyfix try to show users their value to companies, and a recent study suggested that free Internet services offer $2,600 in value to users in exchange for their data.

Practice 4-3

Imagine you are planning body paragraphs for each of the following thesis statements. Complete the following outlines.

Preparing for the College Entrance Examination is very demanding.

Topic sentence of body paragraph 1: When preparing for the College Entrance Examination, you have to tackle strong peer pressure.

Topic sentence of body paragraph 2: 1. _____

_____

Topic sentence of body paragraph 3: 2. _____

Preparing for the College Entrance Examination is an instructive experience.

Topic sentence of body paragraph 1: You can learn how to manage time through preparing for the College Entrance Examination.

Topic sentence of body paragraph 2: 3. _____
_____

Topic sentence of body paragraph 3: 4. _____
_____

Practice 4-4

Write a proper topic sentence for the following paragraphs. The first word of each paragraph has been given. Then share your sentences with a partner.

1. Clothes _____.
   Hollander once observed that the same person may exhibit different gestures and manners of talking when wearing different clothes. This person talks very confidently and acts promptly when in his suit and ties, but very liberal and feeble after changing into his jeans. When asked, he explains his "suit feelings" as empowered and "jean feelings" as relaxed. It looks like people's perception of themselves can be very predicted based on the clothes they wear.

2. Clothes _____.
   The clothes speak about one's self-perception: How I feel about myself. An investigation made by Hollander records the words of an interviewee: If I am wearing a neat business suit, I feel empowered; if I am wearing some baggy clothes, I feel slouchy or relaxed. Clothes can also reflect one's taste, social level, financial status, and many other aspects. When carrying such abundant messages about himself, the wearer is communicating without uttering words and people would respond to the clothes. The

response can be acceptance, rejection, or a misunderstanding, and then a decision in how to approach the wearer.

2.2 Writing supporting sentences with proper reasoning

Core knowledge input

 Micro-lecture How to Reason with Supporting Sentences
MOOC Lesson 4

How to Reason with Supporting Sentences

In a paragraph, writers use supporting sentences to justify the topic sentence. And the strength of such justification shows the **supportiveness** of a paragraph. To improve supportiveness, writers use both reasons and evidence.

Use reasons as logical support.

In an argument, a **reason** is a statement we use to tell why we believe a thesis to be true. It is normally an opinion, serving as a logical answer to the question "Why do you think so?". In a body paragraph, one or more reasons may be offered to tell why the writer believes the claim of the topic sentence. The underlined sentence in the example below is a reason supporting the topic sentence.

> Writing academic paragraphs should be the first skill students learn in college <u>because it is the most frequently required skill in academic writing</u>. [Research by the Association of Essay Writing in five universities shows that students are required to write academic paragraphs in 90% of their assessment tasks.]

Use evidence as proof.

Evidence is the facts that we use to show the truthfulness of the thesis and the reasons. It comes in different forms: examples, case studies, narratives, statistics, testimonies, common knowledge, research findings, etc. In the above example, the bracketed sentence presents a research finding as evidence to support the truthfulness of the reason.

As reflected in the quotation at the beginning of the chapter, evidence is an indispensable element of reasoning. A convincing line of reasoning always consists of evidence because facts (evidence) are more persuasive than opinions (reasons and thesis) by nature. For this, some paragraphs may have only evidence as premises (e.g. paragraphs in Model 4-2).

Model 4-3

Reasons and evidence in body paragraphs

Read the following paragraphs and notice the analysis of their reasoning.

thesis reason [evidence] research findings	**Carbon dioxide gets most of the attention, but unless methane (甲烷) emissions are limited, there is little hope of stabilizing the climate.** Although human activity emits far less methane than carbon dioxide, methane packs a heavier punch. [According to research, over the course of 20 years, a ton of the gas will warm the atmosphere about 86 times more than a ton of CO_2. As a result, methane is responsible for 23% of the rise in temperatures since pre-industrial times.]
reason [evidence] a specific example thesis	So far, smart technologies are playing essential roles in protecting China's ecosystem. [For example, a nature reserve in northwest China's Gansu Province has installed an artificial intelligence-enabled video monitoring system that aids researchers in collecting real-time data on wildlife without disrupting the natural settings of these wild animals. For more than two years now, the AI-enabled video monitoring system, which takes images of all the 110 giant pandas together with other wildlife in the reserve via about 300 infrared cameras, has been helping researchers to monitor the health and safety of these wild animals.] **Therefore, smart technology should be advanced to complement China's efforts in protecting biodiversity.**
thesis reasons ①②③④ [evidence] specific examples	**Lily is a lovely woman.** ①She knows how to enjoy life. [On a rainy summer afternoon, she would arrange a tea set and suiting flowers and idle away the afternoon with a pleasant chat with her husband.] ②She is also an expert in cooking. [She can magically transform an ordinary eggplant into a very tempting stew. Wherever she goes, she carries around her an aroma of delicious food.] ③[What is more, she appreciates beautiful objects, beautiful words, beautiful colors, beautiful shapes. She would be elated at the sight of the wide expanse of water, and thrilled by some medieval manuscripts.] Truly she is a woman of sophisticated taste. ④And yet she is also cultivated, gentle, and kind. [She would put a blanket around the guest who falls asleep while she is discussing painting and literature in her womanish manner with her husband.]

Chapter 4 — How to write a body paragraph?

Practice 4-5

Work in pairs. Tell if the following paragraphs contain reasons and evidence. If yes, check the boxes in front, underline the reasons, and bracket the evidence. If not, cross the boxes in front.

1. ☐ Decisive efforts in global cooperation are of top urgency today for global vaccine equity. Governments, world business communities, and other global foundations should play a greater role in donating vaccines.

2. ☐ It does not make much business sense to have employees working so long that they only get to sleep five hours a night. They can hardly be operating at full efficiency when they are dog-tired.

3. ☐ While the number of deaths is increasing due to faster population aging, the national death rate was 7.18 per thousand in 2021, putting the natural population growth rate at 0.34 per thousand. When the population growth rate drops to below 0.5 per thousand, it is defined as zero growth zone. Thus, the population growth is at a great turning point in history in that it came to a stop, entering into a new stage of long-term decline.

4. ☐ It is important that pregnant women become aware of the potential risks posed by cats. Cats are hosts to infectious toxoplasma gondii, a protozoa that causes the disease, toxoplasmosis, in mammals such as humans. Adult humans rarely show signs of significant disease if they become infected. However, if pregnant women become infected, the fetus can become infected by parasites and suffer serious congenital damage. In the worst cases, infants may lose their eyesight and acquire motor deficits. The symptoms of the disease are not evident in cats so there is no way of knowing if a particular cat is a risk.

5. ☐ The world of business is one area in which technology is isolating us. Many people now work alone at home. With access to a large central computer, employees such as secretaries, insurance agents, and accountants do their jobs at display terminals in their own homes. They no longer have to see the people they're dealing with. In addition, employees are often paid in an impersonal way. Workers' salaries are automatically credited to their bank accounts, eliminating the need for paychecks. Fewer people stand in line with their coworkers to receive their pay or cash their checks. Finally, personal banking is becoming a detached process. Customers

interact with machines rather than people to deposit or withdraw money from their accounts. Even some bank loans are approved or rejected, not in an interview with a loan officer, but by a computer program.

6. ☐ A little bit of work may be satisfying but too much is not. An enterprising junior analyst at Goldman Sachs recently surveyed his peers and fashioned his report in the style of a research presentation from the investment bank itself. The survey found those first-year analysts had worked an average of 98 hours a week since the start of 2021, and only managed five hours of sleep a night. It found that 77% of them had been the subject of workplace abuse, that 75% had sought, or considered seeking, counseling, and that, on average, the cohort had suffered sharp declines in mental and physical health. Unsurprisingly, the analysts thought it was unlikely they would still be working at the bank in six months.

Practice 4-6

Work with the same partner. Develop an argument for each of the theses below. Provide two reasons in support of the thesis and at least one piece of evidence for each reason. Then write a complete body paragraph based on either of the diagrams.

Tips

Consider the following prompt questions when developing your arguments.
- Why do you believe the ideas conveyed in the thesis?
- What facts can support the thesis, such as examples, your own experiences, some events, statistics, etc.?

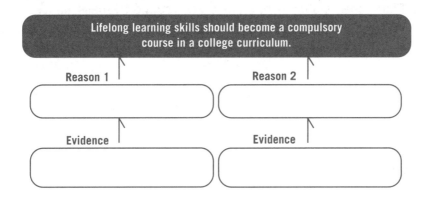

Trust begets social prosperity.

Reason 1

Reason 2

Evidence

Evidence

Write your paragraph here. _____

_____

_____

_____

_____

_____

3. How to evaluate the quality of a body paragraph?

How do we evaluate the quality of the body paragraphs we wrote in the previous section? Four aspects should be considered: supportiveness, unity, coherence, and cohesion. We have discussed supportiveness in the previous section. But there is more we can do.

3.1 Unity of a paragraph

Micro-lecture Maintaining Unity in a Paragraph
MOOC Lesson 4

Maintaining Unity in a Paragraph

An important element in judging the quality of a paragraph is **unity**, which means that a paragraph discusses one and only one main idea. There are two aspects to look into when improving the unity of a body paragraph.

- A paragraph has only one topic sentence.
- All the other sentences are directly supportive of the topic sentence.

For example, if we write a paragraph advancing the idea that red-light running is a deadly crime, we shall focus the discussion on the act being deadly and causing serious damages; do not discuss how difficult it is to control traffic, or how severe the punishment should be.

Model 4-4

Positive and negative examples of unity

Read the paragraphs and study the analysis below.

Colors create biological reactions in our bodies and thus change our behavior. In one study, prisoners were put in a pink room, and they underwent a drastic decrease in muscle strength and hostility within 2.7 seconds. In another study, athletes needing short bursts of energy were exposed to red light. Their muscle strength increased by 13.5 percent, and electrical activity in their arm muscles increased by 5.8 percent. Athletes needing more endurance for longer performances responded best when exposed to blue light. Other studies have shown that the color green is calming. **Green is very popular in many cultures. Many religious temples throughout the world use green and blue to balance heavenly peace with spiritual growth.** To sum up, color influences us in many ways.

The paragraph above lacks unity. The sentences in bold are irrelevant information and they fail to support the topic sentence that "Colors create biological reactions in our bodies and thus change our behavior."

Colors create biological reactions in our bodies and thus change our behavior. In one study, prisoners were put in a pink room, and they underwent a drastic decrease in muscles strength and hostility within 2.7 seconds. In another study, athletes needing short bursts of energy were exposed to red light. Their muscle strength increased by 13.5 percent, and electrical activity in their arm muscles increased by 5.8 percent. Athletes needing more endurance for longer performances responded best when exposed to blue light. Other studies have shown that the color green is calming. After London's Blackfriars Bridge was painted green, the number of suicides decreased by 34 percent. These and other studies clearly demonstrate that color affects not only our moods but behavior as well.

This paragraph has unity because every supporting sentence works in the same direction — to justify the topic sentence.

Practice 4-7

Work in pairs. Decide whether the following paragraphs have unity. If yes, check the boxes in front. If not, cross the boxes and explain the problems.

1. ☐ Colors create biological reactions in our bodies. These reactions, in turn, can change our behavior. In one study, athletes needing short bursts of energy were exposed to red light. Their muscle strength increased by 13.5 percent, and electrical activity in their arm muscles increased by 5.8 percent. Athletes needing more endurance for longer performances responded best when exposed to blue light. Blue is not a good color for dinnerware, however. Food looks less appetizing when it is served on blue plates, perhaps because very few foods in nature are of that color. Other studies have shown that the color green is calming. After London's Blackfriars Bridge was painted green, the number of suicides decreased by 34 percent. It is clear that color affects

not just our moods but our behavior as well.

2. ☐ I think the popularity of horror films with teens is due to teenagers' desires to test their limits in the real world, to see how far they can go before they get scared. Horror films allow teens to test their limits in the safety of the movie theater, where they can put themselves in the position of the teenagers in the film without any real danger to themselves. Last week, I went to see the sci-fi and horror film *Alien* and got so scared anticipating the alien's attack on the crew that I had to leave the theater. My friends didn't seem as scared, so I felt kind of stupid, but for me, that film was a bit more horrifying than I could take. Children obviously would find horror films too scary; everything would seem too real, too possible, so that small children could end up with horrifying nightmares.

3. ☐ Competition is a powerful force to urge people to excel themselves. Without competition, there would be no challenge and we would not test our limits or even go beyond them. If, in a sports game, two or more persons are in a competition, athletes have to bring their A-game to outplay the opponent. If, unfortunately, one loses the game, he must set his heart and mind to get better to win the next competition. In this way, the athletes are driven to improve themselves. In addition, competition is a catalyst to boost innovation. For example, in Silicon Valley, many new technologies are released on a daily basis. No company could afford to slacken and relax in their innovative undertakings. Subject to the competitive industry environment, they have to come up with new, distinctive, and unique ideas to survive. Owing to this, we enjoy many benefits brought by their cutting-edge design and invention, which resulted from the competition.

4. ☐ The art in scientific thinking — whether in physics, biology, or economics — is deciding which assumptions to make. Suppose, for instance, that we were dropping a beach ball rather than a marble from the top of a building. Our physicist would realize that the assumption of no friction is far less accurate in this case: Friction exerts a greater force on a beach ball than on a marble. The assumption that gravity works in a vacuum is reasonable for studying a falling marble but not for studying a falling beach ball.

3.2 Coherence of a paragraph

Core knowledge input

Micro-lecture How to Achieve Coherence
MOOC Lesson 4

How to Achieve Coherence

Besides supportiveness and unity, **coherence** is the third factor to consider when you arrange the materials of a paragraph. Coherence means good organization. The supporting sentences are organized so well that it is very easy for readers to follow the writer's line of reasoning. This good organization can be achieved in two steps.

1. Divide the supporting material into different topical chunks.

Review the third paragraph in Model 4-3. To show that Lily is a lovely woman, the author offers four chunks of premises: knowing how to enjoy life, being good at cooking, having a sophisticated taste, and being kind. Reasons and evidence of the same topic are grouped within the same chunk.

2. Put the topical chunks in order.

After dividing the material into neat chunks, the next job for the writer is to put the chunks in order. In the same example in Model 4-3, the author orders the chunks into four parallel aspects. This is a random order: It does not matter which one goes first and which one goes last. However, this is a rare case. More often, we are advised to adopt one of the following orders: time order, space order, and degree order.

If we want to list the steps of a certain process, or introduce a series of events, we can use time order; if we are to discuss an issue where location elements are involved, we can try space order: inside-outside, front-middle-back, east-west, far-near, etc. Sometimes, a certain chunk deals with a more important issue than others do; in this case, we discuss the more important first, and leave the less important to the secondary or last place. This is called degree order.

Model 4-5

Coherence achieved by organizing the premises

Read the following paragraph and notice the analysis about its coherence.

The process of machine translation of languages is complex. To translate a document from English into Japanese, for example, the computer first analyzes an English sentence, determining its grammatical structure and identifying the subject, predicate, object(s), and modifier(s). Next, the words are translated by an English-Japanese dictionary. After that, another part of the computer program analyzes the resulting awkward jumble of words and meanings and produces an intelligible sentence based on the rules of Japanese syntax and the machine's understanding of what the original English sentence meant. Finally, a human bilingual editor polishes the computer-produced translation.

The topic sentence of this paragraph is the first sentence. The rest of the sentences are descriptions of a process, and therefore we get the chunks of step 1, step 2, step 3, and step 4 of the machine translation process. The chunks are neatly divided, and they are organized in a time order. We would say this paragraph has good coherence.

Practice 4-8

Work in pairs. Read the following paragraphs and decide if they are coherent. If yes, check the boxes in front. If not, cross the boxes and revise the paragraph.

Tips

Evaluate their coherence by considering the following prompt questions.

- What are the reasons and evidence offered in the paragraph?
- Does the author group the reasons and evidence into topical chunks?
- What order does the author use to organize the reasons and evidence?

1. ☐ French and U.S. business managers have decidedly different management styles. French meetings, for example, are long and rambling and rarely end on time.

Furthermore, meetings often end without closure. Managers in the United States, on the other hand, make an effort to start and stop a meeting on time, and North American business meetings typically end with decisions and action plans. Another difference involves documentation. North Americans adore documentation; they have a procedure manual for everything. The French, in contrast, think this is childish. French managers find it difficult to stick to a schedule, but U.S. managers are intolerant of delays. In addition, the French prefer to work alone, whereas North Americans like to work in teams. Another major difference in management style is that in French companies, authority comes from the top. French managers do not share information with subordinates and make decisions with little participation by employees beneath them. In U.S. companies, however, top managers share information and frequently solicit input from subordinates.

2. ☐ The Cass School summer carnival in January is a special event everyone should attend. There are activities for everyone. Each room gives prizes like yo-yos, bug-eyed glasses, and light-up pens. This year, one classroom had a fishpond for little kids. Another room painted a clown with a huge mouth on a board for a beanbag toss. Other rooms had shoe scrambles and relay races. Winning a prize always adds a little excitement to each activity. For a little summer fun, the Cass School carnival is worth a visit.

3.3 Cohesion of a paragraph

Core knowledge input

MOOC Lesson 4

How to Achieve Cohesion

Once coherence is achieved, the next goal is to glue the neatly-divided and well-ordered topical chunks together so that readers can have a smooth reading experience. This smoothness is called **cohesion**. Cohesion means the ideas flow smoothly from one to the next. If coherence guarantees smooth logical progression of ideas, cohesion tackles the smoothness of the textual presentation of those ideas. The following techniques are helpful to achieve cohesion.

1. Connectives

Connectives are words or phrases that link sentences and paragraphs. They indicate the relation between ideas so that there are no abrupt jumps or breaks between ideas. They act like signposts offering directions to readers so that they can easily follow the writer's line of reasoning. There are several types of connectives.

Common Connectives in Writing	
Giving a similar idea	and, also, too, as well, both … and, not only … but also, another, as well as, either…or, neither … nor, likewise, similarly
Giving a further idea	indeed, in fact, particularly, especially, still, besides, furthermore, in addition, moreover, an additional …, another
Giving a different idea	but, yet, or, however, on the other hand, nevertheless, nonetheless, while, although, even though, though, despite, in spite of, in contrast, instead, on the contrary, rather, whereas, alternatively, otherwise
Giving an explanation	in other words, more specifically, that is, for example, for instance, such as, to exemplify
Giving a reason	for, because, since, as, due to, as a result of, for this reason, according to
Giving a result	so, as a consequence, as a result, consequently, hence, therefore, thus
Concluding signal	all in all, in brief, in short, to conclude, to summarize, in conclusion, in summary, in a word
Degree signal	first, first of all, first and foremost, second, more important, most important, more significantly, above all, most of all, the best / worst …
Time signal	first, first of all, second, third, next, then, after that, meanwhile, in the meantime, finally, last of all, subsequently, before, while, when, since
Space signal	next to, across, on the opposite side, to the left, to the right, above, below, near, nearby, beside, on top of, under, over, underneath, far from

2. Repetition of key words

Repeating key words in a paragraph is an important technique for achieving cohesion. Of course, careless or excessive repetition is boring. But used skillfully and selectively, as in the paragraphs in Model 4-7 below, this technique can hold sentences together and secure readers' attention on the central idea.

Chapter 4   How to write a body paragraph?

Synonyms and pronouns can help alleviate any awkwardness caused by repeating the exact same words.

Model 4-6

Cohesion achieved with connectives

Study the following two paragraphs and see how connectives help with cohesion.

As a result of[1] economic reforms in the past 10 years, state-owned, private, and foreign-funded market entities have reinforced the three growth drivers – consumption, investment, and export. Since[2] 2012, China's market entities grew significantly in both number and size. In 2020[3], among all corporate legal entities, state-owned, private, and foreign-funded ones accounted for 1.2 percent, 98 percent, and 0.8 percent respectively. In 2021[4], of the 150 million market entities nationwide, over 100 million were individually owned businesses. In the same year[5], private investment registered a 7 percent growth, higher than the national level of 4.9 percent.	[1] indicating a reason [2] a time signal [3] [4] [5] showing a development of time
In 2021, China became the world's second largest research and development (R&D) spender with a total R&D expenditure of 2.44 percent of its GDP, and[6] 6.09 percent of such spending going to basic research, marking a year-on-year growth of 15.6 percent. Meanwhile[7], the turnover of China's technology contracts exceeded 3.7 trillion yuan and the number of its domestic patents granted and of international patents filed under the Patent Cooperation Treaty ranked first worldwide. Moreover[8], China also leads the world in terms of the numbers of its internationally published science and technology related papers and citations. All of these[9], together with nearly $980 billion worth of high-tech product exports, have made China a science and technology backbone for the world.	[6] [7] indicating a similar idea [8] indicating a further idea [9] indicating a summary

Model 4-7

Cohesion achieved by repeating key words

Study the following paragraphs and notice how the authors make them cohesive by repeating the key words and using synonyms and pronouns.

<u>repetition and synonyms</u> <u>of the key words</u> <u>"economic recession"</u> [repetition and synonyms of the key word "restaurant industry"]	Many problems in the economy are impacting the [restaurant industry]. The factor responsible for most of these negative impacts is the <u>economic recession</u>. Due to <u>weak economic conditions</u>, the U.S. [food service industry] revenues will only rise 2.5% in 2008, compared to the 4.6% increase in 2007; the National Restaurant Association reports this to be among the poorest sales performances by the domestic [restaurant industry] in nearly four decades. In response to the <u>weak economic conditions</u>, [restaurants] are increasing prices only enough to offset higher costs, rather than to expand profit margins. Also, unemployment in the United States affects [restaurants] with rates reaching 5.3% in 2008 compared to 4.6% in 2007. The government has also increased operating costs for [restaurants] by increasing the federal minimum wage to $7.25 in 2009. Finally, consumers are traveling less which is lowering [restaurant] sales; travelers and visitors accounted for a median of 15% of sales at quick service [restaurants]. At this time, the <u>weak economic conditions</u> have had a major impact on the [food service industry].
<u>repetition of the key word</u> <u>"rewarding"</u> [repetition and pronouns of the key words "scientific experiments"]	Doing [scientific experiments] is not always <u>rewarding</u>. Frequently, [they] do not work out as expected. In such cases, [they] are considered failures until some other scientist tries [them] again. [Those] that work out better the second time, however, are the [ones] that promise the most <u>rewards</u>.

Practice 4-9

Work in pairs. Compare the following pairs of paragraphs. Underline the words or phrases used by the authors to achieve cohesion. Explain to each other how they make one paragraph more cohesive than the other.

1. One difference among the world's seas and oceans is that the salinity varies in different climate zones. The Baltic Sea in northern Europe is only one-fourth as salty as the Red Sea in the Middle East. There are reasons for this. In warm climates, water evaporates rapidly. The concentration of salt is greater. The surrounding land is dry and does not contribute much freshwater to dilute the salty seawater. In cold climate zones, water evaporates slowly. The runoff created by melting snow adds a considerable amount of fresh water to dilute the saline seawater.

One difference among the world's seas and oceans is that the salinity varies in different climate zones. For example, the Baltic Sea in northern Europe is only one-fourth as saline as the Red Sea in the Middle East. There are two reasons for this. First of all, in warm climate zones, water evaporates rapidly; therefore, the concentration of salt is greater. Second, the surrounding land is dry; consequently, it does not contribute much freshwater to dilute the salty seawater. In cold climate zones, on the other hand, water evaporates slowly. Furthermore, the runoff created by melting snow adds a considerable amount of fresh water to dilute the saline seawater.

2. School should be able to provide students with abundant opportunities to develop their abilities and show their talents. There is a great variety of student associations, regular sports meetings, as well as evening parties. Students can organize them, advertise them, and participate in them. They develop the ability and show themselves, which they cannot achieve at home.

School should be able to provide students with abundant opportunities to develop their abilities and show their talents. These opportunities include, for instance, a great variety of student associations, regular sports meetings, as well as evening parties. When students organize or advertise them, they acquire relevant skills or abilities, be it leadership, communication skills, marketing strategies, or digital competence. And when students participate in these activities, they are also able to show themselves in front of others, which will boost their confidence. All of this, however, cannot be achieved simply by studying at home.

Model 4-8

Body paragraphs in a critical essay
Study the model essay and pay attention to the supportiveness, unity, coherence, and cohesion of the body paragraphs.

Kids Should Not Have Social Media

thesis statement	❶ Social media has become a huge part of children and teen lifestyles in recent years. Social media has helped children develop communication skills, spread ideas, and allowed them to make friends online. However, **social media is also highly detrimental to the livelihood of our children.**

1st body paragraph	❷ ①*Growing up* with the constant influence of social media, children focused their lives on living up to the unrealistic standards social media present them with. **Many children have been forced to grow up.** [They change the clothes they wear, the way they look, their views and judgments, and their lifestyle as a whole in order to establish a more favorable image.] ②People's identity development follows biological rules, and violation of this natural development would probably incur unfavorable effects. However, most of the children, being immature and ill-informed, do not know the future effects of being forced to *grow up*.

topic sentence
reasons ①②
[evidence]
specific examples

connectives

repetition of key words

2nd & 3rd body
paragraphs as one
contributing argument

topic sentence
reason
[evidence]
① research findings
② testimony
repetition of key words
connectives

interpretation of
evidence ② as the
concluding sentence

4th body paragraph
topic sentence
reasons ①②
repetition of key words
connectives
[evidence] testimony

conclusion

❸ **Besides** affecting *children's* outside image, social media also affects *children's* mental health. *Those* who grew up on social media are more susceptible to anxiety, depression, and other psychological disorders. ①[Studies have shown that *those* who spend more time on social media are more likely to feel jealous as they compare their lifestyles to people on social media.]

❹ ②["*Children* do not understand that people on social media only show highlights of their lives and most of it is fake," says Belinda Miguel, a student at Huntington Beach High School. "Because of this, *children* put more pressure on themselves to become someone they are not."] This pressure of having a "perfect" life affects *children's* lifestyles and ultimately ruins their childhood as they are constantly focused on how many likes or followers they have.

❺ **Not only** do children compare themselves to other people on social media, **but** they are **also** more prone to cyberbullying. ①Many people throughout their lives have experienced *bullying*, but even more have experienced *cyberbullying*. ②Social media is an easy way to spread rumors and judge one another. ["Being behind a screen makes it easier for one to say things they wouldn't say to one's face," says Tyler Durrant, a student at Huntington Beach High School.]

❻ Ultimately, kids should spend time with their friends, family, or go outside, instead of going on social media as they should not need to worry about how they appear toward others, or have the pressure of having a perfect life, or have to confront an overwhelming amount of judging eyes, or become the victim of cyberbullying. One isn't a kid for long and instead of trying to meet the various demands and face the unfair harms imposed by social media, kids should be given the opportunity to enjoy a pure and carefree childhood.

Practice 4-10

Work in pairs. Exchange the paragraphs you wrote in Practice 4-6. Evaluate them against the four criteria of supportiveness, unity, coherence, and cohesion. Revise them for your partner if necessary.

From reading to writing

■ Reading
Read the essay and finish the tasks.

What China Reveals About the Future of Business Innovation

❶ When many Western consumer companies develop a new product, they set out on a long, slow process with an uncertain outcome. That's because innovation typically starts internally, with ideas that flow from the business to the consumer (B2C). A full rollout could take several months, and during that period, executives are haunted by a single question: "I wonder if this thing will sell?" All too often, it won't because by the time the product is finally available, the market has already moved on.

❷ In the current business environment, this model for innovation no longer works, and China is at the forefront with a new approach: using customer insights, largely generated through digital interactions, to inform product development. We call it customer-to-business (C2B) innovation.

❸ C2B innovation is becoming the norm in China. By closely following customer trends via e-commerce platforms, social media, and current events, Chinese companies can design new products that better reflect customers' needs. These products are then quickly produced and distributed through a few select channels. Winning products are rapidly scaled up, those that do not catch on are quickly withdrawn, and the company regroups to focus on a new opportunity. The entire process, from idea to launch, takes weeks rather than months.

❹ Four aspects of the market allow China to lead in C2B innovation.

❺ Customer data. Chinese consumers typically spend more time online than people in most of the other markets, and they spend that time on a concentrated set of e-commerce sites. Rather than merely listing product features and ratings, these e-commerce sites in China include entertainment, social sharing, and community options, along with accurate recommendations based on a customer's profile. Each experience, therefore, is personalized and allows the customer to offer feedback.

❻ The bottom line is that companies operating in China have access to far more data, from a wide range of sources, along the entire path to purchase, and they are able to integrate it all into a single, coherent view of individual consumers. Every day in 2016, for example, users on a typical Chinese e-commerce site shared 20 million product reviews and posted 2 million questions about products to Q&A forums. Leading companies are effectively using bots and machine learning to track and process large volumes of real-time customer input from social media, transaction data, and customer feedback. This efficiently turns rich data into insights about consumers' preferences and unmet needs.

❼ Increasingly, this data is being used to shape new product launches. For example, a famous Chinese durable-goods manufacturer, designed a new dishwasher on the basis of consumer insights captured from consumer data. The dishwasher, which launched in 2015, sold 38,000 units in 2016.

❽ Access to distribution. According to Alex Rampell, a general partner in the venture capital firm Andreessen Horowitz, "The battle between every startup and incumbent comes down to whether the startup gets distribution before the incumbent gets innovation." E-commerce, however, largely solves the distribution challenge for companies. With penetration rates that are higher than anywhere else in the world, and less retail infrastructure to manage, companies in China don't have to spend much time thinking about distribution. Most online purchases go through one of a small number of very dominant online platforms, giving large and small brands an easy and economical means of getting new products in front of consumers nationwide.

❾ For example, a privately owned dairy company in China, has been using data from marketplace forums to better understand customer demands and inform all stages of the innovation cycle, from research to manufacturing to distribution. Data insights help the company to identify unmet needs, test formulations and packaging, and more precisely target customers. As a result, the company has reduced the time required for development of the initial concept to full launch from a year and a half to just three months. Furthermore, the company is on track to launch three times as many products in 2017 as it did in 2016, many of which are distributed only online.

⑩ Flexible manufacturing. Companies operating in China can readily tap into the country's strong manufacturing base and take advantage of flexible approaches, such as small-volume runs and frequent changes to production lines. Geographic proximity helps as well: Companies are simply closer to their production facilities, reducing transit time and logistics. The fashion industry is at the forefront of this shift to faster distribution. In China, "fast-react" suppliers enable fashion companies to sell products before they are even manufactured. Sale to delivery takes place within three days.

⑪ Agile product development. When e-commerce emerged, China's consumer companies were less mature than their competitors in the West. That immaturity, which initially seemed like a hindrance, has quickly become an advantage: These companies do not have a decades-long legacy of physical retail operations and habits to unravel. Instead, a flood of newer brands and more entrepreneurial companies have emerged, with faster decision making, diminished bureaucracy, and less institutional inertia — leading to a far more vibrant market in which speed is a key differentiator.

⑫ For example, another brand, which sells packaged nuts, is China's first — and currently largest — online-only snack foods company. In 2015, just three years after launch, the brand's revenue reached $319 million. This was mostly due to smaller, agile teams that closely follow market developments and quickly adjust the product attributes in response, without having to unwind entrenched legacy processes.

⑬ This approach to innovation — faster product launches fueled by consumer insights and agile processes — will soon become the norm worldwide. And Western companies can adapt what is happening to China in their home markets.

Writing technique questions

Based on what you have learned in this chapter, consider the following questions. Then discuss with your group your answers and seek a consensus.

1. What is the thesis of this essay? Where does the author state it?
2. There are four contributing arguments in the body paragraphs. Locate them.
3. What is the topic sentence for each of the contributing arguments? Underline them in the paragraphs or summarize them in your own words.
4. Study Paras. 5 and 7 closely. Consider the following questions.
   1) What reasons and evidence are offered?
   2) How are the reasons and evidence grouped into topical chunks?
   3) What techniques are used to achieve cohesion?

Critical thinking questions

Consider the questions below and finish the tasks.

1. How have you benefited from the e-commerce innovation in China? Give personal experiences to showcase the benefits.
2. Share your answers to the questions above with your group.
3. Focus on two of the benefits most frequently mentioned by your group members. Then discuss the following questions.
   3.1 Why do you think e-commerce innovation brings about those benefits? Give one reason for each.
   3.2 What news, reports, examples, events, or statistics besides your own experiences can support your reasons? Give one piece of evidence for each of your reasons.

Chapter 4 How to write a body paragraph?

■ **Writing**
Based on your answers to the critical thinking questions, write a body paragraph following the template below. Mind the suppotiveness, unity, coherence, and cohesion.

E-commerce innovation in China has [one the benefits your group has

worked on] _____

A reason for me to think so is that_____

_____

[Provide 2 pieces of evidence: your own experience + one from

Exercise 3.2 of the critical thinking questions]_____

_____

_____

_____

_____

_____

_____

_____

_____

REFLECTION

This chapter discussed how to incorporate reasoning into body paragraphs. Now it's time to review and reflect on what you have learned. Work in pairs and take turns to answer the following questions. Check them as you answer each one.

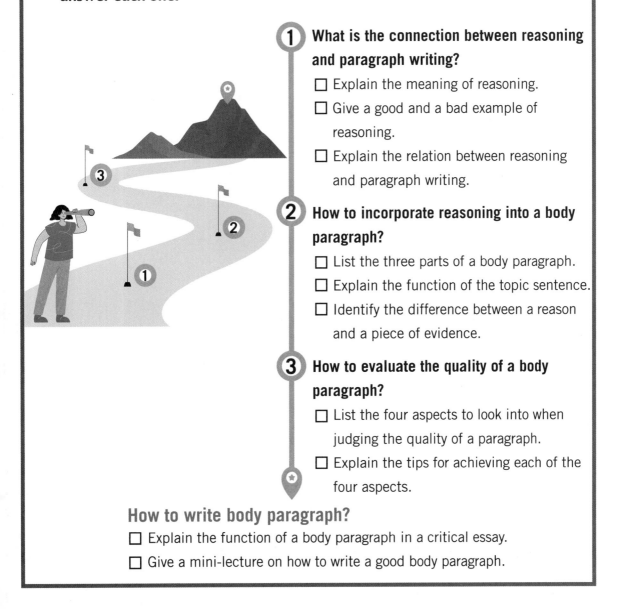

1 **What is the connection between reasoning and paragraph writing?**
- ☐ Explain the meaning of reasoning.
- ☐ Give a good and a bad example of reasoning.
- ☐ Explain the relation between reasoning and paragraph writing.

2 **How to incorporate reasoning into a body paragraph?**
- ☐ List the three parts of a body paragraph.
- ☐ Explain the function of the topic sentence.
- ☐ Identify the difference between a reason and a piece of evidence.

3 **How to evaluate the quality of a body paragraph?**
- ☐ List the four aspects to look into when judging the quality of a paragraph.
- ☐ Explain the tips for achieving each of the four aspects.

How to write body paragraph?
- ☐ Explain the function of a body paragraph in a critical essay.
- ☐ Give a mini-lecture on how to write a good body paragraph.

Chapter 5

How to apply deductive reasoning to writing?

以类取，以类予。

——《墨子·小取》

Through kinds choices are made; through kinds inferences are drawn.

——"Choosing the Lesser," *The Mozi*

Chapter roadmap

1. What is deductive reasoning?

2. How to develop deductive arguments with principles?

3. How to develop deductive arguments with definitions?

How to apply deductive reasoning to writing?

Learning outcomes

At the end of this chapter, you will be able to

- use proper examples to explain what deductive reasoning is;
- understand the deductive reasoning strategies of applying a principle and applying a definition;
- develop deductive arguments with the two strategies above;
- compose deductive essays.

From reading to writing

Identify how Chinese wisdom can contribute to humanity's development and write a deductive essay on this topic.

1. What is deductive reasoning?

The classic quote from *The Mozi* at the beginning of this chapter indicates two major types of reasoning: deductive reasoning and inductive reasoning. This chapter deals with the former one, leaving the latter for Chapter 6.

Deductive Reasoning: What and Why

What is deductive reasoning?

Deductive reasoning, or deductive logic, is a type of argument used in both academia and everyday life. In a valid deductive argument, if all the premises are true, then the thesis must be true. Deductive reasoning allows for certainty as long as certain rules are followed.

Here is a valid deductive argument:

Premise 1: If it's sunny in Shanghai, then he won't be carrying an umbrella.

Premise 2: It's sunny in Shanghai.

Thesis: So, he won't be carrying an umbrella.

In the example above, the author provides two premises to guarantee the truth of the thesis. If the two premises are both true, the thesis cannot be false. Thus, it is called a deductively valid argument.

Why do we need deductive reasoning?

Deductive reasoning proves highly useful during discussions, speeches, writings, and literary pieces. Since the logic of deductive reasoning is such that if the premise is true, it is impossible for the thesis to be false, the written pieces using it are often very persuasive and convincing. Moreover, deductive reasoning allows writing and speaking to be clear, rhetorical, and effective. It removes ambiguities and confusions in the arguments and helps a person become a fluent and eloquent speaker and writer.

Chapter 5 How to apply deductive reasoning to writing?

Model 5-1

Examples of deductive reasoning

- Red meat has iron in it, and beef is red meat. Therefore, beef has iron in it.
- My boss said the person with the highest sales would get a promotion at the end of the year. I generated the highest sales, so I am looking forward to a promotion.
- The use and disinfection of masks are necessary to prevent infection. We want to prevent infection. Therefore, it is important for us to wear a mask and disinfect it.
- One of our customers was unhappy with his experience solely because he waited long for a return phone call. Had we provided a quicker response, he would have been more satisfied.
- We invest in people who make the biggest sales for our company. And we know that our biggest sales come from executives who live in our company's home state. Therefore, we should allocate more of our marketing dollars to targeting executives in that state.

Practice 5-1

Which argument from each of the following pairs is a deduction? Circle the letter in front of it.

1. A: My mother is Irish. She has blond hair. Therefore, everyone from Ireland has blond hair.

   B: Everyone from Ireland has blond hair. My mother is Irish. Therefore, my mother has blond hair.

2. A: Most of our snowstorms come from the north. It's starting to snow. This snowstorm must be coming from the north.

   B: All of our snowstorms come from the north. It's starting to snow. Therefore, the storm is coming from the north.

3. A: All lipsticks in my bag are red. The first lipstick I pulled from my bag is red. Therefore, the second lipstick I pull from my bag will be red, too.

   B: The first lipstick I pulled from my bag is red. The second lipstick I pulled from my bag is red. Therefore, all the lipsticks in my bag are red.

Practice 5-2

Read the following arguments. Underline the premises and bracket the theses. Then work in pairs. Take turns to explain how each of the arguments complies with the logic of deduction.

1. All cats have a very developed sense of smell. Garfield is a cat. Garfield has a well developed sense of smell.

2. Gravity attracts objects to the center of Earth. Apples are subject to gravity. Therefore, apples fall.

3. Our marketing team performed market research related to how much time professional women who are also mothers have to spend on their makeup each day. They discovered that professional women who are also mothers rarely have more than 10 minutes each day to put on their makeup due to family responsibilities. Since our advertising campaign is always based on our market research, we should advertise that our makeup product can be put on in under ten minutes, leaving ample room for other activities involved in the morning.

4. Red meat is nutritious and enables people to keep a balanced diet. Vegetarianism, however, is the practice of abstaining from the consumption of meat (red meat, poultry, seafood, and the flesh of any other animal). Therefore, people should not be encouraged to become vegetarians in order to protect their health.

Practice 5-3

Choose the right thesis based on the premises.

1. Cathy is my friend. She got either an "Excellence" or a "Merit" on her first annual assessment in the company; and I found out she didn't get a "Merit." So _____.
   A. everyone in the company didn't get a "Merit" on the annual assessment
   B. everyone in the company got an "Excellence" on the annual assessment
   C. Cathy didn't get an "Excellence" on her first annual assessment
   D. Cathy got an "Excellence" on her first annual assessment

2. Cathy is my friend. She got an "Excellence" on the annual assessment if she got an "Excellence" on all of the weekly assignments; and she got an "Excellence" on all of the weekly assignments. As such, _____.
   A. Cathy didn't get an "Excellence" on the annual assessment
   B. Cathy got an "Excellence" on the annual assessment
   C. Cathy got an "Excellence" on every assignment
   D. someone didn't get an "Excellence" on the annual assessment

3. Cathy is my friend. She got an "Excellence" during her probation period if she got an "Excellence" on all of the weekly assignments; but she didn't get an "Excellence" during the probation period. So _____.
   A. Cathy didn't get an "Excellence" on all of the weekly assignments
   B. Cathy got an "Excellence" on all of the weekly assignments
   C. Cathy didn't get an "Excellence" on any assignment
   D. no one got an "Excellence" during the probation period

4. Martin got an "Excellence" on Mr. Moon's first test if he worked with Danny; and he worked with Danny if he got Saturday off from his part-time job. Therefore, _____.
   A. if Martin got Saturday off from his part-time job, then he got an "Excellence" on Mr. Moon's test
   B. Martin didn't get an "Excellence" on Mr. Moon's first test if he didn't get Saturday off from his part-time job
   C. Martin got Saturday off from his part-time job if he got an "Excellence" on Mr. Moon's first test
   D. Martin got Saturday off from his part-time job only if he got an "Excellence" on Mr. Moon's first test

Practice 5-4

Think of a decision or judgment you made in life which is based on deductive reasoning. Share it with a partner.

2. How to develop deductive arguments with principles?

Depending on the types of premises used, deductive arguments are applied to writing in two major ways: applying a principle and applying a definition. In this section, we will first look into the former.

Applying a Principle in Deductive Arguments

Applying a principle refers to the deductive reasoning strategy of constructing arguments based on general principles. It is the most frequently used way to conduct deductive reasoning in writing practices. When applying a principle, the key premise in the deduction is a principle. The fundamental logic is that since a principle is true, and a specific case A falls into or out of the principle, then A must be or cannot be like what is prescribed in the principle. The following steps can usually be found in an argument using such a strategy.

Step 1	Present a principle. All plants perform photosynthesis.
Step 2	Explain how the specific case discussed in the thesis embodies (or violates) the principle. (This step is sometimes combined into Step 1 or 3.) A cactus is a plant.
Step 3	State the thesis. A cactus performs photosynthesis.

A principle is a general rule that can apply to many different specific scenarios. For example, "One must wear a seat belt while driving any vehicle." is an overarching principle, which applies to many individual cases: George must wear a seat belt while driving his truck; Tonia must wear a seat belt while driving her sedan; Dianne must wear a seat belt while driving her coupe, etc.

> It may take the form of a law, a policy, a regulation, an established precondition, an antecedent, or a commonly-accepted idea, etc. It may also be an ethical one like "One should treat others as they would wish to be treated."; a scientific one like "Any object that's partially or wholly immersed in a fluid encounters a buoyant force that is equal to the weight of the displaced fluid."; or a logical one like "Two contradictory statements can't be true at the same time."

Model 5-2

Examples of arguments with a principle

Step 1: The whole is of necessity prior to the part.

Step 2: The state is the whole, while the family and the individual are the part.

Step 3: Therefore, the state is by nature clearly prior to the family and to the individual.

This argument uses an ideological belief (Step 1) as a principle, and then says that it applies to the relation between the state and the family or the individual (Step 2). So, the thesis that the state is prior to the family and to the individual naturally follows.

Step 1: Everyone should have the right to marry the person whom he or she chooses.

Step 2 & 3: So, there is no reason for Nancy's parents to force her to marry the billionaire who she does not love.

The argument uses a commonly-accepted idea as a principle (Step 1). The principle is about everyone, and it applies to Nancy, so Nancy should be allowed to marry the person she chooses instead of being forced to marry a man she does not love (Step 2 & 3).

Step 1: If one is able to register 2,000 new voters, then he or she will win the election.

Step 2: Tom has registered more than 2,000 new voters.

Step 3: Therefore, Tom will win the election.

This argument uses an antecedent (Step 1) as a principle and then says that the voting situation with Tom meets the antecedent (Step 2). So, the thesis that Tom will win the election cannot be false.

Step 1: Either your stomach trouble is caused by what you are eating, or it is caused by nervous tension.

Step 2: You told me that you have been taking special care with your diet.

Step 3: Therefore, your stomach trouble is caused by nervous tension.

In this argument, the principle is an either-A-or-B-type precondition (Step 1). Step 2 eliminates the possibility of A, so B must be the case.

Practice 5-5

Identify the three steps in each of the following arguments. Rearrange them in an order of deductive reasoning. Then work in pairs. Compare your answers and explain to each other how the truthfulness of the theses is demonstrated.

1. I must have lost my wallet. I either left it on my dresser or have lost it. It turned out I didn't leave it on my dresser.

   Step 1: _____

   Step 2: _____

   Step 3: _____

2. We should keep away from anything that is a threat to our physical safety. Bungee jumping is a threat to our physical safety. So, we have to be very cautious of it.

   Step 1: _____

   Step 2: _____

   Step 3: _____

3. Lazy people don't deserve handouts. Cecelia and street people like her who don't have regular jobs are lazy. So, you shouldn't give her any pocket change when you see her begging for a handout.

   Step 1: _____

   Step 2: _____

   Step 3: _____

4. Everyone who installs attic insulation runs the risk of inhaling potentially harmful dust and fiberglass particles. Angela and Jennifer install attic insulation. This means that both of them run that risk.

   Step 1: _____

   Step 2: _____

   Step 3: _____

5. We interviewed three people, and each one was very personable. I think that the first person had the strongest résumé. But the second person seemed very creative. I liked the enthusiasm and energy that the third person had, but that person never worked for an organization like ours before. It's a tough choice. But I'm thinking that probably the second person would be the best of the three for us to hire since innovative ideas are more important to us than experience or enthusiasm.

   Step 1: _____

   Step 2: _____

   Step 3: _____

Practice 5-6

Complete the following arguments.

1. Step 1: Throughout my life, I've always been interested in all kinds of electricity.
   Step 2: Now that there is a job offer for me in the field of electrical engineering.

   Thesis: _____

2. Step 1: Citizens in a country should be able to think critically about important social and political issues to keep the country functioning effectively.

   Step 2: Education plays a key role in developing critical thinking abilities.

   Thesis: _____

3. Step 1: Either your anxiety is coming from your workload, or it is coming from your long-lasting tension.

   Step 2: _____

   Thesis: So, your tension produces your anxiety.

4. Step 1: All Chinese had benefited from the country's development.

   Step 2: _____

   Thesis: I have enjoyed benefits of various aspects from China's fast development.

Practice 5-7

Read the experience about Daisy's choice of college. Finish the following tasks.

When deciding which colleges to include on her application list, Daisy researched university mission statements and found that College X, a small private college with a cost of attendance of $50,000 per year, was dedicated to producing compassionate and curious leaders. College Y, a large public university with a cost of attendance of $35,000 per year, promoted itself as a leading scientific research facility.

Daisy's future goals include working as an executive of a nonprofit organization designed to provide assistance to underrepresented populations. Therefore, she decided to apply to College X rather than College Y.

1. Which of the following statements does Daisy's decision most closely conform to?

   A. A direct relationship exists between a college's cost and the quality of the education it provides.

   B. Students should apply to smaller colleges that offer more personalized attention from professors.

   C. A large research university cannot prepare students for a career as a nonprofit executive.

D. Students should apply to colleges with mission statements that align with their goals.

E. The best way for students to know which college is the best fit for them is by researching each college's mission statement.

2. Imagine you are Daisy and you need to persuade your parents about your choice of college. Use the statement you choose from the question above as a principle to write an argument. Then work in pairs. Exchange your arguments and mark the three steps as you did in Practice 5-5.

_____

_____

_____

_____

_____

_____

3. Reflect on your own choice of college and major. Why did you choose your current major? If you were given a second chance, which major would you apply for. Why? First share your ideas with your partner. Then organize your ideas into an argument using the strategy of applying a principle. Write it down below.

_____

_____

_____

_____

_____

3. How to develop deductive arguments with definitions?

Another strategy of deductive reasoning is to apply a definition. How is this strategy used? This is what we will discuss in this section.

Applying a Definition in Deductive Arguments

When **applying a definition** to develop a deductive argument, we use a definition as the key premise to construct an argument. For instance, imagine that someone wants to argue that embryonic stem cell research is doing research on human beings, three steps are involved, as illustrated below.

Step 1	Present the definition. Human embryos are discrete entities and will become humans.
Step 2	Show how the specific case A which is discussed in the thesis fits (or fails to fit) the definition. (This step is sometimes combined into Step 3.) Embryonic stem cell research uses human embryos.
Step 3	Conclude that case A belongs to (or does not belong to) the class specified by the definition. Embryonic stem cell research is then doing research on human beings.

Normally, to make our arguments convincing, we are suggested to use established definitions, namely those made by authoritative parties and well recognized by the target reader. In case we sometimes do need to compose an original definition, the following types could be useful.

Formal definitions

It is based upon a concise, logical pattern that includes as much information as possible within a limited space. It consists of three parts — the term to be defined, the class of object or concept to which the term belongs, the differentiating characteristics that distinguish it from all others of its class. Study the examples below.

- Water is a liquid made up of molecules of hydrogen and oxygen in the ratio of 2 to 1.
- Cruel and unusual punishment is any punishment that is extremely excessive in relation to the crime, shocking to ordinary sensibilities, or equivalent to torture.
- Freedom is the power or right to act, speak, or think as one wants without hindrance or restraint.

Operational definitions

X must satisfy a set of requirements in order to be considered a part of category Y.

- Aggression refers to any instance of intentional forceful contact with sufficient force to leave a mark or make a sound audible from three feet away.
- Laundry is not complete unless it is folded and put away.

Informal definitions

We can use known words or examples to explain an unknown term.

- Freedom, also referred to as liberty or independence, is a state people reach when they are free to think and do whatever they please.
- Cruel and unusual punishments, such as water torture, temperature extremes, and sensory overloads, are punishments that prisoners are subjected to, which people may find shocking.

Model 5-3

Examples of arguments with a definition

Step 1: Plagiarism is presenting someone else's work or ideas as your own, with or without their consent, by incorporating it into your work without full acknowledgment.

Step 2: In his final essay for the history course, Tom copied some phrases and ideas from different sources without any reference.

Step 3: Thus, Tom committed plagiarism.

Step 1: By definition, if a person enters this country illegally, that person is breaking the law. All lawbreakers are criminals.

Step 2 & 3: Therefore, those refugees who entered the country without official permission should be regarded as criminals.

Step 1: If someone is bossy, he acts impolitely, likes shouting at people, and tells people what to do.

Step 2 & 3: Ken is such a person as he always sends his colleagues on all sorts of errands without their consent.

Model 5-4

A model deductive essay

A deductive essay is a form of critical essay in which deductive reasoning is taken as the overall logic. Study the model deductive essay and notice the analysis of its writing characteristics.

Should Celebrities Enter Politics?

Step 1: State the definition of politics (3 criteria for judging if celebrities can be politicians).

thesis statement

❶ Politics is all about connecting and identifying with the needs of the common people. ①Addressing their difficulties, ②identifying with them, and ③instilling hope is all that counts. **Any celebrity that takes this philosophy into account and addresses these grievances can use the platform of their fame to vie for a public office.**

Step 2 (Paras. 2–4): Show how celebrities entering politics fits the definition.
Celebrities meet the first criterion: addressing the difficulties confronting the common celebrities.

❷ Celebrities often desire to resolve the difficulties their neighborhood is faced with and then support developments. They commonly seek advancements in the areas they grew up in and the areas they reside. Their desire for a better society is what drives them to politics. On the other hand, critics argue that these celebrities are hugely wealthy and do not know the feelings associated with the struggling middle class. However, what these critics should understand is that many celebrities grew up in average families. This fact, together with the need to promote their social images, provides them with a strong incentive and will to change the society for the better. And that also explains why they seek an avenue to address societal needs.

Chapter 5 How to apply deductive reasoning to writing?

Celebrities meet the second criterion: identifying with the voters.

❸ The fame of celebrities helps create a personal connection with voters. We have seen people like Ronald Reagan entering politics and excelling. He used his masculinity and heroic nature that the voters identified with to win the elections. He excelled over his competitors since the voters had his success in mind as they have been watching him act for years. Seeing these celebrities in television, movies, and magazines has earned them a social relationship and confidence that people can identify with. This brings a feeling to the voters that they have a personal connection with the celebrities, thus considering them as friends. Critics to this fact argue that stars ought to keep away from politics as it divides their audience. What they do not understand is that being a star creates a connection with the people which in no way divides them.

Celebrities meet the third criterion: instilling hope.

Note: This paragraph itself uses the strategy of applying a principle.
[the principle]

how the principle applies to celebrities

❹ [Also, in the implementation of policies and as a strategy to maintain success while in offices, the leaders ought to be able to instill hope in the constituents and solicit for their support.] Celebrities perform well here with two advantages. First, their ability to conduct themselves in a composed manner while addressing their audiences can do them good. The celebrities have been in the glare of publicity for a long time, and thus they impress with the way they deliver speeches as well as how they answer queries satisfactorily after careful scrutiny. Second, as seen in the leadership of Arnold Schwarzenegger, Ronald Reagan, Jesse Ventura, and Fred Thompson, celebrities portrayed themselves as selfless figures, thus restoring faith in politicians. This is seen in the high voter turnout which saw the election of these celebrities. Most young people are seem to withdraw from politics, but since the emergence of their favorite celebrities in the field, they have made a comeback since these celebrities are seen as relevant and in touch with the general populous.

❺ Some people argue that celebrities should stick to what they do best and forsake politics since they cannot possibly deliver in the realm of governance. This is a myopic viewpoint, since celebrities have enormous experience within the public realm. In this lifestyle, they have interacted with the most knowledgeable and experienced people who have helped them maintain the right perspective. Therefore, being a celebrity in politics can be quite beneficial. It is amazing to see that most politicians want to be celebrities due to the associated benefits.

Step 3: State the thesis again.	❻ To sum up, as long as their policies and ideologies are aimed at meeting the needs of the common people, celebrities running for elected offices should be given an equal chance as anyone else.

Practice 5-8

Complete the following arguments.

1. Step 1: The insurance industry does not consider water damage to houses caused by hurricane storm surges as insurable under hurricane insurance policies; instead, the homeowners need flood coverage.

   Step 2: Apparently, the damage to Mr. McConnell's house was caused by the hurricane storm surge last month.

   Thesis: _____

2. Step 1: The career counseling center is a college department that provides free résumé reviews to students who are about to graduate.

   Step 2: I am a senior at this university and looking for a job.

   Thesis: _____

3. Step 1: The "Chinese dream" is to build a moderately prosperous society and achieve the great rejuvenation of the Chinese nation.

   Step 2: _____

   Thesis: So, the construction of the China Space Station is a milestone in fulfilling the Chinese dream.

4. Step 1: Welfare dependence refers to a situation where the proportion of income from welfare programs in household income, or the welfare replacement rate, exceeds 50 percent.

   Step 2: _____

   Thesis: China's poverty alleviation efforts do not create welfare dependence.

Use the strategy of applying a definition to make an argument to justify each of the following theses. The terms in bold are what you can define.

1. *Alien* is a **horror movie**.

   _____

   _____

   _____

   _____

2. FB Limited is by no means a **socially responsible company**.

   _____

   _____

   _____

   _____

3. My ex-boyfriend posted many embarrassing photos of me on social media without my permission. This is definitely **cyberbullying**.

   _____

   _____

   _____

   _____

From reading to writing

■ Reading
Read the essay and finish the tasks.

World Hungry for Change

❶ From July 26 to 28, 2021, 500 delegates and 150 leaders met in Rome, accompanied by 20,000 virtual delegates for the hybrid (offline and online) UN Food System Pre-Summit to set out what sustainable and equitable food systems could look like and how to make this transformation happen. After three days of plenaries, panel discussions, and side events, several consensus themes emerged: the need for nationally-led action, the need for innovative and sustainable financing, and the need to overcome difficulties. These are the three critical aspects of efforts toward a sustainable and equitable food system. And China, a country that has fed nearly 20 percent of the world's population using only 8 percent of the world's arable land and 5 percent of global freshwater, has demonstrated great success in food system transformation with her achievements in the three aspects above.

❷ China has a national and integrated approach to food security. It has created a sequential policy and investment environment that sees agricultural productivity and nutrition as a question of economic development. The household contract responsibility system introduced in 1978 is often regarded as the start of China's food system transformation, triggering growth in agricultural output and productivity and increasing food supply. It was followed by market reforms in the 1980s and agricultural trade reforms in the 1990s which furthered productivity and economic development. Recently China has integrated human and environmental health into its development agenda. Collectively, the 14th Five-Year Plan (2021–2025) for National Economic and Social Development, and the Long-range Objectives Through the Year 2035, Healthy China 2030 Plan, and Anti-Food Waste Law target awareness of public consumption, low-carbon rural development, healthy and balanced diets, food safety, and environmental degradation related to livestock wastes, agricultural plastics, and fertilizer use.

❸ But policy is not enough on its own. China has also invested significantly in rural public infrastructure, agricultural research and developmen, and innovation to improve food accessibility, off-farm employment, and resilience building. We cannot underestimate China's leadership in e-commerce which has helped smallholder farmers overcome market access barriers. Finance and investment are key to any successful food system transformation.

❹ Despite this progress, some critics still assert that China's food system is facing a set of emerging challenges. Climate change, for example, poses a very serious threat to a safe food system, as the extreme weather events of this year illustrate. However, China has made important commitments to overcoming the challenges, like reaching peak carbon before 2030 and being carbon neutral before 2060. Food and land use change will play a key role in realizing these goals, and they need to be considered in any future emissions policies — a shift toward more sustainable and healthy diets could reduce agricultural greenhouse gas emissions by 18 to 25 percent by 2030.

❺ China has made tremendous progress in building a sustainable and equitable food system that will have positive global ripple effects. The international community must learn from and work with China.

Writing technique questions

Based on what you have learned in this chapter, consider the following questions. Then discuss with your group your answers and seek a consensus.

1. What is the thesis statement of the essay?
2. In order to justify the thesis, the author lays down a principle in Para. 1. What is the principle?
3. What is the thesis of Para. 2? What evidence is offered?
4. What is the thesis of Para. 3? What evidence is offered?
5. What is the overall reasoning strategy of this essay? Complete the reasoning outline below.

    Step 1: _____

Step2: _____

Thesis: _____

Overall reasoning strategy: _____

Critical thinking questions

Consider the questions below and finish the tasks.

1. Food challenges have been a critical issue for the entire world, and according to the author, China's efforts in building a sustainable and equitable food system will set a positive example for the world. What other major challenges do you think the world is faced with? Which one is the most urgent? Why?

2. Share your answers to the questions above with your group, and try your best to persuade them that the challenge you talk about is the most urgent one.

3. Group vote on the most urgent challenge the world is confronted with. Then discuss the following questions.

   3.1 Why do you think it the most urgent challenge for the world?

   3.2 How does China address it? What initiative, policy, strategy, or philosophy, etc. has China applied?

   3.3 What positive effects have China's efforts had on the world?

4. Present your ideas to the class.

■ Writing

Based on your answers to the critical thinking questions, write a deductive essay entitled "_____ Is China's Wisdom for the World." The following outline is given to you as a prompt. You may also review the essay "World Hungry for Change" and the one in Model 5-4 as examples.

[Step 1: Establish a principle by stating why the challenge you discussed in Exercise 3 of the critical thinking questions is the most urgent one.]

_____

_____

[Step 2: Explain how one of China's initiatives, strategies, philosophies, etc. embodies the principle, namely, addressing the challenge successfully.]

_____

_____

[Step 3: Conclude that the initiative / strategy / philosophy you argued for above is China's wisdom for the world.]

_____

_____

REFLECTION

This chapter discussed how deductive reasoning strategies can be used in writing. Now it's time to review and reflect on what you have learned. Work in pairs and take turns to answer the following questions. Check them as you answer each one.

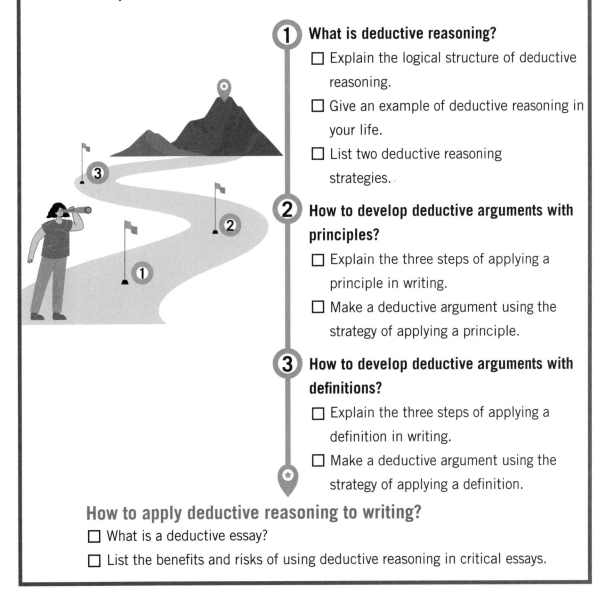

1 What is deductive reasoning?

☐ Explain the logical structure of deductive reasoning.

☐ Give an example of deductive reasoning in your life.

☐ List two deductive reasoning strategies.

2 How to develop deductive arguments with principles?

☐ Explain the three steps of applying a principle in writing.

☐ Make a deductive argument using the strategy of applying a principle.

3 How to develop deductive arguments with definitions?

☐ Explain the three steps of applying a definition in writing.

☐ Make a deductive argument using the strategy of applying a definition.

How to apply deductive reasoning to writing?

☐ What is a deductive essay?

☐ List the benefits and risks of using deductive reasoning in critical essays.

Chapter 6

How to apply inductive reasoning to writing?

谋而不得，则以往知来，以见知隐。谋若此，可得而知矣。

——《墨子·非攻》

"If you plan and are unsuccessful, then use the past to predict the future, and use the manifest to know the hidden. If you plan like this, you can succeed and know."
—"Condemning Offensive Warfare," *The Mozi*

Chapter opener

When a mom and her son returned home, they found their living room in a big mess.

Mom, what happened? Why is the room in such a mess?

It must be the dog! He messed up the house last time we left him at home alone!

It must be! Bad dog!

Chapter roadmap

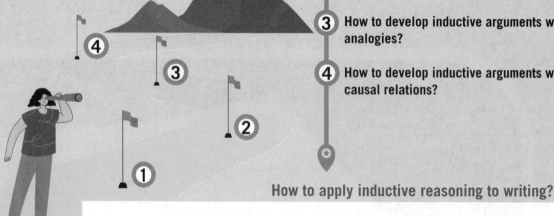

1. What is Inductive reasoning?
2. How to make inductive generalizations?
3. How to develop inductive arguments with analogies?
4. How to develop inductive arguments with causal relations?

How to apply inductive reasoning to writing?

Learning outcomes

At the end of this chapter, you will be able to

- use proper examples to explain what inductive reasoning is;
- understand the inductive reasoning strategies of inductive generalizations, analogical reasoning, and causal reasoning;
- apply the above three strategies to make inductive arguments;
- compose inductive essays.

From reading to writing

Analyze the necessity of sustainable transportation and write an inductive essay on this topic.

1. What is inductive reasoning?

Inductive reasoning has long been used in China, dating back to Pre-Qin Period. But what is it? How does it differ from deductive reasoning? You may find the answers in this section.

Core knowledge input

Micro-lecture Inductive Reasoning: What and Why
MOOC Lesson 6

Inductive Reasoning: What and Why

There is one logic exercise we do nearly every day, though we're scarcely aware of it. When making a decision, we typically go through a subconscious process of filtering observations through our past experiences. For example, if we look outside and see a sunny sky, it's reasonable to think we will not need an umbrella. Because many past sunny days have proven this thinking correct, it is a reasonable assumption. This thought process is an example of **inductive reasoning**.

Inductive reasoning involves drawing conclusions from facts and experiences. It can be understood as the logic in which if the premise is true, the thesis is probably true. The aim for an inductive argument is not certainty but inductive strength, meaning that the premises of the successful argument make the conclusion highly probable. The argument below exemplifies such logic.

Alice has taken four philosophy courses during her time in college. She got an A in all four. She has signed up to take another philosophy course this semester. I predict she will get an A in that course, too.

Task >>>>

Complete the following diagram.

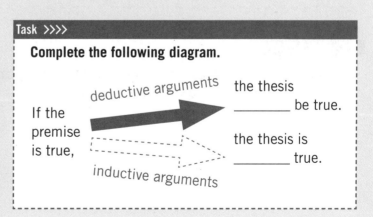

In this example, Alice's future performance is predicted based on her past performances in similar courses. But will Alice definitely get an A in the new course? There is still a chance that she may get a lower grade.

Model 6-1

Examples of inductive reasoning

1. **Premises:** The carpet is ruined, the walls are unpainted, and the building needs a new roof.

   Thesis: The owners are not taking good care of the building.

2. **Premise:** I noticed that all freeway off-ramps were paired with on-ramps in the opposite direction.

   Thesis: The next exit is paired with an on-ramp in the opposite side.

3. **Premise:** The flowers in Stella's garden bloom every year.

   Thesis: They'll bloom again this year.

4. **Premises:** Dylan is a man. He is 99 and is in a coma.

   Thesis: Dylan will not finish the marathon tomorrow.

5. **Premises:** Pigs are just as smart, cute, and playful as dogs and dolphins. Nobody would consider eating those animals.

   Thesis: Eating pork is immoral.

Practice 6-1

Think of two examples of using inductive reasoning in your everyday life or study. Then share your examples in pairs.

Inductive Argument Theses Are NOT Always True

When we reason deductively, if the premise is true the thesis cannot be false. As is discussed in the previous chapter, deductive reasoning is black and white; a thesis is either true or false and cannot be partly true or partly false. When we reason deductively, we try to prove or demonstrate a thesis.

When we reason inductively, however, we try to support a thesis. Inductive arguments are "stronger" or "weaker" depending on how much support the premise provides for the thesis.

Deductive vs Inductive Reasoning

	Deductive reasoning	Inductive reasoning
Feature	The thesis MUST be true if the premise is true.	The thesis is LIKELY to be true if the premise is true.
Pro	Truth-preserving	Generates new theories, new predictions, new relations, etc., since the thesis is not contained in the premises
Con	Does not generate new ideas since the thesis is contained in the premise	Not truth-preserving
Examples	Premises: All dogs have ears; golden retrievers are dogs. Thesis: Golden retrievers have ears.	Premise: In the past, the swans came to this lake every winter. Thesis: They will come to the lake this winter. Premises: Many children like cats as they are cute. Dogs are also cute. Thesis: Children like dogs.

Model 6-2

Analysis of inductive reasoning

1. **Premises:** The lights in my friend's house are out. The curtains are drawn. No one is answering the phone.

   Thesis: My friend must be away.

   Analysis: The thesis is a reasonable prediction, but not necessarily a correct one. The friend may indeed be away, but other inferences are possible: The friend may be sick, or just hiding.

2. **Premises:** I spent 10 minutes looking for a restaurant in San Mateo that was open at 2 p.m., but didn't find one.

   Thesis: There are NO restaurants open past 2 p.m. in San Mateo.

   Analysis: The thesis is an inductive generalization about all the restaurants based on one's experience with some restaurants in San Mateo. It is very weak as the generalization is based on one single experience which is possibly not the usual or general situation.

3. **Premises:** Plastic bags have been banned in many countries as plastic is hard to degrade. Shampoo bottles are also always made of plastic.

   Thesis: Plastic shampoo bottles should be banned.

   Analysis: The premise that plastic is hard to degrade is widely accepted. The thesis about shampoo bottles is drawn on a comparison with plastic bags which share the same property. Thus, the thesis is very likely to be true.

4. **Premises**: Mathew has severe acne. He drinks milk every day and studies suggest drinking milk may cause acne.

   Thesis: Mathew's acne is caused by milk.

   Analysis: The thesis is only highly probable though it is drawn on a cause-effect premise that has been proven by studies. Mathew's acne may also be caused by pressure, insomnia, or other reasons.

Read the following arguments. Underline the premises and bracket the theses. Then work in pairs. Take turns to explain why the theses in these arguments are PROBABLY true.

1. My mobile slipped into the swimming pool. Mobiles are easily damaged by water. My mobile must be broken.

2. Monkey physiology is similar to humans'. This study finds that drug X does not cure liver cancer in monkeys. Thus, drug X will not cure liver cancer in humans, either.

3. There is a lot more lawbreaking in Eureka than in San Francisco, as everyone I've met through work has been in trouble with the law since I moved to Eureka, but when I lived in San Francisco, no one I met through work was in trouble with the law.

Practice 6-3

Read the following statements. Decide whether they are fact statements (F), inductive arguments (I), or deductive arguments (D)? Write down the corresponding letter in the parentheses.

1. You will have trouble parking at North Beach as I went to North Beach several times this year and parking was terrible. (   )

2. Parking at North Beach is also terrible. So, you will find parking in Green Street which is in the center of North Beach is also terrible. (   )

3. Smokers have yellow fingers. Janine is a smoker. I bet he must have yellow fingers, too. (   )

4. Ever since Artie started drinking wine every night about ten years ago, he has been suffering from insomnia. The wine must be causing him to sleep badly. (   )

5. Writers have lively imaginations. So when our neighbor, a novelist, told us that she had seen a ghost, we just assumed she was making it up. (   )

6. It has never snowed in the mountains here. I don't think it will snow here this year. (   )

7. My husband had a severe sore throat. But the problem couldn't be strep throat; strep throat always causes a fever, and he didn't have a fever. (   )

8. Every time I call Jo, he's at the store. I guess he loves shopping. (   )

9. Having spent at least ten years touring the world, eating in homes, restaurants, villages, and cities in every part of the globe, I conclude that of all cuisines, Chinese cuisine is the most varied. (   )

10. Ostriches do not hide their head in the sand. (   )

2. How to make inductive generalizations?

Inductive generalizations is a form of inductive reasoning frequently used in daily life and scientific research. What is inductive generalization? How is it inferred? The answers are the focuses of this section.

Core knowledge input

Micro-lecture Inductive Generalization
MOOC Lesson 6

Inductive Generalization

Inductive generalization is a form of inductive reasoning that supports a thesis based on recurring patterns or repeated observations. To generalize, one must observe multiple specific instances, find common qualities or behaviors, and then make a broad or universal statement — a generalization — about them. For example, if every dog I see chases squirrels, then I would probably generalize that all dogs chase squirrels. Or imagine if you go to a certain business and get bad service once, you may not like it. If you go back and get bad treatment again, you probably won't go back again because you have concluded "Business X always treats its customers badly." This thesis is generalized from two previous experiences.

Task >>>>

Draw a diagram to illustrate the reasoning logic of inductive generalization. Then explain your diagram to a partner. Scan the QR code for more diagrams.

Examples of inductive generalization

1. **Premise**: Every time I've eaten oysters I've been sick.

   Thesis: I must be allergic to oysters.

2. **Premises**: Mary has had several quizzes in the course *Economics*. All of them were easy.

   Thesis: The quizzes in this course are all easy.

3. **Premise**: Data on pulmonary, respiratory, and cardiac conditions among smokers are not as good as those among non-smokers.

   Thesis: Smoking represents a serious health risk.

4. **Premise**: According to a survey by the American Association of Mad Scientists, 98% of the survey participants admitted that they enjoy reading, filling out, and returning random surveys.

   Thesis: Americans love to fill out surveys.

5. **Premises**: I've taken vacations to Florida six times before, and I've enjoyed each visit.

   Thesis: I believe Florida is a good destination for a vacation.

Practice 6-4

Read each of the following arguments, underline the premises, and bracket the theses (which is a generalization). Then share your answers with a partner.

1. Mercury, Venus, and Earth are all known planets and move around the sun from west to east. Therefore, all the known planets move around the sun from west to east.

2. Sam will probably win the election as the poll indicates 80% of voters will vote for him.

3. According to a survey about students' satisfaction with the school, 70% of the students who filled out the survey are satisfied with their school. So students are satisfied with the school.

4. The traffic is terribly heavy at this time every day because I was stuck on the road for over an hour three times last week when I drove back home at about the same time of

the day.

5. China has delivered on all its commitments to UN peacekeeping. Over the past three decades, China has participated in more than 20 UN peacekeeping operations. In maritime escort missions, humanitarian relief operations, anti-terrorist exercises, and anti-pandemic cooperation, Chinese troops have fulfilled their obligations commensurate with China's global standing.

Practice 6-5

Can you think of more examples of inductive generalization based on observations or past experiences in your everyday life or study? Recall such an example and share it with a partner.

Model 6-4

A paragraph based on inductive generalization

premises: specific instances ①②③④⑤	①A recent outbreak of Mad Cow Disease has resulted in, according to an English report, losses of more than three billion dollars due to the necessity of destroying herds and the import restrictions that almost all European countries have placed on English beef imports. ②As people avoid beef and substitute other alternatives both in Great Britain and in other European countries, sales of fish and poultry are skyrocketing. ③Because nervous French shoppers are suspicious of beef, butchers who sell horse meat are experiencing a huge increase in business. ④Thousands of American tourists are reluctant to order beef in restaurants all over Europe. ⑤Even across the Atlantic, the effects of the disease are apparent: Imports of European cheese, meats, and dairy products are now prohibited in the United States. ⑥People everywhere are now quite anxious not only about the beef they are eating today but also about the beef they have eaten in the past since it sometimes takes up to thirty years for human beings to show signs of infection. Clearly, **widespread fear of consuming beef has produced many economic and emotional changes all over the world.**
thesis: a generalization	

Practice 6-6

Read the following paragraph and answer the corresponding questions.

AllGood is a store for everyone because people of all genders and ages can shop there. If you are a young mother searching for baby clothes, you can find a wide variety of cotton outfits for infants and toddlers. If you are a teenager looking for a backpack, you can select from many sizes and styles. If you are a middle-aged woman shopping for photography equipment, housewares, CDs, or videotapes, the merchandise is there. If, on the other hand, you are a man in your thirties looking for garden supplies or tools, you can browse through fertilizers, hand drills, and socket wrenches. Finally, if you are a senior citizen searching for a birthday toy for a grandchild or an inexpensive pair of khakis, you will discover both items stocked in the aisles.

1. The thesis of the paragraph is _____.
2. The thesis is supported by five specific instances which are the premises. They are

   Premise 1: _____

   Premise 2: _____

   Premise 3: _____

   Premise 4: _____

   Premise 5: _____

Practice 6-7

Work in pairs. Think of at least two possible premises to support the following generalized inference. Then write down a paragraph using the strategy of inductive generalization.

The library is the most popular place for study among students at our university.

_____

_____

_____

3. How to develop inductive arguments with analogies?

Another common type of inductive reasoning is analogical reasoning, or the argument by analogy. This section explains what an analogy is, what analogical reasoning is, and how it is achieved.

Core knowledge input

Micro-lecture Analogy and Analogical Reasoning
MOOC Lesson 6

Analogy and Analogical Reasoning

What is an analogy?

An **analogy** is a comparison between two objects, or systems of objects, that highlights respects in which they are thought to be similar. A sparrow is very different from a car, but they are still similar in that they can both move. A washing machine is very different from a society, but they both contain parts and produce waste.

What is analogical reasoning?

Analogical reasoning is any type of reasoning that relies upon an analogy as its key premise. In general, when we make use of analogical arguments, it is important to make clear in what ways two things are supposed to be similar. Our logic here is since A is similar to B and A has a certain feature X, then B should also have the feature X. For example, we can say every choice you make is like spinning the wheel of fortune — sometimes you will get the result that you desire, while other times you will end up with something you always hoped to avoid. By pointing out the shared feature between choice and wheels of fortune, that is, the unexpected results, the thesis "Every choice has a different consequence." may be supported.

How is analogical reasoning used?

Analogies are widely recognized as aids to discovery. The explicit use of analogical arguments, since antiquity, has been a distinctive feature of scientific, philosophical, and legal reasoning. A very familiar example is animal testing in medical research where an analogy is drawn between humans and animals.

Task >>>>

Draw a diagram to illustrate the logic of analogical reasoning. Then explain your diagram to a partner. Scan the QR code for more diagrams.

Model 6-5

Examples of analogical reasoning

1. Given enough time, water can cut through the toughest rocks. So in life, all problems can be resolved as long as we persist and do not give up.

   Analogy:

   A & B: Tough rocks and problems are similar in that they are hard to cut / resolve.

   Feature X: Given enough time, water can cut through the toughest rocks.

   Thesis:

   As long as we persist and do not give up, all problems can be resolved.

2. Without inspiration, we're all like a box of matches that will never be lit.

   Analogy:

   A & B: We (humans) and matches are similar in that both can shine.

   Feature X: Matches will not shine unless they are lit.

   Thesis:

   We won't shine without inspiration.

3. There might be life on Europa because it has an atmosphere that contains oxygen just like Earth.

   Analogy:

   A & B: Europa and Earth are similar in that they are both planets and have an atmosphere containing oxygen.

   Feature X: There is life on Earth.

   Thesis:

   There might be life on Europa.

4. Evolution is a blind giant who rolls a snowball down a hill. The ball is made of flakes — circumstances. They contribute to the mass without knowing it. They

adhere without intention, and without foreseeing what is to result. When they see the result they marvel at the monster ball and wonder how the contriving of it came to be originally thought out and planned. Whereas there was no such planning, there was only a law: The ball once started, all the circumstances that happened to lie in its path would help to build it, in spite of themselves. (Mark Twain, *Tales of Wonder*)

Analogy:

A & B: Evolution and a blind giant rolling a snowball down the hill are similar in that they are both made of circumstances / snowflakes, which both contribute to the mass without knowing it.

Feature X: The ball once started, all the circumstances that happened to lie in its path would help to build it, the result of which cannot be foreseen.

Thesis:

The results of evolution are not planned; they are the results of natural laws.

Practice 6-8

Work with a partner. Complete the analyses of the following analogical arguments. Refer to the analyses in Model 6-5 as examples.

1. This novel has a similar plot to the other one we have read, so probably it is also very boring.

    Analogy between A & B: _____

    Feature X: _____

    Thesis: _____

2. In my opinion, machine translation is not a substitute for human translation. Fast as robot journalists may be, they cannot produce reports as thought-provoking and profound as the human ones. Several robot journalists have been employed to write financial reports in America for more than a year. They can be accurate in data, fast in speed, coherent in arrangement, but they can never produce reports as insightful as a human's. For the same reason, it is quite hard for machine translation to reproduce the

delicate beauty of languages and the profound significance of original works. Thus, human translation will not easily be replaced by machine translation.

Analogy between A & B: _____

Feature X: _____

Thesis: _____

Practice 6-9

Read the following statement. In what aspects is the virtual society on the Internet similar to the actual society? Think of at least two similar features. Then write a short paragraph with the following statement as the topic sentence and the analogies you just made as premises.

The Internet is not a territory where rules do not apply.

_____

_____

_____

_____

_____

_____

_____

_____

_____

Model 6-6

A critical essay with analogical reasoning

Study the model critical essay and pay attention to the analysis about the analogical reasoning used.

Is Economics a Science?

introduction
[thesis statement]

❶ To beginners, it can seem odd to claim that [economics is a science]. After all, economists do not work with test tubes or telescopes. The essence of science, however, is the scientific method which is as applicable to studying a nation's economy as it is to studying the earth's gravity or a species' evolution.

analogical reasoning 1
(Paras. 2–3)

analogy:
A & B: Economics is compared to physics in that they both make assumptions as a research method to simplify problems.

Feature X: Physics' research method is a scientific one.

thesis:
Economics' research method is also a scientific one.

❷ If you ask a physicist how long it would take for a marble to fall from the top of a ten-story building, she will answer the question by assuming that the marble falls in a vacuum. Of course, this assumption is false. In fact, the building is surrounded by air, which exerts friction on the falling marble and slows it down. Yet the physicist will correctly point out that friction on the marble is so small that its effect is negligible. Assuming the marble falls in a vacuum greatly simplifies the problem without substantially affecting the answer.

❸ Economists make assumptions for the same reason: Assumptions can make the world easier to understand. To study the effects of international trade, for example, we may assume that the world consists of only two countries and that each country produces only two goods. Of course, the real world consists of dozens of countries, each of which produces thousands of different types of goods. But by assuming two countries and two goods, we can focus our thinking. Once we understand international trade in an imaginary world with two countries and two goods, we are in a better position to understand international trade in the more complex world in which we live.

analogical reasoning 2
(Paras. 4–5)
analogy:
A & B: Economics is compared to physics in that they both use different assumptions to answer different questions.

❹ The art in scientific thinking — whether in physics, biology, or economics — is deciding which assumptions to make. Suppose, for instance, that we were dropping a beach ball rather than a marble from the top of a building. Our physicist would realize that the assumption of no friction is far less accurate in this case: Friction exerts a greater force on a beach ball than on a marble. The assumption that gravity works in a vacuum is reasonable for studying a falling marble but not for studying a falling beach ball.

Feature X: Physics' research method is a scientific one.	❺ Similarly, economists use different assumptions to answer different questions. Suppose that we want to study what happens to the economy when the government changes the number of dollars in circulation. An important piece of this analysis, it turns out, is how prices respond. Many prices in the economy change infrequently; the newsstand prices of magazines, for instance, are changed only every few years. Knowing this fact may lead us to make different assumptions when studying the effects of the policy change over different time horizons. For studying the short-run effects of the policy, we may assume that prices do not change much. We may even make the extreme and artificial assumption that all prices are completely fixed. For studying the long-run effects of the policy, however, we may assume that all prices are completely flexible. Just as a physicist uses different assumptions when studying falling marbles and falling beach balls, economists use different assumptions when studying the short-run and long-run effects of a change in the quantity of money.
thesis: Economics' research method is also a scientific one.	
conclusion [restate the thesis]	❻ Like mathematicians, psychologists, lawyers, and physicists, [economists apply the logic of science to examine how an economy works. It is a science.]

Practice 6-10

Work on the following tasks. Then write an analogical argumentative paragraph with the given topic sentence.

Task 1: Think about a subject / skill that you excel at and recall the learning strategies that help you effectively learn it.

Task 2: Then think of a subject / skill that you are not yet good at. Identify some common features in these two subjects / skills to form an analogy.

Task 3: Consider how you can use any one of the learning strategies mentioned in Task 1 to help you improve your performance in the subject / skill you are not yet good at.

Task 4: Write an analogical argumentative paragraph on what you just considered. The topic sentence is given to you.

My performance in _____ [subject / skill you are not yet good at]

may be improved by _____ [a strategy or strategies you think useful]

_____

_____

_____

_____

_____

_____

_____

_____

_____

_____

_____

_____

Core knowledge input

MOOC Lesson 6

Analogy, Simile, or Metaphor?

Analogies, similes, and metaphors are all literary devices used to create comparisons between different entities. However, they are actually very different. While similes and metaphors are figures of speech that are generally quite short and simple, analogies are usually arguments or parts of an argument that are more elaborate and explanatory.

	Analogy	Simile	Metaphor
Common feature	compare different ideas, concepts, and experiences		
Definition	an argumentative comparison using familiar ideas to explain unfamiliar ideas	a figure of speech that describes something by comparing it with something else using words including *as*, *like*, *seem*, etc.	a figurative language to describe something by comparing two usually unrelated things and stating that one is the other
Purpose	to make or support an argument	to describe or help understand	
Examples	• Time is like a thief in that thieves steal physical objects and time steals moments of our lives. • Life is just like a garden — it is ever-growing and changing, needing care and dedication, and always filled with beautiful surprises.	• Time is like a thief. • Life is like a garden.	• Time is a thief. • Life is a garden.

Practice 6-11

Read the following statements. Decide whether they are analogies (A), similes (S), or metaphors (M). Write down the corresponding letter in the parentheses.

1. America is a melting pot. (   )
2. Our soldiers are as brave as lions. (   )
3. Eyes are the windows to the soul. (   )
4. A good book is a friend. It provides entertainment and insight. It keeps you company and helps you feel connected to others. (   )
5. "A room without books is like a body without a soul." — Marcus Tullius Cicero (   )
6. "Life is like a box of chocolates. You never know what you're gonna get." — Forrest Gump (   )

4. How to develop inductive arguments with causal relations?

On a daily basis, we seek to understand why events occurred by identifying the factors that led up to them. This is a causal reasoning process. Then what is causal reasoning? How to make causal arguments?

Core knowledge input

Micro-lecture Causal Reasoning: What, Why, and How
MOOC Lesson 6

Causal Reasoning: What, Why, and How

What is causal reasoning?

Causal reasoning is the process of identifying causality: the relationship between a cause and its effect. It is a form of inductive reasoning we use all the time without even thinking about it. When we read about environmental problems such as the depletion of the ozone layer, we wonder "Why is this happening?". Whenever we make decisions in our daily lives, we ask ourselves, "Why should I do this?" People routinely make such efforts because detecting causal connections among events helps them to make sense of the constantly changing flow of events.

Why do we need causal reasoning?

The philosopher John Mackie described causal reasoning as "the cement of the universe." Because it enables people to find meaningful order in events that might otherwise appear random and chaotic, causal understanding helps people to plan and predict the future. With causal reasoning, we can

- gain a complete picture of how and why something happened by looking for its multiple causes and understanding the different roles each of them plays, be it background conditions, trigger factors, or catalysis;
- decide who is responsible by assessing how much responsibility each of the multiple causes bears;
- figure out how to make something happen or not happen by zeroing in on a factor

or factors that will push the event forward;

- predict what might happen in the future by showing that all the causes needed to bring about an event are in place or will fall into place.

How do we develop causal arguments?

So how do we write an argument to say that one thing causes another? Here are some tips.

1. **Identify possible causes.**

    If other writers have already identified possible causes, our argument simply needs to refer back to those and add in any that have been missed. If not, the writer can put themselves in the role of a detective and imagine what might have caused the event.

2. **Determine which factor is most correlated with the effect.**

    If we think that a factor may cause an event, the first question to ask is whether they go together. To do so, we may use some of "Mill's methods."

    - Method of Agreement: If an event is repeated and every time it happens, a common factor is present, that common factor may be the cause. For example, a family went out together for a buffet dinner but afterward felt sick and experienced stomach aches. The easiest way to determine the cause of the illness is by comparing the food eaten by each family member and finding out which foods everyone ate.
    - Method of Difference: We take two things and make sure they are exactly the same in all relevant respects, except for one key difference. If one thing experiences the phenomenon in question and the other doesn't, then that one key difference is likely the cause of the phenomenon.
    - Method of Concomitant Variation: According to this method, if holding other factors constant, an increase or decrease in some causal factor A is always accompanied by a corresponding increase or decrease in some phenomenon X. We conclude that A and X are causally related.

3. **Explain how the factor could have caused the effect.**

    This means analyzing how one thing causes another. For example, a scientific writer may tell how carbon dioxide in the atmosphere could effectively trap heat and warm the planet.

4. **Eliminate alternate explanations.**

    Correlation is not causation. So, if we have found a strong correlation, we need to consider other possible explanations and argue that the one we support is the most plausible one. Proving causality is tricky, and often even rigorous scientific studies can do little more than suggest that causality is probable or possible. But we can do a better job of assessing causes if we develop the habit of looking for alternate explanations.

Model 6-7

Examples of causal reasoning

1. **Premises:** Stella decides that for this year's Gardening Day she would finally determine what effect Kwik-Gro fertilizer has on her primroses. She has two rows of these plants, each acquired from the same stock of primroses sold at the same store, and bought on the same day. She gives them all the same amount of water; the sunlight is the same for each row; the soil is the same. Dressed appropriately for the day, she applies Kwik-Gro to one row, but not to the other. The row receiving Kwik-Gro soon dries up and dies, leaving a grub-infested, gooey mess where once were thriving primroses.

   Thesis: Kwik-Gro kills primroses.

   Analysis: The premises describe what Stella does to determine the effect of Kwik-Gro fertilizer has on her flowers. Mill's method of difference is applied here. The thesis is the effect she discovers. In this way a cause-effect relationship is established between the Kwik-Gro fertilizer and the growth of primroses, thereby deciding the role of this fertilizer.

2. **Premises:** A farmer noticed a marked increase in crop yields for the season. He started using a new and improved fertilizer that year, and the weather was particularly ideal — just enough rain and sunshine. Nevertheless, the increase was greater than could be explained by these factors. So he looked into it. He discovered that his fields had been colonized by hedgehogs, who prey on the kinds of insect pests that usually eat crops.

   Thesis: Hedgehogs in his fields had contributed to the marked increase of his crop yields.

   Analysis: The premises include more than one cause for the effect that the crop yields markedly increased. By eliminating all the other alternatives, the factor of hedgehogs was discovered as a key cause for the marked increase. The thesis in this way specifies one of the causes.

3. **Premises**: A pediatric oncologist was faced with a number of cases of childhood leukemia over a short period of time. Puzzled, he conducted thorough examinations of all the children, and also compared their living situations. He was surprised to discover that all of the children lived in houses that were located very close to high-voltage power lines.

   Thesis: Exposure to electromagnetic fields causes cancer.

   Analysis: This argument uses Miller's method of agreement to identify that the factor which is present in all the cases of childhood leukemia is the fact that they all lived in houses that were located very close to high-voltage power lines.

Practice 6-12

Explain to a partner how the following causal relationships are justified in the arguments. Refer to the analyses in Model 6-7 as examples.

1. According to the newly revised Henan Provincial Population and Family Planning Ordinances, only–child employees, with hospitalized, aged parents who are above 60 years old, can enjoy up to 20-days paid leave every year to take care of their parents. Without paid leave, the only-child employees, who are the breadwinners of their families, are forced to take unpaid leave, reducing their already limited salaries. Most of them would rather work than spend those hours with their parents. Without paid leave, elderly parents will suffer from a lack of care and contact by their children, which is harmful for the family as a whole. Therefore, offering paid leave to only-child employees will go someway to addressing potential parent-child issues in these families.

2. The remarkable development of the swimsuit industry in Huludao, China's Liaoning Province is a result of the country's reform and opening-up policy. Before the reform and opening-up, Huludao was just a tiny fishing village. But today it has risen in status as the global hub for the swimsuit business. By 2018, Huludao has more than 1,200 swimsuit firms, with an annual output of 190 million suits and an output value of more than 14 billion yuan. Every one out of four swimsuits sold in the world comes from Huludao.

Practice 6-13

Think of two more examples of causal reasoning in your everyday life or study. Then share your examples with a partner.

Model 6-8

A critical essay with causal reasoning

Study the model critical essay and pay attention to the analysis about the causal reasoning used.

	Shyness
introduction thesis statement	❶ If you suffer from shyness, you are not alone, for shyness is a universal phenomenon and social scientists are learning more about its causes. **In fact, shyness in an individual can result from both biological and environmental factors**.
causal reasoning 1 (Para. 2) <u>thesis</u> premises ①②③ using research findings to support the causal relation between shyness and biological factors	❷ <u>Recent research reveals that some individuals are genetically predisposed to shyness.</u> In other words, some people are born shy. ①Researchers say that between 15 to 20 percent of newborn babies show signs of shyness: They are quieter and more vigilant. ②Researchers have identified physiological differences between sociable and shy babies that show up as early as two months. ③In one study, two-months-old who were later identified as shy children reacted with signs of stress to stimuli such as moving mobiles and tape recordings of human voices: increased heart rate, jerky movements of arms and legs, and excessive crying.
	❸ However, environment can, at least in some cases, triumph over biology. A shy child may lose much of his or her shyness. On the other hand, many people who are not shy as children become shy as adults, a fact that points to environmental or experiential causes.
causal reasoning 2 (Para. 4) <u>thesis</u> premises ①supporting the correlation between shyness and family life ②explaining how small family size can cause shyness	❹ <u>The first environmental cause of shyness may be a child's home and family life.</u> ①Children who grow up with a difficult relationship with parents or a dominating older sibling are more likely to be inhibited in social interactions. ②Another factor is the fact that today's children are growing up in smaller and smaller families, with fewer and fewer relatives living nearby. Growing up in single-parent homes or in homes in which both parents work full time, children may not have the socializing experience of frequent visits by neighbors and friends. Because of their lack of social skills, they may begin to feel socially inhibited, or shy, when they start school.

causal reasoning 3 (Para. 5)
thesis

premises
using Mill's method of
difference

❺ A second environmental cause of shyness in an individual may be one's culture. In a large study conducted in several nations, 40 percent of participants in the United States rated themselves as shy, compared to 57 percent in Japan and 55 percent in Republic of Korea. Of the countries participating in the study, the lowest percentage of shyness was found in Israel, where the rate was 31 percent. Researchers Henderson and Zimbardo say, "One explanation of the cultural difference between Japanese and Israelis lies in the way each culture deals with attributing credit for success and blame for failure." In Japan, an individual's performing success is credited externally to parents, grandparents, teachers, coaches, and others, while failure is entirely blamed on the person. Therefore, Japanese learn not to take risks in public and rely instead on group-shared decisions. In Israel, the situation is entirely reversed, according to Henderson and Zimbardo. Failure is externally attributed to parents, teachers, coaches, friends, anti-Semitism, and other sources, while all performance success is credited to the individual's enterprise. The consequence is that Israelis are free to take risks since there is nothing to lose by trying and everything to gain.

causal reasoning 4 (Para. 6)
thesis

premises ①②③④⑤
using several specific
instances to explain how
technology can cause
shyness

❻ In addition to family and culture, technology may play a role as well. ①Watching television, playing video games, and surfing the Web have displaced recreational activities that involve social interaction for many young people. ②Adults, too, are becoming more isolated as a result of technology. Face-to-face interactions with bank tellers, gas station attendants, and store clerks are no longer necessary because people can use machines to do their banking, fill their gas tanks, and order merchandise. ③College students take online courses. ④Telecommuters work from home, giving up daily contact with coworkers. ⑤Everyone texts, E-mails, and converses anonymously in online chat rooms. As a result, people have less opportunity to socialize in person, become increasingly awkward at it, and eventually start avoiding it altogether. In short, they become shy.

conclusion
restate the thesis

❼ To sum up, shyness has both genetic and environmental causes. Some people come into the world shy, while others become shy as a result of their experiences in life. It appears that most people have experienced shyness at some time in their lives, and recent research indicates that the number of shy people is increasing. Therefore, if you are shy, you have lots of company.

Practice 6-14

Read the following paragraph. Underline the premises and bracket the thesis. Then work with a partner. Compare your answers and explain to each other how the causal relationship is established.

One common effect of video game addiction is isolation and withdrawal from social experiences. Video game players often hide in their homes or in Internet cafés for days at a time — only reemerging for the most pressing tasks and necessities. The effect of this isolation can lead to a breakdown of communication skills and often a loss in socialization. While it is true that many games, especially massive multiplayer online games, involve a very real form of e-based communication and coordination with others, and these virtual interactions often result in real communities that can be healthy for the players, these communities and forms of communication rarely translate to the types of valuable social interaction that humans need to maintain typical social functioning. As a result, the social networking in these online games often gives the users the impression that they are interacting socially while their true social lives and personal relations may suffer.

Practice 6-15

Can you think of other effects of video game addiction? Work in groups. Brainstorm and list the effects. Then select one cause-effect relationship to make an argument about. Write a short paragraph of about 80–100 words on your own. Hint: You may take Paras. 2 & 4 of the essay in Model 6-8 as examples.

_____

_____

_____

_____

_____

_____

Read and analyze the following arguments. Identify if they are inductive generalizations (I), analogical (A), or causal reasoning (C). Write down the corresponding letter in the parentheses. Then explain your answers to a partner.

1. His performance on this test was bad because he didn't read the textbook fully. So, preparation for exams will pay off. (   )

2. Boxing is a dangerous sport, and like all dangerous sports, it's a lot of fun to watch. (   )

3. This company is like a racehorse. It has run fast and won the race, and now it needs feed and rest for a while. (   )

4. A survey found out that more than 90% of the students at the university usually stay up late. Therefore, most university students often stay up late. (   )

5. Most of the top-performing employees at the company attended a certain university. So the company should target that university more for recruiting efforts. (   )

6. The top-3 computer manufacturers all produce notebook computers with built-in cameras. Because these companies are a representative sample of all major computer manufacturers, it follows that all major computer manufacturers probably manufacture notebook computers with built-in cameras. (   )

7. In the last five years, there has been a significant increase in the consumption of red wine. During this same time, there have been several major news reports about the beneficial long-term effects on health that certain antioxidants in red wine can provide. Thus, the increase in red wine consumption can be directly attributed to consumers' recognition of the beneficial effects of antioxidants. (   )

8. Privacy should be honored by all people. Otherwise, tragedy might follow. Take Princess Diana as an example. She was killed in a car crash, which was caused by tabloid reporters relentlessly chasing her. This tragedy is a wake-up call for all the media and the Internet users who tend to abuse their power and pry into the private lives of public figures. There are many other examples of such kinds. (   )

From reading to writing

■ Reading

Read the essay and finish the tasks.

Sustainable Mobility: China's Efforts Inspire Emulation

❶ Around the globe, policymakers are leveraging technological innovation to transform the transport sector, progressively shifting away from fossil fuel consumption to clean energy to achieve sustainable mobility. China is a trailblazer in this field, commendably serving as the major driver of the world's sustainable transport transition and also sharing technical expertise and innovation with the rest of the world.

❷ A critical examination of the country's contribution towards achieving sustainable transport indicates that apart from the fact that China accounts for about 90 percent of the world's electric buses, trucks, and almost all two- and three-wheelers as of July 2021, the country has also installed 2.015 million public charging stations, representing the largest electric vehicle charging network in the world. Furthermore, China dominates the global electric vehicle supply chain, which includes contributing 60 percent of the battery component manufacturing and commanding a whopping 80 percent of raw material refining, together with almost 500 world-class Chinese electric vehicle manufacturers that are competing for the top spot. Thus, China's exports and contribution in this field are the main drivers that underpin progress in the global sustainable transport transition.

❸ While China has the broadest model offering for electric vehicles, the country is also promoting the use of bicycles, which is another means of transport that is economical for short distances, reduces congestion particularly in urban areas, being environmental, and offers many health benefits. As the world's largest exporter of bicycles, China is once again contributing considerably to improving access to affordable and clean transportation to the world. According to data from the China Bicycle Association, from January to September 2020 alone,

China had exported more than 40 million bicycles. This quantity is almost four times the European Union's yearly production of bicycles.

❹ By providing the world with millions of bicycles and manufacturing a wide range of different electric vehicles to suit all forms of travel on roads, China is on course to reducing global carbon emissions. While available data reveal that the transport sector accounts for one-fifth of the world's carbon dioxide emissions, road travel alone contributes three-quarters of the total emissions from the transport sector — the largest share of the carbon emissions is produced by passenger vehicles such as buses and cars as they account for 45.1 percent whiles trucks carrying freight contribute 29.4 percent. This shows that by contributing more than any other country in transforming road transport, which is by far the largest carbon emitter, China is hitting the nail on the head in the country's policy approach to boost global sustainable transport transition.

❺ Again, the Belt and Road Initiative (BRI), China's massive transport infrastructure project that is connecting Asia with Africa and Europe through land and maritime networks is advancing efforts towards sustainable mobility — this tremendous infrastructure investment is seeking to connect more than 60 percent of the world's population. By building roads, airports, railroads, ports, bridges, and other relevant transport facilities, the BRI which is the world's largest infrastructure project is filling the infrastructure gap in cities and rural areas across several regions as it is scaling up the required climate-resilient infrastructure needed to support sustainable transportation worldwide.

❻ In a nutshell, China has demonstrated beyond reasonable doubt that the country's people-centered approach to providing sustainable mobility transcends national or regional borders. This supports the argument that China's commitment is worthy of emulation and also requires the cooperation of all countries to build the much-needed climate-resilient and robust global sustainable transport sector.

Writing technique questions

Based on what you have learned in this chapter, consider the following questions. Then discuss with your group your answers and seek a consensus.

1. What is the essay's thesis statement?

2. The thesis statement contains also a roadmap indicating that the essay is going to

   be developed into two lines of reasoning: 1)_____

   _____; and 2) _____.

3. Which paragraphs are contributing arguments comprising the first line of reasoning, and which the second line of reasoning?

4. In Para. 2, the author attempts to justify that _____

   _____

   _____. The following evidence is provided:

   Evidence 1: _____.

   Evidence 2: _____.

   Evidence 3: _____.

   Evidence 4: _____.

   Evidence 5: _____.

   This is a typical type of inductive reasoning strategy called _____.

5. What is the thesis of Para. 4? What inductive reasoning strategy is used to justify it?

6. What is the overall reasoning strategy used to support the thesis statement? Why do you think so?

Critical thinking questions
Consider the questions below and finish the tasks.

1. Why is sustainable mobility critical for the development of human society? What

positive effects will it produce? What potential risks do you anticipate if no efforts are made to promote it?

2. Share your answers to the questions above with your group.

3. Discuss with your group to categorize all the positive and negative impacts that you shared in Exercise 2. Draw a mind map to show your ideas.

sample

4. Present your mind map to the class.

Chapter 6　How to apply inductive reasoning to writing?

■ Writing

Based on your answers to the critical thinking questions, write an essay on the topic "Why Sustainable Transportation Matters?". Apply at least one of the inductive reasoning strategies learned in this chapter.

REFLECTION

This chapter discussed how inductive reasoning strategies can be used in writing. Now it's time to review and reflect on what you have learned. Work in pairs and take turns to answer the following questions. Check them as you answer each one.

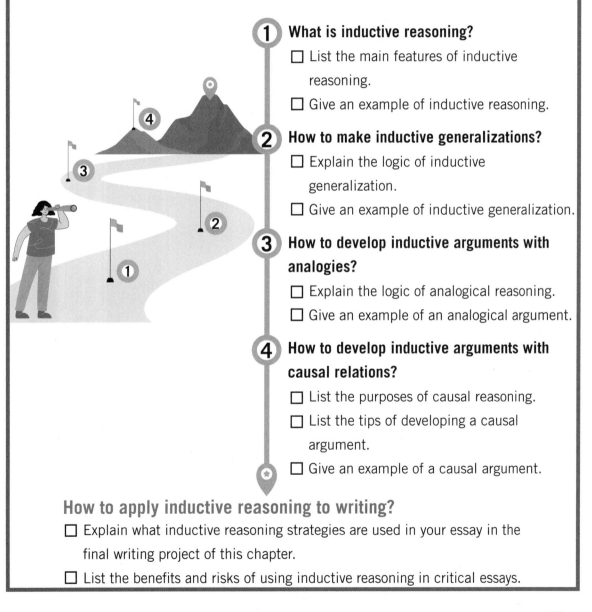

1 What is inductive reasoning?
- ☐ List the main features of inductive reasoning.
- ☐ Give an example of inductive reasoning.

2 How to make inductive generalizations?
- ☐ Explain the logic of inductive generalization.
- ☐ Give an example of inductive generalization.

3 How to develop inductive arguments with analogies?
- ☐ Explain the logic of analogical reasoning.
- ☐ Give an example of an analogical argument.

4 How to develop inductive arguments with causal relations?
- ☐ List the purposes of causal reasoning.
- ☐ List the tips of developing a causal argument.
- ☐ Give an example of a causal argument.

How to apply inductive reasoning to writing?
- ☐ Explain what inductive reasoning strategies are used in your essay in the final writing project of this chapter.
- ☐ List the benefits and risks of using inductive reasoning in critical essays.

How to revise an essay?

彼以此其然也，说是其然也。我以此其不然也，疑是其然也。

——《墨子·经说下》

Another, on the basis of these being so, says this is so. I, on the basis of these not being so, call in question this being so.

——"Canons and Explanations B," *The Mozi*

T: So far, we've learned 5 reasoning strategies: applying a principle, applying a definition, inductive generalization, analogical reasoning, and causal reasoning.

S: I'm ready to produce a good critical essay.

2

T: Well, the strategies are powerful, but are you sure you can use them effectively to produce strong arguments?

3

S: Er... Then how do I improve the strength of my arguments?

4

Chapter roadmap

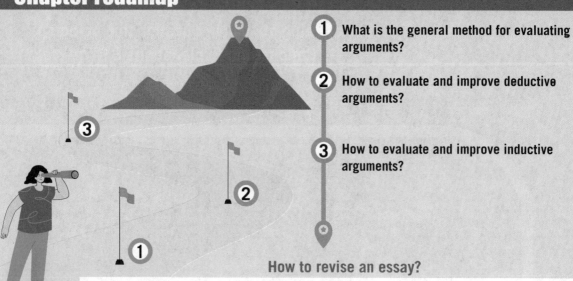

1. What is the general method for evaluating arguments?

2. How to evaluate and improve deductive arguments?

3. How to evaluate and improve inductive arguments?

How to revise an essay?

Learning outcomes

At the end of this chapter, you will be able to

- understand the two essential concerns of argument evaluation;
- list the right evaluation questions for different types of arguments;
- evaluate different types of arguments by asking and answering proper questions;
- improve the strength of different types of arguments in critical writing.

From reading to writing

Consider the effectiveness of China's poverty alleviation policies and improve an argument on this topic.

1. What is the general method for evaluating arguments?

We are always told that good writing is a result of continuous revision. But besides editing the language, what can we do to improve the content of our essays? As the quote at the beginning of this chapter says, to question the rightfulness of an idea is an important step towards improving it. In this section, we will address this issue.

Core knowledge input

MOOC Lesson 7

Two Essential Concerns over Argument Evaluation

There are two essential concerns regarding the soundness or strength of an argument: truthfulness and validity. When an argument includes both true premises and a valid structure, the argument is sound.

Truthfulness: How true are the premises?

In dealing with this first concern, you need to consider certain questions: Does each premise make sense? Is it based on a source that can be trusted? What evidence is being offered as part of each premise?

Validity: To what extent does the thesis follow the premises?

Evaluating arguments also involves investigating the relationship between the premises and the thesis. Do the premises sufficiently support the thesis? Is it the case that if the premises are true, the thesis will (very likely to) be true? If yes, the argument is valid. Otherwise, it is invalid.

Model 7-1

Evaluating truthfulness and validity of arguments

Read the following arguments and study their evaluation.

Premises:	Anything that is a threat to our health should not be legal. Smoking is a threat to our health.
Thesis:	Therefore, smoking should not be legal.
Truthfulness:	**How true are the premises?**
	While it has been quite sufficiently proven that smoking is a threat to our health, it is too absolute to say "Anything that is a threat to our health should not be legal." The author simply makes this assertion without offering any evidence.
Validity:	**To what extent does the thesis follow the premises?**
	If indeed anything that is a threat to our health should not be legal and smoking is truly a threat to our health, then we must admit that smoking should not be legal. Even though we think the first premise is not true, the structure of the argument is valid because if we assume that the premises are true, then the thesis necessarily follows.
Overall evaluation:	The argument, though valid, is not sound in that one of its premises is not true.
Premises:	Mr. Jia believes that it is vital for our national security that we develop alternative sources of energy. Mr. Jia is the mayor of our city.
Thesis:	Therefore, we should develop alternative sources of energy.
Truthfulness:	**How true are the premises?**
	The premises are open information, so they are most likely to be true.

Validity: **To what extent does the thesis follow the premises?**

This argument is not valid because even if we assume that the premises are true, the conclusion does not follow. Although Mr. Jia is the mayor, that fact does not give him any special expertise in alternative sources of energy. For a topic of such complexity and global significance, one person's opinion is far from enough, no matter who that person is.

Overall evaluation: The argument is not sound, though the premises are true.

Practice 7-1

Underline the premises and bracket the theses of the following arguments. Then work in pairs and take turns to say if the premise of each argument is true or how you can verify its truthfulness.

1. Parents should take their kids to regular music lessons because playing a musical instrument improves kids' brains.

   Truthfulness: _____

   _____

2. In a complete educational system, social interaction should be involved. If we acknowledge this principle, and since taking MOOCs lacks social interaction, traditional classes are obviously irreplaceable.

   Truthfulness: _____

   _____

3. Traditional classroom teaching is instrumental to fostering students' learning habits and qualities. Since classroom teaching obliges students to attend classes on time, it will improve their responsibility and diligence.

   Truthfulness: _____

   _____

Practice 7-2

Work with the same partner. Read the following arguments. Underline the premises and bracket the theses. Take turns to explain whether they are valid.

1. All birds fly. Tracy can fly. So, Tracy is a bird.

   Validity: _____

   _____

2. Whenever we are confronted with trouble, the first people we turn to are our parents. They will then advise us on how to solve our problems based on their own life experience. So, parents are the best teachers in our lives.

   Validity: _____

   _____

3. In Volume II, Chapter IX of *Frankenstein*, the creature argues with Victor Frankenstein like this: You created me and so are obliged to me as your creature. This obligation is in part to improve my lot as father. A companion would best improve my lot. Therefore, you must create a companion for me.

   Validity: _____

   _____

2. How to evaluate and improve deductive arguments?

Truthfulness and validity are two general concerns of argument evaluation. But do you feel like you need more specific instructions, especially when evaluating arguments using different reasoning strategies? In this section, we will first take a closer look at the evaluation and improvement of deductive arguments.

2.1 Evaluating and improving arguments with a principle

Micro-lecture **Specific Evaluation Questions for Arguments with a Principle**
MOOC Lesson 7

Specific Evaluation Questions for Arguments with a Principle

When evaluating arguments based on reasoning with a principle, ask the following check-up questions.

1. **Is the principle true or widely accepted? (truthfulness concern)**
    Some principles, such as the law of gravitation or a provision from *The Civil Code of the People's Republic of China*, can be clearly verified as true or not. Other principles, however, such as moral standards or professional ethics, are more of shared conceptions of a certain group of people. When evaluating the truthfulness of such principles, we consider whether the principle is widely accepted by the reader group.

2. **Are the other premises true? (truthfulness concern)**
    Review Section 1 of this chapter.

3. **Are the premises directly relevant to the thesis? (validity concern)**
    The relevance of the premises to the thesis can be understood as whether the thesis would be different if the premises are different or not available. Compare the following examples.

Principle used: People need to improve their understanding of how language works so that they can use it more effectively.	
A relevant thesis (if no other premises offered) People who have difficulty using a second language should be encouraged to study the grammar rules of that language.	**An irrelevant thesis (if no other premises offered)** People who only speak one language should be encouraged to study a second language.

Model 7-2

Evaluating and improving arguments with a principle

Only when people have an adequate understanding of how language works can they use it effectively. Some studies have found that many people cannot describe the different grammatical components of their own language, and a surprising number of people cannot even remember the rules of their mother tongue. Therefore, people who cannot use their mother language effectively should be encouraged to study a second language.

Step 1 **Analyzing the argument**	**Reasoning strategy used:** Applying a principle **Thesis:** Therefore, people who cannot use their mother language effectively should be encouraged to study a second language. **Principle used:** Only when people have an adequate understanding of how language works can they use it effectively. **Other premises offered:** Some studies have found that many people cannot describe the different grammatical components of their own language, and a surprising number of people cannot even remember the rules of their mother tongue.
Step 2 **Asking the evaluation questions**	**1. Is the principle true?** The principle is widely accepted according to our common sense. **2. Are the other premise(s) true?** This can be verified true or not by consulting the related studies or investigations. **3. Are the premises directly relevant?** No. The research findings that many people are poor at their own language could be understood to suggest that they need to improve the proficiency of their first language before learning a second. Although it seems relevant to the topic of this argument, it fails to build the connection between the principle and the thesis.
Step 3 **Revising the argument by correcting the problem(s) found**	**Suggested improvements:** Look for other research findings that can support the connection between learning a second language and improving one's understanding of their mother language. For example, a recent research shows that the study of a foreign language provides a way of comparing different language structures and thus improves our understanding of how our mother languages work.

All eight-year-olds should be in bed by 9:30 p.m. You are an eight-year-old child. Therefore, you should be in bed by 9:30 p.m.

Step 1 Analyzing the argument	**Reasoning strategy used:** Applying a principle **Thesis:** You should be in bed by 9:30 p.m. **Principle used:** All eight-year-olds should be in bed by 9:30 p.m. **Other premises offered:** You are an eight-year-old child.

Step 2 Asking the evaluation questions	1. **Is the principle true?**
	   Although children are suggested to have enough sleep, it is not a widely accepted rule.
	2. **Are the other premise(s) true?**
	   This can be easily verified.
	3. **Are the premises directly relevant?**
	   Yes.

Step 3 Revising the argument by correcting the problem(s) found	**Suggested improvements:** Use another principle or talk about how children benefit from receiving enough sleep.

Practice 7-3

Evaluate and improve the following arguments by filling out the evaluation tables. Then work in pairs. Compare your answers and discuss it where you disagree.

1. Society must condemn actions (even if peaceful) that precipitate violence. Violence will lead to bigger problems instead of solving them. Therefore, society must condemn private gun ownership.

Step 1 Analyzing the argument	**Reasoning strategy used:** Applying a principle **Thesis:** 1) _____ **Principle used:** 2) _____ **Other premises offered:** 3) _____

(Continued)

Step 2 **Asking the evaluation questions**	**1. Is the principle true?** 4) _____ **2. Are the other premise(s) true?** 5) _____ **3. Are the premises directly relevant?** 6) _____
Step 3 **Revising the argument by correcting the problem(s) found**	**Suggested improvements:** 7) _____ _____

2. The regulation says we should accept the lower price quote for our staff uniforms. The price quote from Company ABC is now lower than the price quote from Company LMN. Therefore, we will get the uniforms for our staff from Company ABC.

Step 1 **Analyzing the argument**	**Reasoning strategy used:** Applying a principle **Thesis:** 1) _____ **Principle used:** 2) _____ **Other premises offered:** 3) _____
Step 2 **Asking the evaluation questions**	**1. Is the principle true?** 4) _____ **2. Are the other premise(s) true?** 5) _____ **3. Are the premises directly relevant?** 6) _____
Step 3 **Revising the argument by correcting the problem(s) found**	**Suggested improvements:** 7) _____ _____

3. A medical technology ought to be funded if it has been used successfully to treat patients. Adult stem cells are being used to treat patients successfully in more than sixty-five new therapies. Adult stem cell research and technology should be funded.

Step 1 **Analyzing the argument**	**Reasoning strategy used:** Applying a principle **Thesis:** 1) _____ **Principle used:** 2) _____ **Other premises offered:** 3) _____

Step 2
Asking the evaluation questions
	1. Is the principle true?
	   4) _____
	2. Are the other premise(s) true?
	   5) _____
	3. Are the premises directly relevant?
	   6) _____

Step 3 **Revising the argument by correcting the problem(s) found**	**Suggested improvements:** 7) _____ _____

2.2 Evaluating and improving arguments with a definition

Core knowledge input

Micro-lecture Specific Evaluation Questions for Arguments with a Definition
MOOC Lesson 7

Specific Evaluation Questions for Arguments with a Definition

When evaluating arguments based on reasoning with a definition, ask the following check-up questions.

1. Is the definition true or appropriate? (truthfulness concern)

When we use a definition as a premise to support the thesis, we often cite a well-recognized one from dictionaries, books, formal reports, or other authoritative sources. In this case, evaluating the truthfulness of the definition means to go to the cited source and check if it has been reported accurately. But there are also situations where we have to establish a definition on our own, and then being a true definition can be interpreted as that the definition is appropriate in the way that it covers all the essential features of the subject being defined.

2. **Are the other premises true? (truthfulness concern)**
Review Section 1 of this chapter.

3. **Are the premises directly relevant to the thesis? (validity concern)**
For example, when arguing that XYZ University is a world-class university, a definition of a world-class university is clearly more relevant to the thesis than a definition of a good university.

Model 7-3

Evaluating and improving arguments with a definition

An international talent is an individual who has superior professional skills in a certain field and essential transferable skills needed to solve problems in different situations. Therefore, our teaching program, which aims at cultivating international talents for the country, should focus on developing students' professional skills and transferable skills.

Step 1 Analyzing the argument	**Reasoning strategy used:** Applying a definition **Thesis:** Our teaching program, which aims at cultivating international talents for the country, should focus on developing students' professional skills and transferable skills. **Definition used:** An international talent is an individual who has superior professional skills in a certain field and essential transferable skills needed to solve problems in different situations. **Other premises offered:** None.

Step 2 Asking the evaluation questions	**1. Is the definition true?** No. First, no source is offered to help us verify the truthfulness. Second, this definition fails to address a key feature of international talents, i.e. being capable of international communication. **2. Are the other premise(s) true?** N/A **3. Are the premises directly relevant?** Yes.
Step 3 Revising the argument by correcting the problem(s) found	**Suggested improvements:** Provide a qualified definition. For example, an international talent is an individual who has regional knowledge, language skills, international contacts, and inter-cultural experiences in addition to superior professional skills in a certain field and essential transferable skills.

Plagiarism is presenting someone else's work or ideas as your own, with or without their consent, by incorporating it into your work without full acknowledgment. Any student who commits plagiarism should be expelled from school.

Step 1 Analyzing the argument	**Reasoning strategy used:** Applying a definition **Thesis:** Any student who commits plagiarism should be expelled from school. **Definition used:** Plagiarism is presenting someone else's work or ideas as your own, with or without their consent, by incorporating it into your work without full acknowledgment. **Other premises offered:** None.
Step 2 Asking the evaluation questions	**1. Is the definition true?** Yes. **2. Are the other premise(s) true?** N/A **3. Are the premises directly relevant?** No. The definition of plagiarism can help decide what behavior is recognized as plagiarism or plagiarism is not a moral behavior. It cannot justify the thesis that students committing it should be expelled from school.

(Continued)

Step 3 Revising the argument by correcting the problem(s) found	**Suggested improvements:** Cite the school rules about when a student can be expelled, and judge if plagiarism violates the rules.

Practice 7-4

Evaluate and improve the following arguments by filling out the evaluation tables. Then work in pairs. Compare your answers and discuss it where you disagree.

1. Writing is the language skill of communicating to an unknown audience with a pen or a keyboard. So, to develop your writing skill you should first prepare a good pen and then keep your audience in mind.

Step 1 Analyzing the argument	**Reasoning strategy used:** Applying a definition **Thesis:** 1) _____ **Definition used:** 2) _____ **Other premises offered:** 3) _____

Step 2
Asking the
evaluation
questions
	1. Is the definition true?
	    4) _____
	2. Are the other premise(s) true?
	    5) _____
	3. Are the premises directly relevant?
	    6) _____

Step 3 Revising the argument by correcting the problem(s) found	**Suggested improvements:** 7) _____ _____

2. Vegetarianism is the practice of abstaining from the consumption of meat (red meat, poultry, seafood, and the flesh of any other animal), and it may also include abstention

from by-products of animal slaughter. Ming is a vegetarian. So, she is living a healthy life.

Step 1 Analyzing the argument	**Reasoning strategy used:** Applying a definition **Thesis:** 1) _____ **Definition used:** 2) _____ **Other premises offered:** 3) _____

Step 2 Asking the evaluation questions	**1. Is the definition true?**
	   4) _____
	2. Are the other premise(s) true?
	   5) _____
	3. Are the premises directly relevant?
	   6) _____

Step 3 Revising the argument by correcting the problem(s) found	**Suggested improvements:** 7) _____ _____

3. How to evaluate and improve inductive arguments?

When evaluating deductive arguments, we examine the relevancy of the premises to the thesis as well as the truthfulness of the premises. Is it the same with evaluating inductive arguments? This is what we will discuss in this section.

3.1 Evaluating and improving arguments with inductive generalization

Core knowledge input

Micro-lecture Specific Evaluation Questions for Arguments with Inductive Generalization
MOOC Lesson 7

Specific Evaluation Questions for Arguments with Inductive Generalization

When evaluating arguments based on inductive generalization, ask the following check-up questions.

1. **Are the premises true? (truthfulness concern)**
   Review Section 1 of this chapter.

2. **Are the premises directly relevant to the thesis? (validity concern)**
   For example, car accidents that happened because of the use of cell phones when driving are relevant to the generalization that using cell phone technology while driving is associated with a greater risk of automobile accidents. In contrast, people's views on using cell phones when driving are not relevant in supporting the same generalization.

3. **Are the premises sufficient to support the thesis? (validity concern)**
   We examine the sufficiency of the premises from three perspectives:
   - **Quantity:** How broad the generalization is? How many specific examples or cases should be offered to support it adequately?
   - **Typicality:** Are the specific examples or cases offered typical ones? For example, when investigating if college students carry laptops to classes, computer science majors would not be considered as typical cases because their classes tend to use computers more frequently.
   - **Coverage:** Can the specific examples or cases offered cover all the key aspects of the generalization? For example, simply using statistics about annual household income is not sufficient to support a thesis about happiness, as happiness also includes other aspects like health, relations, security, etc.

Model 7-4

Evaluating and improving arguments with inductive generalization

My boyfriend has never shown any real concern for my feelings. My conclusion is that men are insensitive, selfish, and emotionally superficial.

Step 1 Analyzing the argument	**Reasoning strategy used:** Inductive generalization **Thesis:** Men are insensitive, selfish, and emotionally superficial. **Premises:** My boyfriend has never shown any real concern for my feelings.
Step 2 Asking the evaluation questions	**1. Are the premises true?** Not sure. No evidence is offered as this sentence itself is a generalization about the boyfriend's usual attitude to the author. **2. Are the premises relevant?** Yes. The boyfriend is a man. **3. Are the premises sufficient?** No. There's only one example offered, and it is unclear how typical it is because we don't know what kind of a man the boyfriend is. Also, it is only about the boyfriend's attitude to the author not covering the other aspects of a man's emotional intelligence, such as empathy to other people. This is over-generalizing.
Step 3 Revising the argument by correcting the problem(s) found	**Suggested improvements:** The thesis is a generalization about all men, which makes it extremely hard to look for sufficient specific cases. If the author insists on justifying such a thesis, statistical results about men's EQ (compared with that of women) from reliable investigations may be more adequate than a few individual cases.

Another Ice Age in coming. Winters in Toronto were extremely cold in the past three years. And opinion polls also show that most people think there is a new Ice Age on the way.

Step 1 Analyzing the argument	**Reasoning strategy used:** Inductive generalization **Thesis:** Another Ice Age in coming. **Premises:** Winters in Toronto were extremely cold in the past three years. And opinion polls also show that most people think there is a new Ice Age on the way.

(Continued)

Step 2 **Asking the** **evaluation** **questions**	**1. Are the premises true?** They are likely to be true because such information can be easily verified. **2. Are the premises relevant?** That the past three winters in Toronto were cold is relevant, but people's ideas from the opinion polls are subjective beliefs, which are not relevant evidence of global cooling. **3. Are the premises sufficient?** No. Even if the first premise is true, it only offers temperature changes in the past three winters in Toronto, not including those changes in other seasons or other areas of the world.
Step 3 **Revising the** **argument by** **correcting the** **problem(s) found**	**Suggested improvements:** 1. Provide evidence about temperature changes around the world in different seasons. 2. Provide evidence about other indicators of global cooling.

Practice 7-5

Evaluate and improve the following arguments by filling out the evaluation tables. Then work in pairs. Compare your answers and discuss it where you disagree.

1. I must have met five or six students from N University at the philosophy conference over the break, and they were all really smart. That must be an amazingly smart student body up there at N University!

Step 1 **Analyzing the** **argument**	**Reasoning strategy used:** Inductive generalization **Thesis:** 1) _____ **Premises:** 2) _____
Step 2 **Asking the** **evaluation** **questions**	**1. Are the premises true?** 3) _____ **2. Are the premises relevant?** 4) _____ **3. Are the premises sufficient?** 5) _____

| Step 3 Revising the argument by correcting the problem(s) found | Suggested improvements:
 6) _____
 _____ |

2. E-books are more convenient than paper books. For example, you can carry books and magazines with you. Books and magazines weigh tens of grams at least and a few kilograms at most. If there are many books, it is difficult to carry them.

Step 1 Analyzing the argument	**Reasoning strategy used:** Inductive generalization **Thesis:** 1) _____ **Premises:** 2) _____
Step 2 Asking the evaluation questions	**1. Are the premises true?** 3) _____ **2. Are the premises relevant?** 4) _____ **3. Are the premises sufficient?** 5) _____
Step 3 Revising the argument by correcting the problem(s) found	**Suggested improvements:** 6) _____ _____

3. College education entitles a graduate to more choices of lifestyle. When still in college, one can positively choose the activity or work that one is interested in. In contrast, a non-college student's life is decided by his / her boss. When graduating from college, one can choose to be a senior executive or start up a business. On the contrary, a non-college student can only labor or set up a small stand that may go bankrupt easily. With a college education, we can choose our own life.

Step 1 Analyzing the argument	**Reasoning strategy used:** Inductive generalization **Thesis:** 1) _____ **Premises:** 2) _____

Step 2
Asking the
evaluation
questions
	1. Are the premises true?
	  3) _____
	2. Are the premises relevant?
	  4) _____
	3. Are the premises sufficient?
	  5) _____

Step 3 Revising the argument by correcting the problem(s) found	**Suggested improvements:** 6) _____ _____

3.2 Evaluating and improving analogical arguments

Core knowledge input

 Micro-lecture Specific Evaluation Questions for Analogical Arguments
MOOC Lesson 7

Specific Evaluation Questions for Analogical Arguments
When evaluating analogical arguments, ask the following check-up questions.

1. **Are the premises, especially the analogy, true? (truthfulness concern)**
   By true analogy, we mean the similarities between the two things compared, which are used as the basis of the thesis, are true. Revisit this example in Model 6-5: There might be life on Europa because it has an atmosphere that contains oxygen just like Earth. Here the similarity used to support the thesis is both Europa and Earth have an atmosphere that contains oxygen. So, to test the truthfulness, we may ask if there is truly oxygen in the atmosphere of Europa.

2. **Are the premises, especially the analogy, directly relevant to the thesis? (validity concern)**

   The author uses the similarities between two things to support the thesis. But are the similarities relevant to the thesis? Can we say since both students wear spectacles, their academic performances must be equally good? The similarity in sight is not relevant to academic performance.

3. **Are the premises, especially the analogy, sufficient to support the thesis? (validity concern)**

   This can be examined from two aspects:

   - How strong are the similarities? For instance, how much oxygen is there in the atmosphere of Europa? Is it close to the amount of oxygen in Earth's atmosphere?
   - Do the similarities cover all key aspects contributing to the thesis? Or does the argument overlooks significant differences between the two things compared? For example, is oxygen content the only key factor influencing life on a planet? Are there similarities in other aspects, such as water, climate, etc., between the two planets?

Model 7-5

Evaluating and improving analogical arguments

"Mama always said life was like a box of chocolates. You never know what you're gonna get!"—*Forrest Gump*

Step 1 **Analyzing the argument**	**Reasoning strategy used:** Analogical reasoning **Thesis:** You never know what you're gonna get! **Premises:** Analogy: Life is similar to a box of chocolates.
Step 2 **Asking the evaluation questions**	1. **Are the premises true?** No. We are not told in which way life is similar to a box of chocolates. 2. **Are the premises relevant?** Not sure, since no specific similarity is offered. 3. **Are the premises sufficient?** No.

Chapter 7 How to revise an essay?

(Continued)

Step 3 Revising the argument by correcting the problem(s) found	**Suggested improvements:** Specify the similarities between life and a box of chocolates, use evidence to support them, and make sure the similarities are key to the thesis about the uncertainty of life.

The early bird gets the worm. Birds are like job applicants and worms are like good jobs: The former are many in number and the latter is scarce. Early applicants probably get the best jobs.

Step 1 Analyzing the argument	**Reasoning strategy used:** Analogical reasoning **Thesis:** Early applicants probably get the best jobs. **Premises:** Analogy: Job-hunting is similar to birds looking for worms in that birds and job-hunters are many but worms and jobs are scarce.
Step 2 Asking the evaluation questions	1. **Are the premises true?** This similarity in quantity may be true, as there are indeed many birds and job-hunters compared to the number of worms and jobs available. 2. **Are the premises relevant?** Yes. The quantity of a thing has something to do with the probability of getting it. 3. **Are the premises sufficient?** No. It overlooks a significant difference: Success in job-hunting is largely determined by if an applicant's competence matches the demand of the job, which is not a key factor in worm-hunting.
Step 3 Revising the argument by correcting the problem(s) found	**Suggested improvements:** Use a different analogy or support the thesis with a different reasoning strategy, such as early application allows better preparation, which may lead to a better chance of winning the job.

Practice 7-6

Evaluate and improve the following arguments by filling out the evaluation

tables. Then work in pairs. Compare your answers and discuss it where you disagree.

1. Pupils are more like oysters than sausages. The job of teaching is not to stuff them and then seal them up, but to help them open and reveal the riches within.

Step 1 Analyzing the argument	**Reasoning strategy used:** Analogical reasoning **Thesis:** 1) _____ **Premises:** 2) _____

Step 2
Asking the
evaluation
questions
	1. Are the premises true?
	   3) _____
	2. Are the premises relevant?
	   4) _____
	3. Are the premises sufficient?
	   5) _____

Step 3 Revising the argument by correcting the problem(s) found	**Suggested improvements:** 6) _____ _____

2. If one were to listen to only one kind of music or eat only one kind of food, it would soon become tasteless or boring. So it seems to me that a life-long career does not promise very much excitement or enrichment.

Step 1 Analyzing the argument	**Reasoning strategy used:** Analogical reasoning **Thesis:** 1) _____ **Premises:** 2) _____

Step 2
Asking the
evaluation
questions
	1. Are the premises true?
	   3) _____
	2. Are the premises relevant?
	   4) _____
	3. Are the premises sufficient?
	   5) _____

(Continued)

Step 3 Revising the argument by correcting the problem(s) found	**Suggested improvements:** 6) _____ _____

3. Addiction to smartphones will eventually ruin one's life. We have seen many addictions, such as drug addiction or alcoholism, destroying people's health and eventually ruining their lives. Thus, becomming addicted to your phone is no exception.

Step 1 Analyzing the argument	**Reasoning strategy used:** Analogical reasoning **Thesis:** 1) _____ **Premises:** 2) _____
Step 2 Asking the evaluation questions	**1. Are the premises true?** 3) _____ **2. Are the premises relevant?** 4) _____ **3. Are the premises sufficient?** 5) _____
Step 3 Revising the argument by correcting the problem(s) found	**Suggested improvements:** 6) _____ _____

4. We should not blame the media for deteriorating moral standards. Newspapers and TV are like weather reporters who report the facts. We do not blame weather reporters for telling us that the weather is bad.

Step 1 Analyzing the argument	**Reasoning strategy used:** Analogical reasoning **Thesis:** 1) _____ **Premises:** 2) _____

(Continued)

Step 2
Asking the
evaluation
questions
	1. **Are the premises true?**
	   3) _____
	2. **Are the premises relevant?**
	   4) _____
	3. **Are the premises sufficient?**
	   5) _____

Step 3 Revising the argument by correcting the problem(s) found	**Suggested improvements:** 6) _____ _____

3.3 Evaluating and improving causal arguments

Core knowledge input

Micro-lecture Specific Evaluation Questions for Causal Arguments
MOOC Lesson 7

Specific Evaluation Questions for Causal Arguments

When evaluating causal arguments, ask the following check-up questions.

1. **Are the premises true? (truthfulness concern)**
   Review Section 1 of this chapter.

2. **Are the premises sufficient to support the causal relationship? (validity concern)**
   To answer this question, we need to consider the following three questions at the same time:
   - Can the premises prove that the proposed cause happens before the proposed effect?
   - Can the premises sufficiently confirm a correlation between the proposed cause and the proposed effect?
   - Can the premises sufficiently disconfirm alternative explanations? This can be

understood as that 1) the correlation is not due to some mutual cause, 2) the correlation is not due to chance, and 3) there is no other cause (or effect) that is more sufficient.

Model 7-6

Evaluating and improving causal arguments

Most young criminals watch violent movies before they commit their crimes. Obviously, violent movies lead to juvenile delinquency.

Step 1 **Analyzing the argument**	**Reasoning strategy used:** Causal reasoning **Thesis:** Violent movies lead to juvenile delinquency. **Premises:** Most young criminals watch violent movies before they commit their crimes.
Step 2 **Asking the evaluation questions**	1. **Are the premises true?** Not sure, since no evidence is offered. 2. **Can the premises prove that the proposed cause happens before the proposed effect?** Yes, if it is true. 3. **Can the premises sufficiently confirm a correlation between the proposed cause and the proposed effect?** No. Even if the premise is true, it does not support a correlation between watching violent movies and committing crimes. 4. **Can the premises sufficiently disconfirm alternative explanations?** No. It does not say anything about why other possible effects of watching violent movies do not make sense here.
Step 3 **Revising the argument by correcting the problem(s) found**	**Suggested improvements:** 1. Provide evidence to prove that most young criminals watch violent movies before they commit their crimes. 2. Offer more sufficient premises to justify the correlation between watching violent movies and committing crimes, such as what the criminals say about why they committed crimes. 3. Use premises to tell why other possible effects of watching violent movies, such as relieving one's pressure, should not be considered significant.

Muscle soreness causes muscle growth. You must all have experienced this: When undergoing a body shaping program, you feel muscle soreness, and then later you find your muscles have grown.

Step 1 **Analyzing the argument**	**Reasoning strategy used:** Causal reasoning **Thesis:** Muscle soreness causes muscle growth. **Premises:** When undergoing a body shaping program, you feel muscle soreness, and then later you find your muscles have grown.
Step 2 **Asking the evaluation questions**	1. **Are the premises true?** Yes. 2. **Can the premises prove that the proposed cause happens before the proposed effect?** Yes. 3. **Can the premises sufficiently confirm a correlation between the proposed cause and the proposed effect?** Yes. 4. **Can the premises sufficiently disconfirm alternative explanations?** No. There is actually another factor — exercising the muscle — that causes both the cause and effect in the argument.
Step 3 **Revising the argument by correcting the problem(s) found**	**Suggested improvements:** Recognize the effect of exercising on both muscle soreness and growth and revise the causal relationship.

Practice 7-7

Choose the best evaluation of the following causal arguments' strength. Then work in pairs. Compare your answers and discuss it where you disagree.

A. The argument is weak because it neither sufficiently establishes a correlation nor sufficiently rules out plausible alternative conclusions.

B. Though the argument sufficiently establishes a correlation between the proposed cause and effect, the argument is weak because it does not sufficiently rule out plausible alternative conclusions.

C. Though the argument does not sufficiently rule out all of the plausible alternative conclusions, the argument is strong because it sufficiently establishes a correlation between the proposed cause and effect.

Argument 1: Of course John cheated on his first Critical Thinking midterm simply because he thought he could get away with it. After all, he cheated on every question. (   )

Argument 2: I'm convinced John cheated on his first Critical Thinking midterm primarily because he thought he could get away with it. After all, he was talking with his best friend, Melvin, right before taking the midterm; and when Melvin said, "You won't get away with it," John bet Melvin $50 he would get away with cheating on his first Critical Thinking midterm. (   )

Argument 3: I'm convinced John cheated on his first Critical Thinking midterm solely because he thought he could get away with it. After all, he was studying for the midterm during the two hours before he took it; and then, only minutes before the midterm, his best friend bragged that he got away with cheating on the midterm he just took, and said he thought John couldn't get away with cheating. John said, "Yes I can," and bet his best friend $100 he'd get away with cheating on his first Critical Thinking midterm. (   )

Argument 4: I'm convinced John cheated on his first Critical Thinking midterm at least in part because he thought he could get away with it. After all, he was studying for the midterm five hours before he took it, and correctly answered every question he reviewed during that time; and then, only minutes before the midterm, he was studying with a classmate and correctly answered every question they reviewed. Then, only a minute before it was time for him to take the midterm, his best friend teased John for studying so much, bragged that he got away with cheating on the midterm he just took, and said he thought John couldn't get away with cheating. John said, "Yes I can," and bet his best friend $100 he'd get away with cheating on his first Critical Thinking midterm. (   )

Argument 5: Well, I think my sister was shoplifting at her job primarily because her boss treats her like a slave. First, my sister is paid $1 an hour, less than everyone else who has the same job. Second, her boss only lets my sister work night and weekend shifts. Finally, her boss never says "Yes." when my sister asks for a day off. (   )

Argument 6: I think the primary reason James shoplifted was that he was hungry. Think about it. The food he stole was on the back wall of the store, and to get to it he walked past dozens of items he could have easily stolen and sold. Also, remember he walked into the store twice before stealing the food. The first time he walked straight to the food section and immediately left when he saw someone else there. Finally, he didn't even leave the store with the food he stole. He just took it, walked into the store restroom, and ate the food in the restroom. (   )

Argument 7: I'm convinced spending more money on public education helped lower the rate of smoking-related deaths. Over the last ten years, we have steadily increased spending on public education and the rate of smoking-related deaths has steadily declined. (   )

Model 7-7

Evaluating and revising a complete essay

Study the following student essay. Notice the analysis and the evaluation Q & A.

Cell Phones Should Not Be Allowed in the Classroom

theis statement

❶ Technology has taken its toll on the current generation. Children, teens, and young adults are less intent on learning and more interested in their wireless devices. In fact, students now prefer using their cell phones as a means of studying over critical thinking. Although cell phones in the classroom are beneficial in some ways like safety, emergency, and enhancing learning, **cell phones should be banned from classrooms because they cause distraction and promotes cheating.**

Chapter 7 How to revise an essay?

causal reasoning 1
thesis

an untrue premise: no evidence offered

[insufficient premises]: They confirm a correlation between cell phone use and grades rather than distraction.

causal reasoning 2
thesis
[an insufficient premise]: Having access to the resources does not mean students' actual using them.
[an insufficient premise]: It cannot confirm the correlation between using cell phones and cheating, since using phones for texting does not mean texting to cheat.

❷ Cell phones distract students. One of the most popular things that have evolved within technology is social media. Social media is a way for students to participate in online communities. They are able to post, chat, and share images of their daily activities. Most students who bring their cell phones into the classroom spend most of their time posting and sharing on their social media. When they do this, they are unable to learn. The student is unable to understand what the lesson is about at that point in time. [This could ultimately result in low or failed grades. According to Doward Jamie, teenage test scores increased by 6.4% after cell phones were prohibited in the classroom.]

❸ Cell phones in the classroom promote cheating. There are many websites, forums, and tutors available online. These resources allow students to ask a question about their homework and then recieve the answer. [If a student is allowed to bring their cell phone to class, they will have access to these online services.] Another con of having cell phones in the classroom is that if the student has a friend that takes the same class at a different time, they are able to take a picture of the questions or text them the answers to the test. Both of these are a violation of a student code of ethics. [According to Lenhart, Amanda, and others, 54% of teens use their phones for text messages, this can be used as a medium for cheating by texting others for answers during an ongoing test.]

❹ Being able to use cell phones in the classroom does have its benefits. For example, students can use additional resources for a complete understanding of their lessons. But most students use cell phones for bad purposes.

❺ In conclusion, the use of cell phones in classrooms should not be allowed because it affects students negatively.

Evaluation Q & A:
1. **Q:** What is the overall reasoning strategy used to support the essay thesis?
   A: Inductive generalization: Using cell phones in classrooms is bad in two ways, so it is generally bad and should be banned.
2. **Q:** Is the inductive generalization strong?
   A: No. The two proposed negative effects of cell phones are not sufficient in justifying the thesis, since there are other aspects about cell phone use and classroom learning.
3. **Q:** How can it be improved?
   A: Outlining the essential tasks of students learning in a classroom as a principle, and then showing how cell phones affect each of those tasks adversely.

Practice 7-8

Evaluate the following arguments by filling out the evaluation tables. Then work in pairs. Compare your answers and discuss it where you disagree.

1. Six months after Hoover took office in 1929, the stock market crashed and the Great Depression began. He is therefore responsible for this tragic episode in our history.

Step 1 Analyzing the argument	**Reasoning strategy used:** Causal reasoning **Thesis:** 1) _____ **Premises:** 2) _____

Step 2 Asking the evaluation questions	**1. Are the premises true?**
	   3) _____
	2. Can the premises prove that the proposed cause happens before the proposed effect?
	   4) _____
	3. Can the premises sufficiently confirm a correlation between the proposed cause and the proposed effect?
	   5) _____
	4. Can the premises sufficiently disprove alternative explanations?
	   6) _____

Step 3 Revising the argument by correcting the problem(s) found	**Suggested improvements:** 7) _____ _____

2. The decisive reason for us to be addicted to smartphones is that we sometimes don't want to face the reality. Nir Eyal's study shows that people are more likely to check their phones when they are supposed to finish tasks on time. Obviously, playing with a cell phone is a symbol of avoiding reality. Phones present us with an attractive virtual world where we can do what we really want with few restrictions. Consequently, we are stuck in that virtual world and become addicted to our smartphones.

Chapter 7 How to revise an essay?

Step 1 Analyzing the argument	**Reasoning strategy used:** Causal reasoning **Thesis:** 1) _____ **Premises:** 2) _____
Step 2 Asking the evaluation questions	**1. Are the premises true?** 3) _____ **2. Can the premises prove that the proposed cause happens before the proposed effect?** 4) _____ **3. Can the premises sufficiently confirm a correlation between the proposed cause and the proposed effect?** 5) _____ **4. Can the premises sufficiently disprove alternative explanations?** 6) _____
Step 3 Revising the argument by correcting the problem(s) found	**Suggested improvements:** 7) _____ _____

From reading to writing

■ Reading
Read the essay and finish the tasks.

Is Poverty Alleviation Supporting the Lazybones?

❶ I once hosted a group of American college students visiting China. After I introduced the history and experience of China's poverty alleviation, the usual Q & A session took place. What impressed me the most was the question they asked: "Your government has allocated so much fiscal budget to help the poor who are usually the lazy people at the bottom, do taxpayers agree with their money being spent this way?"

❷ Recently, some colleagues from other departments also asked me whether the conditional cash transfer in the poverty alleviation policy to some extent contributed to the inertia of some lazy people. Both of these two questions reflect a social issue — the phenomenon of welfare dependence.

❸ Is China's poverty alleviation creating welfare dependence? Does it support the lazybones? The answer is clearly "no."

❹ In the United States, welfare dependence refers to a situation where the proportion of income from welfare programs in household income, or the welfare replacement rate, exceeds 50 percent. In Europe, when the welfare replacement rate exceeds 80 percent, the beneficiary's labor supply is greatly reduced. In China's targeted poverty alleviation, however, the average welfare replacement rate of the beneficiaries is 13 percent. Furthermore, the transfer payments to the registered poor population are divided into cash transfers and in-kind (以实物形式) transfer payments, which are basically focused on production, including distribution of production materials, such as livestock and fodder, education, medical subsidies, etc.

❺ Empirical research findings also indicate that targeted poverty alleviation in China did not lead to "raising lazy people." In 2015, Martin Ravallion and Chen Shaohua of the World Bank conducted a study on unconditional cash transfer payments in China and found that the project had no significant impact on labor supply. Abhijit Banerjee et al. also conducted a similar study in 2017 and found that the conclusions of the research on the impact of transfer payment welfare policies on labor supply were consistent with Martin and Chen. In fact, a large number of practical transfer payments for targeted poverty alleviation in China, such as providing piglets and cattle to poor households, has increased the labor supply of the poor and helped them achieve the goal of targeted poverty alleviation through livestock raising.

❻ Experts who study poverty all agree that poverty and inequality are closely related. The reason why inequality affects a person's choice is because under unequal conditions, the dominant and wealthy groups systematically monopolize opportunities, resulting in systematic exclusion of opportunities for the poor. Once a person falls into such a poverty trap, it becomes almost impossible to come out. Thus, the real poverty alleviation is about breaking this cycle.

❼ The biggest problem in the life of the poor is the daily difficulties and crises.

Their behavior is mainly driven by more urgent and important motivations. They will take their best and minimum resources at hand to respond to crises. Besides, Nobel Prize laureates in economics, Abhijit Banerjee and Esther Duflo, believe that the first choice for the poor is to make their lives more interesting. The poor are more inclined to buy cigarettes and alcohol when they have money, rather than invest in human capital. The poor often spend money where it shouldn't be spent, which is a typical case of irrational consumption from an economic point of view. In short, the poor may not be unaware of the importance of "long-term investment," but they "cannot wait" for the return on long-term investment.

❽ The Chinese government's poverty alleviation policy is about providing a different way of life and improving the livelihoods of the poor, giving them more opportunities and financial aid, guaranteeing their health, education, and housing, and helping them out of the poverty trap.

❾ In summary, China's poverty alleviation is completely justified, and it is by no means raising the lazybones.

Writing technique questions

Based on what you have learned in this chapter, consider the following questions. Then discuss with your group your answers and seek a consensus.

1. What is the thesis of the essay?
2. In which paragraphs does the author justify the thesis?
3. Read Para. 4 again and consider the questions:
    3.1　What is the thesis of this paragraph?
    3.2　What are the premises?
    3.3　What reasoning strategy is used?
    3.4　What questions can be asked to evaluate this kind of argument? Evaluate the argument by answering the questions.
4. Read Para. 5 again and consider the questions:
    4.1　What is the thesis of this paragraph?
    4.2　What are the premises?

4.3 What reasoning strategy is used?

4.4 What questions can be asked to evaluate this kind of argument? Evaluate the argument by answering the questions.

Critical thinking questions

Consider the questions below and finish the tasks.

1. In Para. 8 of the essay above, the author claims that China's poverty alleviation policy helps the poor out of the poverty trap. Is there any reasons or evidence offered?

2. What practical measures has the Chinese government taken to alleviate poverty? Research such measures.

3. Share your answers to the questions above with your group.

4. Discuss the following questions with your group

    4.1 What is a poverty trap according to Paras. 6 & 7?

    4.2 How do China's measures help the poor population out of the poverty trap?

    4.3 What evidence (i.e. events, statistics, news, testimonies, etc.) can you find to support your answer to the previous question?

Chapter 7 How to revise an essay?

■ **Writing**
Based on your answers to the critical thinking questions, revise the argument developed in Paras. 6–8 of the essay in the previous reading task. The following outline has been given to you as a prompt.

A poverty trap is a vicious cycle in which _____

_____.

Effective poverty alleviation should be able to break this cycle and get

the poor out of the trap. This is exactly what China has been doing.

[Justify the previous sentence with your answers to Exercises 4.2 and

4.3 of the critical thinking questions.] _____

_____

_____

_____

_____

_____

_____

_____

_____

REFLECTION

This chapter discussed practical strategies for evaluating and improving critical essays. Now it's time to review and reflect on what you have learned. Work in pairs and take turns to answer the following questions. Check them as you answer each one.

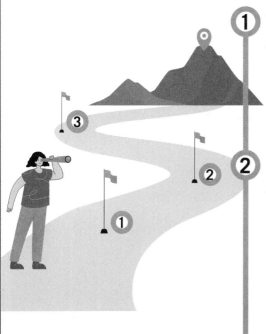

1 **What is the general method for evaluating arguments?**

☐ Name the two essential concerns of argument evaluation.

☐ Give a positive and a negative example to explain each of the two concerns.

2 **How to evaluate and improve deductive arguments?**

☐ Explain with an example each of the specific evaluation questions for arguments with a principle.

☐ Explain with an example each of the specific evaluation questions for arguments with a definition.

3 **How to evaluate and improve inductive arguments?**

☐ Explain with an example each of the specific evaluation questions for arguments with inductive generalization.

☐ Explain with an example each of the specific evaluation questions for analogical arguments.

☐ Explain with an example each of the specific evaluation questions for causal arguments.

How to revise an essay?

☐ Summarize the three basic steps for argument improvement.

Chapter 8

How to respond to opposition by making counterarguments?

彼举然者，以为此其然也，则举不然者而问之。

——《墨子·经说上》

If "that" is raised as being so and taken as the ground for "this" being so, then raise what is not so and question it.

——"Canons and Explanations A," *The Mozi*

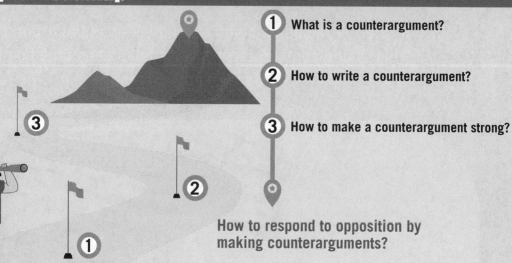

1 What is a counterargument?

2 How to write a counterargument?

3 How to make a counterargument strong?

How to respond to opposition by making counterarguments?

Learning outcomes

At the end of this chapter, you will be able to

- identify a counterargument in a critical essay;
- understand where and why to put a counterargument in a critical essay;
- refute an opposition with adequate strategies;
- write a complete counterargument.

From reading to writing

Analyze efforts needed to promote world peace and write a critical essay with counterarguments on this topic.

1. What is a counterargument?

Considering both the affirmative and the negative sides of an issue before reaching a conclusion is what the quotation at the beginning of this chapter tells us. That is why in Chapter I, we have learned that an important characteristic of critical writing is responding to opposing arguments rather than justifying the thesis merely from our own perspective. But how do we do that? Study this chapter.

1.1 Basics of counterarguments

Micro-lecture **Counterarguments in Critical Essays: What and Why**
MOOC **Lesson 8**

Counterarguments in Critical Essays: What and Why

What is a counterargument?

While we are composing a critical essay, imagine there are some reasonable objectors looking over our shoulder and some fence-sitters who have not decided which side of the argument they will support. They are neutral or skeptical readers of our argument and the audience we should consider to convince. Therefore, we need to anticipate what objections they are most likely to raise and argue against them to strengthen our own argument. When doing so, we are making counterarguments.

A **counterargument** is an argument made to refute an opposing argument. It undermines and weakens the opposing argument by rebutting it with adequate reasoning. Normally, a counterargument begins with a statement of the opposing argument and then moves on to refute it.

Why do counterarguments matter?

Avoiding ideas conflicting with our own gives readers the impression that we may be uncertain, fearful, or unaware of opposing ideas. We might also leave important questions hanging and concerns about our argument unaddressed. In short, our arguments will be weak if we fail to consider opposing arguments.

Including a counterargument in an essay shows readers we understand that alternative positions exist, have considered them, and can respond to them. Therefore, a counterargument is helpful from the following aspects.
- It increases our credibility.
- It allows us to anticipate doubts and pre-empt them.
- It weakens the opposing arguments while strengthening ours.

Model 8-1

A sample counterargument

the opposing argument	The athletic director argues against reducing university support for athletic programs on the grounds that they make money that goes toward academic programs. [It is true that here at Springfield the surpluses from the football and basketball programs have gone into the general university fund, and some of that money may have made it into academic departments (the fund's accounting methods make it impossible to say for sure.] [But the athletic
[refutation]	director misses the point. The problem is not that the athletic programs may cost more than they take in but that they demand too much to begin with. For an institution that hopes to become first-rate academically, too many facilities, too much money, too much energy, and too many people are tied up in the effort to produce championship sports teams.]

Practice 8-1

Which of the following arguments contains a counterargument? Circle the letter in front of it. Then underline the opposing argument and bracket the refutation.

A. Bottled water should be banned because it is too expensive and is an unnecessary cost. A single water bottle costs, on average, $1.45. The total cost of bottled water sold in the United States is $11.8 billion and the global annual cost is $60 billion.

B. Professional note-taking services keep students from developing their own thinking and organizational skills.

C. But volunteerism suggests that you are a team player, a quality many employers will look for in potential hires. Many companies also lead a number of annual volunteer projects on their staffs, so if you are active in community service and applying to work for such an organization, play up that experience.

D. Economists like to claim that the reason jogging becomes popular is that it costs little to buy equipment, but then not jogging costs even nothing. And the scant equipment which jogging demands must make it a marketer's least favored form of recreation.

Practice 8-2

Did you notice the counterarguments in the critical essays in previous chapters? Now revisit the essays in Model 5-4 of Chapter 5 and Model 6-6 in Chapter 6. Identify the counterarguments in the essays. Then work with a partner to point out the opposing argument and the refutation in each of them.

Practice 8-3

Work in pairs. Compare the following two outlines and discuss which one is more convincing and why.

Outline 1
Introduction Paragraph
- Background information
- Thesis statement: Employers should give their workers the option to work from home in order to improve employee well-being and reduce office costs.

Body Paragraph 1
- Topic Sentence: Workers who work from home have improved well-being.
- Supporting details

Outline 2
Introduction Paragraph
- Background information
- Thesis statement: Employers should give their workers the option to work from home in order to improve employee well-being and reduce office costs.

Counter-argument Paragraph
- Opposition: People might argue that working from home could reduce productivity.
  - Distractions at home could make it hard to concentrate.
  - Dishonest / lazy people might work less because no one is watching.

- Refutation: Results in an academic study suggest this is false.
  - Study: Productivity increased by X%
  - other details

Body Paragraph 2

- Topic Sentence: Furthermore, companies can reduce their expenses by allowing employees to work from home.
- Supporting details

Body Paragraph 2

- Topic Sentence: In addition, people who work from home have improved well-being.
- Supporting details

Body Paragraph 3

- Topic Sentence: *Furthermore, companies can reduce their expenses by allowing employees to work from home.*
- Supporting details

Conclusion

- Summary of key points
- Restatement of the thesis

Conclusion

- Summary of key points
- Restatement of the thesis

1.2 Positions of counterarguments in an essay

Core knowledge input

MOOC Lesson 8

Where to Place a Counterargument

Since counterarguments are so essential to strengthening our arguments and increasing our credibility, do we then include as many counterarguments as possible in a critical essay? Where should we put them?

Our answer to the first question is a big "NO." Too many counterarguments in an essay can show a reverse effect and weaken our main argument. However, there is no clear answer as to how many counterarguments are considered proper, either. The bottom line is we make a counterargument when we predict that there is an opposition. In line with this, we can also understand where a counterargument should be placed in a critical essay. A counterargument can be placed anywhere in a critical essay, as long as the author anticipates an opposing idea. Some common places to deploy a counterargument are listed below.

In the introduction of an essay
- **Before proposing the thesis:** A counterargument is placed here because refuting the opposing argument is the motive for this piece of writing. After introducing the opposing argument, it's natural for us to then present readers with our thesis which counters the opposing argument.

In the body of an essay
- **Right after the thesis statement:** When we raise a controversial thesis, a counterargument to a typical opposing argument fits well in the first paragraph of the body part.
- **Within a contributing argument:** If we anticipate some opposition to a contributing argument we make, then we include a counterargument within the same argument, either in the same paragraph or as an independent paragraph.
- **As an independent argument:** To respond to a common opposing idea on the issue rather than one particularly to any of our contributing arguments, we normally make the counterargument an independent body paragraph.

In the conclusion of an essay
- It is also a good idea to use a counterargument to conclude our essay if we predict that our reader may have a general disagreement with our argument. In this case, we may refute this opposition and reemphasize our own thesis in the final lines.

Model 8-2

Examples of counterarguments in different parts of an essay

Counterargument	Television wastes time, pollutes minds, destroys brain cells, and turns some viewers into murderers. Thus runs the prevailing talk about the medium, supported by serious research as well as simple belief. But television has at least one strong virtue, too, which helps to explain its endurance as a cultural force. In an era when people often have little time to speak with one another, television provides replacement voices that ease loneliness, spark healthful laughter, and even educate young children. (Revisit Model 2-2 for the full text.)

Where the counterargument appears:
In the introduction before the thesis statement
Why place the counterargument there:
- Disagreement with the widely-held view about TV's negative impacts is what drives the author to write this essay.
- It's also a technique to attract readers' attention by refuting a commonly-held idea.

Counterargument	If you were to toss, say, a banana peel out of your car while driving along the motorway, that would be a completely harmless action, due to the fact that it's part of a fruit — right? Actually, no. A banana peel can take up to two years to decompose, and with a third of motorists admitting to littering while driving, that's a whole lot of discarded banana peels, or much worse. (Revisit Model 1-5 for the full text.)

Where the counterargument appears:
In the first body paragraph immediately after the thesis statement
Why place the counterargument there:
After raising the essay thesis, the author anticipates an immediate opposition that natural litter such as a banana peel is not harmful. So, she makes a counterargument right after the thesis statement before moving on to justify it.

Counterargument	Celebrities often desire to resolve the difficulties their neighborhood is faced with and then support developments. They commonly seek advancements in the areas they grew up in and the areas they reside. Their desire for a better society is what drives them to politics. On the other hand, critics argue that these celebrities are hugely wealthy and do not know the feelings associated with the struggling middle class. However, what these critics should understand is that many celebrities grew up in average families. This fact, together with the need to promote their social images, provides them with a strong incentive and will to change the society for the better. And that also explains why they seek an avenue to address societal needs. (Revisit Model 5-4 for the full text.)

Where the counterargument appears:
Within a contributing argument
Why place the counterargument there:
After arguing for the essay thesis by saying that celebrities desire to resolve the difficulties for their people, the author predicts that critics may question this idea, so a counterargument follows immediately within the same paragraph to pre-empt oppositions.

Counterartument	Some people argue that celebrities should stick to what they do best and forsake politics since they cannot possibly deliver in the realm of governance. This is a myopic viewpoint, since celebrities have enormous experience within the public realm. In this lifestyle, they have interacted with the most knowledgeable and experienced people who have helped them maintain the right perspective. Therefore, being a celebrity in politics can be quite beneficial. It is amazing to see that most politicians want to be celebrities due to the associated benefits. (Revisit Model 5-4 for the full text.)

Where the counterargument appears:
As an independent argument in the body section
Why place the counterargument there:
When finishing all the contributing arguments from his own perspective, the author anticipates an opposition on the topic of celebrities entering politics rather than to any of his contributing arguments, so he refutes it here to make his own essay stronger.

Counterargument	The value of these replacement voices should not be oversold. For one thing, almost everyone agrees that too much TV does no one any good and may cause much harm. In addition, human beings require the give and take of actual interaction. They need to interact with actual speakers who respond directly to their needs. Replacement voices are not real voices and in the end, can do only limited good. But even limited good is something, especially for those who are lonely or neglected. Television is not an entirely positive force, but neither is it an entirely negative one. Its voices stand by to provide company, laughter, and information whenever they're needed. (Revisit Model 2-2 for the full text.)

Where the counterargument appears:
In the conclusion
Why to place the counterargument there:
The author predicts that after reading the essay, critics may have a general disagreement with the overall argument in the essay, so he makes a counterargument to respond to the opposing view in the conclusion.

Practice 8-4

Bracket all the counterarguments in the essay. Compare your answers with a partner and then discuss why the counterarguments are placed there.

The Locavore Myth: Why Buying from Nearby Farmers Won't Save the Planet

❶ Buy local, shrink the distance food travels, and save the planet. The locavore movement has captured a lot of fans. To their credit, they are highlighting the problems with industrialized food. But many of them are making a big mistake. By focusing on transportation, they overlook other energy-hogging factors in food production.

❷ Take lamb as an example. A 2006 academic study, funded by the New Zealand government, discovered that it made more environmental sense for a Londoner to buy lamb shipped from New Zealand than to buy lamb raised in the U.K. This finding is counterintuitive — if you're only counting food miles. But New Zealand lamb is raised on pastures with a small carbon footprint, whereas most English lamb is produced under intensive factory-like conditions with a big carbon footprint. This disparity overwhelms domestic lamb's advantage in transportation energy savings.

❸ New Zealand lamb is not an isolated case. Take a close look at water usage, fertilizer types, processing methods, and packaging techniques and you discover that factors other than shipping far outweigh the energy it takes to transport food. One analysis, by Rich Pirog of the Leopold Center for Sustainable Agriculture, showed that transportation accounts for only 11 percent of food's carbon footprint. A fourth of the energy required to produce food is expended in the consumer's kitchen. Still more energy is consumed per meal in a restaurant, since restaurants throw away most of their leftovers.

❹ Locavores argue that buying local food supports an area's farmers and, in turn, strengthens the community. Fair enough. Left unacknowledged, however, is the fact that it also hurts farmers in other parts of the world. The U.K. buys most of its green beans from Kenya. While it's true that the beans almost always arrive in airplanes — the form of transportation that consumes the most energy — it's also true that a campaign to shame English consumers with small airplane stickers affixed to flown-in produce threatens the livelihood of 1.5 million sub-Saharan farmers.

❺ Another chink in the locavores' armor involves the way food miles are calculated. To choose a locally grown apple over an apple trucked in from across the country might seem easy. But this decision ignores economies of scale. To take an extreme example, a shipper sending a truck with 2,000 apples over 2,000 miles would consume the same amount of fuel per apple as a local farmer who takes a pickup 50 miles to sell 50 apples at his stall at the green market. The critical measure here is not food miles but apples per gallon.

⑥ The one big problem with thinking beyond food miles is that it's hard to get the information you need. Ethically concerned consumers know very little about processing practices, water availability, packaging waste, and fertilizer application. This is an opportunity for watchdog groups. They should make life-cycle carbon counts available to shoppers.

⑦ Until our food system becomes more transparent, there is one thing you can do to shrink the carbon footprint of your dinner: Take the meat off your plate. No matter how you slice it, it takes more energy to bring meat, as opposed to plants, to the table. It takes 6 pounds of grain to make a pound of chicken and 10 to 16 pounds to make a pound of beef. That difference translates into big differences in inputs. It requires 2,400 liters of water to make a burger and only 13 liters to grow a tomato. A majority of the water in the American West goes toward the production of pigs, chickens, and cattle.

⑧ The average American eats 273 pounds of meat a year. Give up red meat once a week and you'll save as much energy as if the only food miles in your diet were the distance to the nearest truck farmer.

⑨ If you want to make a statement, ride your bike to the farmer's market. If you want to reduce greenhouse gases, become a vegetarian.

2. How to write a counterargument?

Critical essays need counterarguments to be more convincing. But how to make a counterargument? Are there some instructions to follow? In this section, we will provide general guidance on counterargument writing, leaving more specific strategies to the next section.

Model 8-3

Three steps of writing a counterargument

Read the following counterarguments and study the analysis.

Step 1: **introduce an opposing argument** **Step 2:** refute the opposing argument by pointing out its incompleteness **Step 3:** [further support the refutation with reasons and evidence]	Some scholars and researchers claim that technology has negative impacts on a child's developing mind. According to one research, early exposure to purely entertainment content, and media violence in particular, is negatively associated with cognitive skills and academic achievement. <u>Although there is validity to the presented argument, this theory excludes educationally driven programming.</u> [In his eBook *Children's Learning From Educational Television*, Fisch described how some television programs are types of informal education, "much like educational activities that children find in magazines, museums, or after-school programs." Television can be used to supplement the academic experience of a student. When presented in an informal and entertaining way, this supplemental material can help students become more engaged in topics, and more willing to delve into deeper consideration of concepts. Early learners may also be introduced to subject matter that is not typically introduced until later phases of formal schooling. Children and adolescents may also find value in television news programming which provides information on current events, such as the program of *Nick News*.]
Step 1: **introduce an opposing argument** **Step 2 + 3:** refute the opposing argument and further support the refutation	Although some people believe bottled water should be banned because it is unnecessary and expensive, <u>yet there are times, such as during natural disasters, when bottled water is the only safe source for people to drink.</u>

Core knowledge input

Micro-lecture Three Steps of Writing a Counterargument
MOOC Lesson 8

Three Steps of Writing a Counterargument

From the analysis of the counterarguments in Model 8-3, we can see that basically, there are three major steps to follow when composing a counterargument in a critical essay.

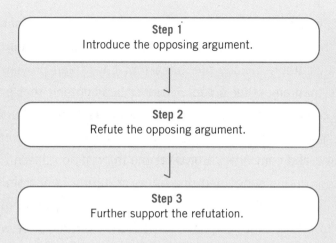

Step 1
Introduce the opposing argument.

Step 2
Refute the opposing argument.

Step 3
Further support the refutation.

Following the three steps, a counterargument can be either as concise as a few sentences or as complete as a few paragraphs. Counterarguements can be divided into two types based on their length and complexity.

- **The petit type**

    We can simply use the sentence patterns, such as "Although ..., yet ..." or "It is true that ..., but ...," to put forward the opposing argument and refute it immediately. Review the second example in Model 8-3.

- **The advanced type**

    This kind of counterargument consists of the opposing argument, which is fully developed with reasons and evidence, the refutation, and the further justification, which is also sufficiently organized. Review the first passage in Model 8-3 for an example of this kind. In some extreme cases, such a counterargument may be stretched into several paragraphs.

Practice 8-5

Identify the three writing steps of the following counterargument. Highlight the sentences composing step 1, underline those of step 2, and bracket those of step 3.

Many people have been reeled in and hoodwinked by misleading media accounts of pit bulls attacking people in public. They contend that any attempt to defend these dogs is irresponsible and inviting disaster. They believe that these dogs should be banned from public spaces. I could not disagree more, but let's take a closer look at some of the concerns about these animals. One common argument that pit bull detractors use is that pit bulls are demonstrably vicious creatures that have been proven to attack people at a much higher rate than any other breed. These critics contend that pit bulls are involved in more than 60% of canine attacks on humans and are therefore untrustworthy. Based on these facts, one might conclude that pit bulls are indeed vicious creatures that need to be carefully monitored and controlled. But what the information doesn't reflect is that most of these attacks occur during scheduled dog fights or during fight training. It's not the breed, but the context in which they are forced to live, train, and perform. If one were to train French poodles to attack other dogs for sport from the time they were puppies, then we would likely hear frequent media reports about the scourge of French poodle attacks in our cities and public spaces. Sure pit bulls bite more people than other breeds, but the information that pit bull detractors fail to divulge when they present their evidence against pit bulls is where and how the attacks are occurring. The attacks are mostly not happening in the places where normal people frequent. Their statistics are not coming from parks or schools or normal neighborhoods. They are mostly taking places in areas where the dogs fight or are training to fight. Omitting this important fact is tantamount to lying. It would seem that those who wish to malign the pit bull breed are not above skewing the data to fit their needs.

Practice 8-6

Work in pairs. Revisit Model 3-7 in Chapter 3. Identify all the counterarguments in the essay "Working at McDonald's." Highlight the sentences composing step 1, underline those of step 2, and bracket those of step 3.

3. How to make a counterargument strong?

This section will further discuss the specific strategies in each of the three steps of writing a counterargument so as to make our counterarguments strong.

3.1 Introducing an opposing argument to a counterargument

MOOC Lesson 8

Step 1: Introduce an Opposing Argument
Two major introduction methods

The first step of constructing a counterargument is of course presenting the opposing argument that we are about to refute. There are two major ways to introduce the opposing argument.

1. **Stating the opposing argument directly as someone else's idea**

   Some scholars and researchers claim that technology has negative impacts on a child's developing mind …

   Many of the concerns surrounding facial recognition stem from reports that facial recognition algorithms are biased and that their use will lead to racial profiling …

2. **Conceding the opposing argument as partly valid or correct**

   It is true that here at Springfield the surpluses from the football and basketball programs have gone into the general university fund, …

   While I understand that advertising prescription drugs on TV should be cautiously considered because it poses a potential risk of drug abuse, …

Tips for introductions

We suggest the following tips for introducing opposing arguments:

- Include not only the thesis but also a key premise, as the premise is the target of our refutation.
- State it briefly to save room for our own argument.
- Use signal words to indicate to our readers that this is the opposition's argument, not our own.

 Scan the QR code for signal words used to introduce opposing arguments.

How to predict an opposing argument

Sometimes, we know clearly what the disagreeing voices are because they somehow inspire us to write. In many other cases, however, we need to consciously predict the opposing views when writing. The following questions can help us anticipate opposing arguments.

- Could someone disagree with our thesis?
- Could someone question any of our premises?
- Could someone draw a different conclusion from any of the premises we present?
- Could someone offer a different explanation of our evidence?
- Is there any evidence out there that could weaken our thesis?

Model 8-4

Examples of introducing opposing arguments

Read the following examples of introducing opposing arguments to counterarguments and notice the analysis of the writing techniques.

signal words **thesis of the opposing argument** a premise supporting the opposing argument	**Making a concession** Although **excessive employment of AI will do harm to society** since it may cause mass unemployment, it cannot be denied that AI robots are highly useful for reducing the risk of humans being killed or injured by replacing them for especially dangerous tasks.
signal words **thesis of the opposing argument** a premise supporting the opposing argument	**Direct statement** Some people may argue that **by kicking students who bully others out of school instead of helping and directing them towards the right path, they will keep getting worse until it's too late.** This will simply shift the problem from bullying within the school to bullying outside the school.

Practice 8-7

Think of two opposing arguments to each of the following thesis statements. Then introduce them as opposing arguments as specified in the "Core knowledge input" on page 221. The first has been done for you as an example.

1. Facts are the currency of the modern world, and students must learn as many facts as possible.

Introducing opposing arguments:

Example: Some people argue that it's more important for students to learn ideas and concepts, so they'll be able to truly understand and use facts.

1) _____

2) _____

2. Social media sites help students do better at school.

Introducing opposing arguments:

1) _____

2) _____

3. AI can improve our standard of living.

Introducing opposing arguments:

1) _____

2) _____

4. School uniforms keep students focused on their education, rather than their clothes.

Introducing opposing arguments:

1) _____

2) _____

3.2 Refuting the opposing argument and giving further justification

Core knowledge input

 Micro-lecture Step 2: Refute the Opposing Argument
MOOC Lesson 8

Step 2: Refute the Opposing Argument

After introducing the opposing argument, we need to refute it. This takes much more work than simply denying it. We will first evaluate it using argument evaluating strategies (review Chapter 7 for more). Then based on our evaluation, the following two common ways to refute an arguement are often adopted.

Two major ways to refute an arguement

1. **Pointing out directly the problem with the opposing argument:** State what problem you have found with the opposing argument after evaluating it, such as false premises, insufficient support, or irrelevancy, etc. Review the example in Model 8-1. Here is another example:

   Many people believe that becoming a vegetarian is a simple way to live a healthy life. It is true that a vegan diet may help lower blood pressure and cholesterol, which in turn will help improve your cardiovascular health. Unfortunately, there are also drawbacks to being a vegetarian. For instance, many vegans are likely to have nutritional concerns that are not as common in people with a balanced, omnivorous diet. (Problem with the opposing argument: insufficient support)

2. **Telling why the opposing argument is not important compared to our argument:** If we find the opposing argument makes sense to some extent, acknowledge it first and then state why it is less important, or less possible for it to be true, by prioritizing alternative inferences, such as other more significant advantages, disadvantages, or possibilities. Review the first example in Model 8-2. Another example is given below:

   It is true, that advertising prescription drugs on TV should be cautiously considered because it poses a potential risk of drug abuse, however the benefits of increased sales for pharmaceutical companies and increased revenue for advertising agencies and television stations outweigh the risks. (Refuting the opposing argument by prioritizing an advantage)

Tips for refutation

Follow the following tips when refuting an opposing argument.

- Use signal words to show readers that we are now refuting the opposing arguement. *But*, *however*, or *yet* are commonly used here.
- Attack it directly instead of merely denying it or emphasizing our own argument. To do so, again we should point out its problem or state why it is less possible. The following is a **bad** example in that it only introduces the opposing argument without responding to it.

Social networking websites are considered by many to have adversely influenced both individuals and communities. However, I believe that the effect of those sites has been mostly beneficial to individuals and society because online socializing has made it possible to use personal connections in three different ways that were inaccessible before.

Step 3: Further Support the Refutation

Our refutation in Step 2 is just a brief attack on the opposing argument. To make the refutation strong, we need to further justify it with reasons and evidence. Review Chapters 4–6 for more information.

Model 8-5

Examples of refutation in counterarguments

Read the following examples of refutation in counterarguments and notice the analysis of the writing techniques.

opposing argument signal word refutation [further support]	**Pointing out the problem directly** **Some argue that SUVs' relatively low mileage increases the nation's dependence on foreign oil.** <u>However</u>, <u>the connection seems to make sense until the data are more closely examined</u>. [First, while SUVs generally consume more gasoline than do cars, they are not the rapacious gas hogs critics suggest.

True, the largest SUVs get, on average, just 17 miles per gallon. But relatively few of these vehicles sell each year. Indeed, the most popular SUVs are midsize ones, which get an average 20.7 mpg, according to the Oak Ridge National Laboratory. That's just 5 mpg less than a large car, and just 3 mpg less than an average minivan. What's more, despite the surge in sales of SUVs over the past ten years, the overall fuel economy on the road has actually improved. Consider: In this decade, SUVs went from 5 percent of all registered cars on the road to 11 percent. Yet fuel economy of all cars on the road climbed nearly 7 percent between 1990 and 2000.

opposing argument signal word refutation [further support]	**Stating why it is less important** **There's little doubt that the necessity of social distancing has contributed to our recent collective loneliness.** But loneliness existed long before the current pandemic. [As a psychologist, I'm privy to many of the beliefs that contribute to feelings of isolation, including the idea that loneliness is necessarily related to the size of our social networks or the extent to which we are surrounded by others. In reality, loneliness has less to do with being alone and much more to do with the experience of feeling unseen. It is the quality, not quantity, of our relationships that fulfills our need for connectedness.]
signal word opposing argument refutation [further support]	**Pointing out the problem directly** But those who argue that **SUVs must change to fix the problem of road hazards** overlook the other possible solution: making smaller cars heavier and more crash-resistant. [That would arguably protect drivers and passengers in these cars not only when they collide with an SUV, but in the many other crashes that involve trucks, buses, or fixed objects.]

Practice 8-8

Evaluate each of the following arguments and then make a complete counterargument.

Example:

Alternative energy can effectively replace fossil fuels because some renewable energies are cheaper than coal and gas.

Evaluation	Thesis: Alternative energy can effectively replace fossil fuels.
	Premises: Some renewable energies are cheaper than coal and gas.
	Reasoning strategy used: inductive generalization (listing some advantages of renewable energies and generalizing that they can replace fossil fuels)
	Evaluation questions to be asked: • Are the premises true? Yes. • Are the premises relevant? Yes. • Are the premises sufficient? No. Besides price, many other factors, such as transmission, also influence the popularity of different fuels.
Counterargument	Some people insist that alternative energy can effectively replace fossil fuels because some renewable energies are cheaper than coal and gas. However, we should not assume that price is the sole decisive factor influencing the popularity of fuels. In fact, another more important concern when choosing which fuel can be used widely and sustainably is transmission, which means the power lines and infrastructure needed to move electricity from where it's generated to where it's consumed. Take wind and solar as examples. Most of what exists today was built to serve large fossil fuel. But wind and solar farms aren't all sited near old fossil fuel power plants. To adequately take advantage of these resources, new transmission infrastructure is needed — and transmission costs money, which means the financing can be significant barriers for the accessibility of alternative energy.

1. People should become vegetarians because it is cruel and unethical to kill animals for food.

Evaluation	Thesis: 1)
	Premises: 2)
	Reasoning strategy used: 3)
	Evaluation questions to be asked: 4)

(Continued)

Counterargument	5)

2. Public school students should be required to wear school uniforms because uniforms help bring equality and a sense of belonging among students.

Evaluation	**Thesis:** 1)
	Premises: 2)
	Reasoning strategy used: 3)
	Evaluation questions to be asked: 4)
Counterargument	5)

Counterarguments in a critical essay
Read the following critical essay, identify the counterarguments, and notice the analysis about the writing techniques.

Social Media Is the New Smoking, and You Are Addicted

❶ Her heart raced so fast that she was sure she was going to have a heart attack. She sped up. She was anxious to get home. One could even see the sweat dripping down her face. In an attempt to take a shortcut, she jaywalked across a wide street, zigzagging her way through it. She almost got hit by a truck, but she didn't care. She was not concerned. She was just a few meters from her place. She had only one goal in mind. She needed it so bad — to plug her phone in and get back to social media. She existed now. She was online again. Lisa won't admit it, but she is addicted to social media.

thesis statement

❷ **Social media giants need to stop pretending they are changing the world into a better place but come forward to admit that they are deliberately selling a product that is, in fact, addictive and harmful for us.**

contributing argument 1 (Paras. 3–4)
Social media is addictive.

❸ Social media is known for having complex algorithms to capture and manipulate our consumption, maximizing the higher amount of engagement possible. There is even a term for this in Silicon Valley: Brain Hacking. Tristan Harris, the former Google design ethicist says that is like having a "slot machine in your pocket." Just like in the gambling business, social media companies use intermittent variable rewards to get their users hooked. Apps and websites sprinkle intermittent variable rewards all over their products because it's "good for business," as Mr. Harris states in his article "How Technology Is Hijacking Your Mind."

❹ According to a recent article by Hacker Noon, people spent over four hours a day on their mobile phones in 2017, and about 5.4 years in a lifetime. That's almost five times more than what one person spent socializing (1.4 years) over their entire life. It's about time that we collectively became aware of this new disease.

counterargument 1 as the 2nd contributing argument (Paras. 5–6)

signal words
① Step 1: introducing the opposing argument (making a concession)
② Step 2: refuting the opposing argument (stating why it is less important)
③ Step 3: further supporting the refutation (negative influences of social media)

counterargument 2 in the 3rd contributing argument (Para. 7)

signal word
① Step 1: introducing the opposing argument (stating it directly)
② Step 2: refuting the opposing argument (stating its problem)
③ Step 3: further supporting the refutation (testimony)

contributing argument 4

❺ ① I agree that social media has enormous benefits: from propelling careers, to effortlessly providing contact with people in developing countries, and helping those without a voice to speak up. ② But we should remain alert to the hidden, malicious influence social media contains.

❻ ③According to some experts, social media may have a major impact on our mental health. People get sucked in by numbers and notifications, pressured by a reward system — which is the core stimuli of most apps. Users get a high rush of dopamine every time they receive a notification, according to one study. The release of dopamine is the basic factor for nicotine, cocaine, and gambling addictions. It's like brain candy for our neurons, meaning that social media imitates natural pleasurable experiences, like eating or doing sports, which makes it very addictive, setting up reinforcement in our brains. Some people might experience social exclusion if they haven't jumped on the bandwagon yet. Just as it happens with social smoking, social media is at times used by individuals who often feel afraid of missing out, while others might feel isolated, depressed, and suffering from anxiety according to a psychological study carried out by the University of Pittsburgh.

❼ The social damage is clearly obvious. Social media has invaded our lives and impacted our routines so significantly. For example, in the case of productivity, it is especially corrosive to focus and deep work, and let's not forget the recent and enormous negative impact on democracy as well. ① The way information is being consumed and how it is affecting the current political landscape is yet to be determined, ② but we are already facing the consequences of an unregulated industry. ③"Everyone who has scrolled through a social media website knows how, instead of imparting wisdom, the system dishes out compulsive stuff that tends to reinforce people's biases," stated *The Economist* last November.

❽ Most powerfully, these companies still have an opportunity to set the record straight. They could put up warnings about excessive usage and consumption, as the food and tobacco companies were required by law to do. Their algorithms are the redeeming feature of their future. They could still adopt them to fight misinformation, the spread of fake news, and protect users from click-baiting malpractices. But these changes are probably cut against their business models designed to compulsively attract attention, which means that they won't step forward, and this probably will lead to the imposition of regulations in the future. Thus, there is a huge need for a solid set of guidelines for responsible regulation.

❾ Connectivity increases with every day that passes, yet somehow our social contact is more broken nowadays than ever before. It makes me wonder, as with smoking, will there be social media tables in restaurants in the future? Will social media consumption in large doses cause some sort of social cancer? Only time will tell how the future landscape will shape up, yet one day social media might have to include mandatory warnings like the ones present on cigarette packages today.

Practice 8-9

Revisit the essay you wrote at the end of Chapter 6. Work in pairs. Check to see if your partner has anticipated and responded to any opposition there. If not, revise the essay by adding at least one counterargument.

From reading to writing

■ Reading
Read the essay and finish the tasks.

A Powerful Chinese Military Contributes to Global Stability

❶ At the founding ceremony of the People's Republic of China in 1949, the weapons showcased were mainly made by other countries. The fly-by was completed by the same group of aircraft flying twice because there were simply not enough military planes. "What are we capable of making now?" Mao Zedong asked in 1954, "a car, a plane, a tank, a tractor, we can make none of these." In 2019, at the military parade commemorating the 70th anniversary of the PRC's founding, Beijing displayed a remarkable array of weapons that operated on land, sea, and in the air, including those that were capable of mounting joint air defense barrages and the Dongfeng series strategic missiles. A total of 32 armament formations joined the parade, making it the largest of its kind in the nation's history, in terms not only of scale but also of the variety of weapons.

❷ Over the course of a few decades, China's armed forces have transformed from a backward military that could barely stage a decent parade to one that is modernized and has made significant strides in all aspects of national defense. The People's Liberation Army is not only charged with the responsibility to defend China's homeland security but also plays a prominent role in safeguarding world peace in the age of globalization.

❸ A country needs powerful military to be strong and secure. Traditional Chinese wisdom holds that those who prefer to wage wars will perish, and those who forget wars will be in danger. China believes that a country needs a powerful military before it can truly be strong and secure, and that China must build fortified national defense and a strong people's military commensurate with its international standing and its security and development interests.

❹ Many western media outlets have been playing up China's military spending, suggesting that China might be a threat to regional stability with its defense budget for 2022 at 1.45 trillion yuan (about $229 billion). However, they are, at the same time, shying away from comparing it with its international counterparts. According to statistics from the Stockholm International Peace Research Institute, China's defense expenditure accounted for 1.7 percent of its GDP, while for Saudi Arabia, the United States, India, and the United Kingdom, the percentages were 8.4 percent, 3.7 percent, 2.9 percent, and 2.2 percent respectively. The difference is more salient in regards to per capita terms. China has a population, which is four times that of the U.S., but its overall military expenditure is only a quarter of its American counterpart. China has also made concrete moves, including military downsizing. But the West chooses to turn a blind eye to this and to the fact that Western countries are pushing up the share of their military spending in GDP.

❺ In addition, more powerful China makes a safer world. Since 2013, on top of its peacekeepers already serving on UN peacekeeping missions in engineer, medical, and transport units, China has dispatched guard contingents, infantry battalions, and helicopter contingents to countries including The Republic of Mali, The Republic of South Sudan, and The Republic of Sudan. Meanwhile, China has more than 2,200 peacekeepers deployed on UN missions in seven mission areas and at the UN headquarters. The country has also completed its registration of a UN standby peacekeeping force comprising of 8,000 troops. China has been playing a crucial role in UN peacekeeping efforts.

❻ China is also a major financial contributor to the UN peacekeeping budget and the biggest provider of troops among permanent members of the UN Security Council for the UN peacekeeping force. Over the past three decades, China has participated in more than 20 UN peacekeeping operations. In maritime escort missions, humanitarian relief operations, anti-terrorist exercises, and anti-pandemic cooperation, Chinese troops have fulfilled their obligations commensurate with China's global standing, repeatedly showing to the world that the Chinese army is a force not only of power, but also of peace and civilization.

❼ In this day and age, peace and development stand at a critical historical juncture as the world heads into a new era of instabilities and transformations. Accordingly, Chinese troops will contribute significantly to world peace, shoulder more peacekeeping responsibilities, and provide stronger support for building a human community with a shared future.

Writing technique questions

Based on what you have learned in this chapter, consider the following questions. Then discuss with your group your answers and seek a consensus.

1. What is the thesis of this essay?
2. What are the two major contributing arguments developed in Paras. 3–6?
3. There is a counterargument in the essay. Where is it? Identify the three steps of counterargument writing.
4. Why does it appear there?
5. How does the counterargument help justify the thesis of the essay?

Critical thinking questions

Consider the questions below and finish the tasks.

1. World peace is the common pursuit of all mankind, but unfortunately conflicts and wars never stop. What are some issues disrupting global stability? Do you think these issues can be successfully tackled? Why or why not?
2. Share your answers to the questions above with your group.
3. Work in a larger group of 6–8 students. Have a debate on the motion "Is world peace possible." Follow the steps below.

   3.1 Divide your group members into two sides: the affirmative and the negative.

3.2 Each side develops at least three arguments for your position, anticipates two arguments against your position, and prepares counterarguments to them.

3.3 Decide the speaker order on your side.

3.4 Debate in the following procedures.

Step 1
- 1st speaker of the affirmative: State your overall argument. (2 min.)
- Last speaker of the negative: Counter the argument. (1 min.)

Step 2
- 1st speaker of the negative: State your overall argument. (2 min.)
- Last speaker of the affirmative: Counter the argument. (1 min.)

Step 3
- 2nd speaker of the affirmative: Further argue for your position. (1 min.)
- 2nd speaker of the negative: Further argue for your position. (1 min.)
- The two speakers counter each other's arguments. (2 min.)

Step 4
- 3rd speakers from both sides (if there is any): Repeat Step 3.

Step 5
- Last speaker of the affirmative: Summarize your arguments. (2 min.)
- Last speaker of the negative: Summarize your arguments. (2 min.)

■ Writing

Based on your answers to the critical thinking questions, write a complete essay on the topic "Is World Peace Possible?". Include at least one counterargument in your essay.

REFLECTION

This chapter discussed practical strategies for making counterarguments. Now it's time to review and reflect on what you have learned. Work in pairs and take turns to answer the following questions. Check them as you answer each one.

① **What is a counterargument?**
- ☐ State what a counterargument is.
- ☐ Explain why a critical essay normally includes some counterarguments.
- ☐ State where a counterargument appears in an essay and why it appears there.

② **How to write a counterargument?**
- ☐ Explain the three steps of writing a counterargument.
- ☐ Use an example to showcase the three steps.

③ **How to make a counterargument strong?**
- ☐ Provide examples to explain the tips for introducing an opposing argument.
- ☐ Provide examples to explain the tips for refuting an opposing argument.

How to respond to opposition by making counterarguments?
- ☐ Name 3 important things you need to do or consider when responding to an opposing argument.

Use verbs effectively

Verbs are essential for sentences. Sentences can do without some parts of speech, but never without verbs. In some cases, we can even use a single verb as a one-word sentence. Well-chosen verbs can deliver a message accurately and forcefully, while casual verb choices may lead to wordy or unclear writing.

Learning outcomes

At the end of this clinic, you will be able to

- use one-word verbs to avoid an informal writing style;
- replace *be* verbs with action verbs for a more direct writing style;
- avoid verb-turned nouns for more forceful writing;
- use active voice and passive voice properly.

Core knowledge input

Micro-lecture Verb Use for Formality and Conciseness

Verb Use for Formality and Conciseness

Language in academic writing is usually described as formal, concise, precise, and neutral. If these characteristics fail to appear in writing, even the most innovative and intelligent ideas might be perceived as simplistic or even be disregarded by a scholarly community. To avoid this situation, writers should polish their sentences. And since verbs are an indispensable part of a sentence, writers should choose verbs with particular care.

The following are some guiding rules on how to use verbs properly to achieve formality and conciseness.

1. Avoid phrasal verbs.

A phrasal verb is a verb made up of two or more words: the main verb and an adverb or preposition, or both. Although phrasal verbs are acceptable in spoken English, they are considered too informal for academic writing. Furthermore, phrasal verbs often have multiple meanings. Our aim is to write essays using simple language that makes our argument clear and concise. It is therefore recommended that we replace phrasal verbs with formal one-word alternatives. You may find some examples in Model LC1-1.

2. Replace *be* verbs with action verbs.

There are two verb types for predicates: *Be* verbs and action verbs. *Be* verbs (is, am, are, was, were, been, be) indicate a state of being; action verbs describe movements. Both verb types are very useful, but too many *be* verbs, which themselves do not carry messages, may make a sentence lifeless. Action verbs, on the other hand, can give a more accurate picture or a stronger message about the subject. Therefore, writers are encouraged to replace *be* verbs with action verbs whenever possible. Study the examples in Model LC1-2.

3. Turn nouns back into verbs.

Many verbs merely <u>serve the function of a predicate</u> without describing a real action.
Many verbs merely <u>function as a predicate</u> without describing a real action.

In the first sentence, the verb "serve" is vague and weak. It does not express an action, while the real action is expressed with the verb-turned noun "function." Why not use the verb directly?

Verbs such as *serve, get, make, have,* together with *be* verbs, are general, weak, colorless words that do not contain a very specific meaning of their own. When they are used in the "verb + noun" pattern, the real action is expressed in the noun. Since such verbs are not contributing much to the message, we can edit them out and turn the noun back into the verb. More examples can be found in Model LC1-3.

4. Use active voice unless passive voice is necessary.

Writers can use action verbs in either an active or passive voice. A verb is active when the subject of the sentence is the doer (or the agent) of the action; it is passive when the subject of the sentence is the receiver of the action. Both active and passive voices are commonly used in different situations.

Active voice, which better suits people's habitual information processing sequence than passive voice, cannot only help produce more direct, forceful, and concise sentences, but also help give clearer information when describing events. That is why writers prefer the active voice, especially in non-scientific writing situations.

However, this does not mean that writers should entirely discard passive voice. Passive voice can be necessary for certain circumstances:

- when it is better not to identify the agent;
- when the performer of the action is unknown;
- when the writer wants to emphasize certain information, while the performer is relatively unimportant;
- in scientific writing to put the emphasis on the experiment or process being described rather than on the researcher.

Model LC1-1

Examples of replaced phrasal verbs in sentences

Read the following pairs of sentences, and notice how the phrasal verbs are replaced.

Sentences with phrasal verbs	Revised sentences
It took her a few minutes to **figure out** the math problem.	It took her a few minutes to **solve** the math problem.
Our financial adviser had **pointed out** the risks of investing in the currency markets.	Our financial adviser had **identified** the risks of investing in the currency markets.
I'm surprised that she's **put up with** him for all of these years.	I'm surprised that she's **tolerated** him for all of these years.
They **carried on** until all the work was finished.	They **continued** until all the work was finished.
Teachers should encourage kids to **find** things **out** for themselves.	Teachers should encourage kids to **discover** things for themselves.
The General sent a message to the enemy, urging them to **give** themselves **up**.	The General sent a message to the enemy, urging them to **surrender**.

Practice LC1-1

Underline the phrasal verb in each of the sentences, and replace it with the correct form of a one-word verb from the box.

understand	leave	become	suit
differentiate	remove	spread	express

1. The irrelevant paragraph was cut out.

2. She was not cut out for the task.

3. Good-bye. I have to cut out now.

4. Nobody could make out exactly what the old man was trying to say.

5. During the strike, rumors were put about that the company was planning to close the factory and build a new one abroad.

6. He's a brilliant artist, but he doesn't put himself across very well in interviews.

7. It is humans' ability to think that sets them apart from other animals.

8. Although very shy as a child, he eventually turned out to be a natural leader.

Model LC1-2

Different effects of *be* verbs and action verbs

Read the following pairs of sentences, and contrast the effects of *be* verbs and action verbs. Notice that the message is much stronger and clearer after the *be* verbs are replaced by actions verbs.

> I **was the boss of** a team of six service employees.
> I **supervised** a team of six service employees.
>
> It **is my intention** to finish the task as soon as possible.
> I **intend** to finish this task as soon as possible.
>
> Biology **is interesting** to me.
> Biology **interests** me.
>
> The bell **is a symbol of** freedom.
> The bell **symbolizes** freedom.

Practice LC1-2

Change the *be* verbs in the following sentences into action verbs. Then write down the revised sentences.

1. His words are making the situation complicated.

_____

2. China is not fearful of a trade war with any country in the world.

_____

3. Negative advertising is influential on voters' perceptions of candidates.

_____

4. Electric car technology was in existence as early as 1830.

_____

5. The idea of remaining true to our original aspiration is inspiring to me.

_____

Model LC1-3

Examples of turning nouns back into verbs

Read the following pairs of sentences, and notice how the second message in each pair is much more concise and effective.

1. The government should **make an improvement** to its public image.

   The government should **improve** its public image.

2. I **made the decision** to leave.

   I **decided** to leave.

3. This event **had an influence** on his values.

   This event **influenced** his values.

4. These rules can **give guidance to** the local economic development.

   These rules can **guide** the local economic development.

Practice LC1-3

Circle the verb-turned noun in each sentence and then convert it back into a verb. Write down the revised sentences.

1. We made an investigation into the spending habits of the elderly.

_____

2. He made an analysis of the causes of local poverty.

_____

3. Young children should be taught to have respect for the elderly.

_____

4. I have a dislike for this type of movies.

_____

5. The local community should provide assistance to the disabled.

_____

6. After dinner, we engaged in a free discussion of our future investment.

_____

7. The People's Bank of China will keep its monetary policy toolbox wide open to achieve the stability of the monetary aggregate.

_____

8. They should carry out a careful examination of the manufacturing process.

_____

9. This is just another trick to entice the army to launch an attack against them.

_____

10. I have the need for his approval.

_____

11. Introducing private investment will give a boost to railway operations in China.

_____

12. G20 members have the power to make transformation of the international system that would bring about long-lasting peace and development.

_____

Model LC1-4

Uses of active voice and passive voice

Read the following pairs of sentences, and notice the analysis.

Active voice used

☺ The committee is considering the action on the bill.

☹ Action on the bill is being considered by the committee.

☺ Johnny shot the bear.
☹ The bear was shot by Johnny.

☺ A recent study found evidence of nonhuman primates (灵长动物) engaging in ritualistic behavior.
☹ Evidence has been found of nonhuman primates engaging in ritualistic behavior.

The first sentence in each pair above is preferred because they sound direct, natural, and easy to understand. Since the doer of the action, such as the committee, is known, there is no need to use passive voice.

Passive voice used

Mistakes were made.

The window was broken.

The oriental rug was made in China.

He was shot in the leg.

In the sentences above, passive voice is needed because the performer of the action is unknown.

The needs of the students should be considered.

The new rule was enacted to tighten security.

By using passive voice, the authors emphasize certain information. In the examples above, "the needs" and "the new rule" were placed at the beginning of the sentences and hence were emphasized.

☺ The solution was heated to the boiling point.
☹ The scientist heated the solution to the boiling point.

☺ The subject was observed.
☹ The researchers observed the subject.

☺ The experiment results were recorded.

☹ The team recorded the experiment results.

In scientific writing, the agent of the action is often omitted to emphasize the research work itself and excludes irrelevant information as shown in the previous pairs. Verbs referring to research activities, such as *examine, observe, measure, record, use,* are usually in passive voice. However, verbs referring to the writer's own thinking activity and result, like *cite, show, inquire,* are often used in active voice.

Practice LC1-4

Read the following sentences. Decide if the voice is used properly. If yes, check the sentence. If not, change it into a proper voice.

1. ☐ The entrance examination was failed by over one-third of the applicants to the school.

   _____

2. ☐ Your bicycle has been damaged.

   _____

3. ☐ No alternative is left to me but to ask you for help.

   _____

4. ☐ Incentives for growth and public goods to the world have been consistently provided by China.

   _____

5. ☐ His writing shows an active imagination.

   _____

6. ☐ Products from all the participating countries are exhibited in the stadium.

   _____

7. ☐ An announcement that there will be stronger supervision of loans to students was issued by the Ministry of Education.

   _____

8. ☐ Millions of years ago, animal and plant life was caused to diversify by the changes in Earth's climate.

_____

Language Clinic 2

Use concrete and specific language

As non-native English writers, we tend to use general, vague, or abstract language in essay writing, probably without knowing it. That is why we need to improve the specificity and concreteness of expressions. But what kind of language is concrete and specific? How can we use such language effectively?

Learning outcomes

At the end of this clinic, you will be able to

- identify concrete, abstract, specific, and general words;
- understand the effects of using concrete and specific language;
- apply 3 methods to improving your language specificity.

Core knowledge input

Micro-lecture Concrete Words, Abstract Words, Specific Words, and General Words

Concrete Words, Abstract Words, Specific Words, and General Words

Concrete words vs abstract words

Concrete words refer to tangible qualities or characteristics, or things we know through our senses, such as things that we can see, smell, touch, taste, or hear. Abstract words refer to intangible qualities, ideas, and concepts. These words refer to things we know only through our intellect.

Concrete words	Abstract words
a new idea	creative
a female president	feminist

Concrete words	Abstract words
handshakes	peace
kisses	love

Specific words vs general words

Specific words designate particular items or individual cases, while general words refer to large classes and broad areas.

Specific words	General words
the Toyota Corolla car	automobiles
chemistry tutor	jobs
Angry Birds	video games

Practice LC2-1

Are the following words or expressions abstract (A), concrete (C), general (G), or specific (S) ones? Write the letter accordingly in each blank.

1. A. kindness _____

   B. a wide grin like spring breeze kissing my face _____

2. A. honor _____

   B. glittering trophies _____

3. A. languages _____

   B. Spanish _____

4. A. skills _____

   B. intercultural communication skills to tell China's stories well to the world _____

Core knowledge input

Micro-lecture Why Use Concrete and Specific Language

Why Use Concrete and Specific Language

Abstract and general language may evoke different meanings based on an individual's subjective interpretation of the words. Concrete and specific words can accurately convey the writer's ideas, and there is little room for subjective interpretation on the reader's part. Therefore, concrete and specific language saves the reader's time in grasping the writer's message, and improves communication efficiency.

Abstract and general language	vs	Concrete and specific language
giving a vague description	giving clear description
ambiguous, open to various interpretations	communicating meaning exactly
probably boring to read	appealing and interesting to read
hard to understand	easy to understand

Model LC2-1

Different effects of the two types of language

Compare the sentences in Paragraphs A and B. Notice the analysis of the effects of the two types of language.

Paragraph A with abstract and general language

Students ① <u>like to get good</u> grades. They ② <u>try hard</u> for the "A" each time. They ③ <u>spend a lot of time</u> on papers or studying for tests. They sometimes ④ <u>stay up all night</u> to finish an essay or to make sure they are ready for their exam.

Analysis:

①② Vague descriptions and boring to read.

③ Ambiguous, and open to various interpretations: How hard they try? How much time has been spent?

---

④ More concrete and specific than the previous sentences. But what is it like when "staying up all night"? It is much better if we say "They sometimes stay up until four in the morning to finish an essay."

It is a "telling" paragraph. It simply gives a sketchy account of the bare facts. The reader cannot get a vivid picture at all.

Paragraph B with concrete and specific language

① Few things are more important in college than a high grade in a class. Since an "A" is the ultimate goal, students ② dive into papers or keep their eyes pried open for a drawn-out study session. ③ The sound of the alarm clock reminds them that they ④ have sacrificed a whole night's rest for those essays and tests.

Analysis:

① Clear descriptions of the importance of getting good grades.

②③ Appealing to sensations by using concrete language like "dive into," "keep their eyes pried open," and "the sound of the alarm clock."

③④ A vivid scene of staying up to study, including a description of what they lost: a night's rest.

It's a "showing" paragraph. The use of concrete and specific language gives more details and thus invites empathy from readers. Consequently, the message "students like to get good grades" can be conveyed in a more lively, memorable, and effective way.

Practice LC2-2

Compare the sentences in each of the following groups. Decide which one is more concrete and specific. Circle the letter in front. Then explain your choices to a partner.

1. A. The boy is a book lover.

   B. Jay has many books on his bookshelf.

   C. Jay has nearly a hundred poetry, science, and psychology books on his bookshelf.

2. A. China aims to do something to protect the environment.

   B. China aims to cut greenhouse gas emissions.

   C. China aims to see its carbon dioxide emissions peak before 2030 and realize carbon neutrality before 2060.

3. A. People may treat some more diseases in the future.
    B. Chinese scientists developed a "detour" therapeutical strategy that may help relieve symptoms of fatty liver in the future.
    C. Some scientists found potential ways to treat liver diseases.

Core knowledge input

3 Methods to Improve Language Specificity

Method 1: The 5W1H method

The 5W1H method is shorthand for "Who, What, When, Where, Why, and How." Answers to these questions provide a basis for digging deeper into details, so as to make language concrete and specific. So, the 5W1H approach can be used as a guideline for improving language specificity.

The 5W1H Method

Method 2: The ladder of abstraction

Most words do not fall neatly into categories; they're not always either abstract or concrete, general or specific. Therefore, we can try classifying words by placing them on a scale: a ladder of abstraction. On this scale, we place a word on a higher or lower level of abstraction. The lower on the scale, the more concrete and specific a word is. We can take a word down several levels of abstraction to make them more concrete and specific.

Example of the Ladder of Abstraction

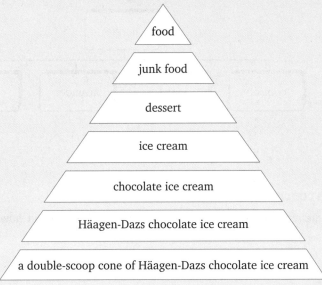

Method 3: Hyponyms

One of the most effective ways for writers to move down the ladder of abstraction is using hyponyms. A hyponym is a word whose meaning is included in that of another word with a broader connotation.

In other words, hyponyms are more specific words that constitute a subclass of a more general word. Nouns, verbs, adjectives all have their hyponyms.

Examples of Hyponyms

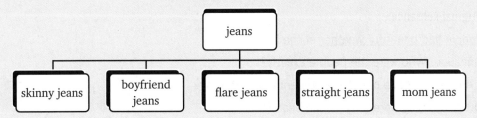

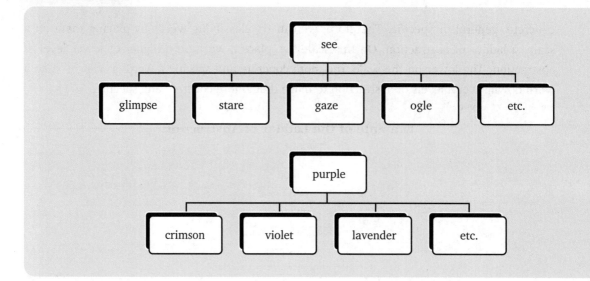

Model LC2-2

Making language concrete and specific

Study the model sentences and notice the series of Q & A. Think about how the underlined parts are revised.

Original sentence:

Like calligraphy, traditional Chinese painting is done in <u>the same way</u>.

Question: What is the specific way of Chinese painting? How is it done?

  Answer: By a brush, on paper or silk.

Question: How is "a brush" used? Can I provide an answer at a lower level of abstraction?

  Answer: A brush is dipped in black ink or colored pigments.

Revised sentence:

Like calligraphy, traditional Chinese painting is done using a brush dipped in black ink or colored pigments, usually on paper or silk.

Original sentence:

<u>People</u> <u>had</u> <u>beautiful weather</u> at the beach.

Question: Who were the people exactly?

  Answer: A group of college students from Beijing.

Question: Why were they on the beach?

Answer: They were on vacation.

Question: What can be seen when the weather is beautiful at the beach?

Answer: The blue sky, white clouds, the sun, and the blue sea.

Question: How can the state and colors of the above elements be presented in a more precise and vivid way?

Answer: The powder-blue sky, puffy and white clouds, the sparkling sun, and the azure ocean water.

Question: How would the students feel? Another word that is at a lower level of abstraction than "had"?

Answer: Enjoyed.

Revised sentence:

On their vacation, a group of college students from Beijing enjoyed the powder-blue sky, the puffy and white clouds, the sparking sun, and the azure ocean water.

Practice LC2-3

Take each of these general or abstract terms down three levels of abstraction.

Example:			
junk food	ice cream	chocolate ice cream	Häagen-Dazs chocolate ice cream

1. learning   _____   _____   _____

2. community   _____   _____   _____

3. healthy   _____   _____   _____

4. nice day   _____   _____   _____

Practice LC2-4

Think of one or more hyponyms for each underlined word and rewrite the sentences.

Example:
The students cooked food. → The international students fried eggs and vegetables.

1. Natural materials are good. → _____ are _____.

2. <u>The building</u> made <u>strange sounds</u>. → _____ made _____.

3. <u>Animals</u> <u>communicate</u> <u>well</u>. → _____ _____ _____.

Practice LC2-5

Revise the following sentences with all three methods you have learned to make them more concrete and specific.

> **Example:**
>
> To become better in college, one will have to work hard. →
>
> <u>To earn higher grades in college, you will need to attend every class, complete all your homework before the deadline, write several drafts for each paper, and review your notes for each class.</u>

1. Students showed their creativity. →

   _____

   _____

2. The environment of my hometown has become better. →

   _____

   _____

3. China is a responsible country. →

   _____

   _____

Language Clinic 3

Use valid parallel structure

Many students often have problems with parallel structure in English writing. What does parallel structure or parallelism mean? How can a parallel structure be effectively written?

Learning outcomes

At the end of this clinic, you will be able to

- identify parallel structure in English writing;
- understand how parallel structure is achieved at three levels;
- recognize how parallel structure is maintained with conjunctions;
- write sentences with valid parallel structures.

Core knowledge input

Micro-lecture Parallel Structure

Parallel Structure

What is parallel structure?

"It was the best of times, it was the worst of times, it was the age of wisdom, it was the age of foolishness, it was the epoch of belief, it was the epoch of incredulity, it was the season of Light, it was the season of Darkness, it was the spring of hope, it was the winter of despair, we had everything before us, we had nothing before us, we were all going direct to Heaven, we were all going direct the other way."

— Charles Dickens, *A Tale of Two Cities*

Parallel structure (also called parallelism or parallel construction) is the repetition of the same grammatical form in two or more parts of a sentence. The excerpt above is such an example. Parallelism is most commonly used in sentences containing elements that appear in a pair or in a series. It is also applied to headings and outlines in academic writing. A parallel structure may happen at various levels from words and phrases to clauses and paragraphs.

1. Parallel words

On the word level, valid parallelism is used to group a noun with another noun, an adjective with other adjectives, and so on. When a series is composed of verbs, do not mix forms. For example, mixing an infinitive (a verb beginning with to) with a gerund (a verb form ending in -ing) breaks parallel structure.

2. Parallel phrases

The parallel structure should be used to balance a series of phrases with the same grammatical structure. For example, avoid mixing noun phrases with verb phrases.

3. Parallel clauses

Parallelism is also applicable to a series of clauses in a sentence.

Effects of parallel structure

Maintaining parallel structure helps you avoid grammatically incorrect sentences and improves your writing style. Although lack of parallelism is not always strictly incorrect, sentences with parallel structures are easier to read and add a sense of balance to your writing.

1. Parallelism can create a sense of rhythm and emphasis, like in the following example.

"… we will pay any price, bear any burden, meet any hardship, support any friend, and oppose any foe in order to assure the survival and success of liberty."

— John F. Kennedy, *Inaugural Address*

2. Parallelism can help writers achieve brevity and simplicity. For instance, the use of participle phrases can help organize a number of different things around one subject, thereby enabling the writer to avoid repeating the subject.

"That's one small step for man, one giant leap for mankind."

— Neil Armstrong

"A fearful man, all in coarse grey, with a great iron on his leg. A man with no hat, and with broken shoes, and with an old rag tied round his head. A man who had been soaked in water, and smothered in mud, and lamed by stones, and cut by flints, and stung by nettles, and torn by briars; who limped, and shivered, and glared and growled; and whose teeth chattered in his head as he seized me by the chin."

— Charles Dickens, *Great Expectations*

Good and bad examples of parallelism

Read the following example sentences which contain parallel structures. Learn how parallel structure is achieved at the three levels.

	Non-Parallel	Parallel
Words	When talking to the customers, the sales manager always speaks sincerely and with passion.	When talking to the customers, the sales manager always speaks sincerely and passionately.
	The participants in the workshop learned how to communicate, negotiate, and the process of working collaboratively for the most effective outcome.	The participants in the workshop learned how to communicate, negotiate, and cooperate for the most effective outcome. The participants in the workshop learned about communicating, negotiating, and cooperating for the most effective outcome.
Phrases	Initial trials showed that exposure to the chemical caused memory problems, intermittent dizziness, and deters sleep.	Initial trials showed that exposure to the chemical caused memory problems, intermittent dizziness, and insomnia.
	Her main duties were answering phone calls, filing records, and to conduct visitor surveys.	Her main duties were answering phone calls, filing records, and conducting visitor surveys.
Clauses	The report card stated that the student often talked in class, that he bullied other students, and rarely finished his homework.	The report card stated that the student often talked in class, that he bullied other students, and that he rarely finished his homework. The report card stated that the student often talked in class, bullied other students, and rarely finished his homework.

Read the following sentences. Decide whether the parallel structure is correctly maintained at the word, phrase, or clause level. If yes, check the boxes in front and underline the parallel parts. If not, cross the boxes and revise them.

1. ☐ Is cable news today reliable, unbiased, and accurate?

2. ☐ Mary loves music, swim, and to read.

_____

3. ☐ We are curious who he is and why he is here.

_____

4. ☐ My parents always support my actions or what I said.

_____

5. ☐ She asked for my mobile number, my address, and what my work is.

_____

6. ☐ Doctors are encouraging patients to consume more water and exercising three times a week.

_____

7. ☐ Have watching television, surfing the Internet, and cell phones negatively impacted our culture?

_____

8. ☐ I realize that I did badly in the module because I missed several lectures, arrived late for most seminars, and I was lacking in motivation.

_____

9. ☐ In some parts of the country, a carbonated beverage is called "soda," whereas "pop" is used in other parts of the country.

_____

10. ☐ According to Kolb, experiential learning consists of having an experience, reflecting on that experience, learning from it, and plan changes for the future.

_____

Parallel structure with conjunctions

The usual way to join parallel structures is to use conjunctions which connect phrases or clauses. Study the following examples and pay attention to the parallelism achieved by conjunctions.

Coordinating conjunctions (such as *for, and, nor, but, or, yet, so,* etc.)

The university library has plenty of resources ***and*** space.

What matters is not what you say ***but*** how you behave.

We should not judge others by their appearance ***or*** wealth.

Correlative conjunctions (such as *not only ... but also, either ... or, neither ... nor, if ... then,* etc.)

Her handwriting is ***both*** legible ***and*** elegant.

The sample population should be ***neither*** too young ***nor*** too old.

Blueberries are ***not only*** delicious ***but also*** rich in antioxidants.

Comparison (such as *over, than, as,* etc.)

I would ***rather*** stay up late ***than*** get up early.

Driving to work is more convenient ***than*** taking a bus.

Listening is ***as*** important ***as*** talking in communication.

Practice LC3-2

Read the following sentences. Highlight the conjunctions. Then think about whether the parallel structure is correctly maintained. If yes, underline it. If not, revise it.

1. He would rather die than to surrender.

   _____

2. We can stay at home or out shopping.

   _____

3. She will not admit it nor will she be apologizing.

   _____

4. They are not only roommates but also best friends.

   _____

5. Cheating can result in a fail or even being expelled from school.

_____

6. This course teaches students to think critically and have better writing.

_____

7. This conclusion is made based on both qualitative and quantitative data.

_____

8. The whole wheat sandwich is healthier than that is made from refined grains.

_____

9. The university is famous for its great teachers, advanced facilities, and beautiful campus.

_____

10. It is vital not only to know the requirements but also complying with them so you can get a high grade.

_____

Practice LC3-3

Translate the following sentences into English using the given conjunctions. Make sure every sentence is parallel in structure.

> **Example:**
> 让所有学生以高分通过考试不仅是可能的，而且是可取的。(not only...but also...)
> It is not only possible, but also desirable, for all students to pass the test with a good grade.

1. 她擅长演奏古典音乐和现代音乐。（as well as）

_____

2. 该公司正在寻找一位坚定（determined）、有条理并且守时的毕业生。（and）

_____

3. 比起浪漫小说，他更喜欢侦探小说。（than）

_____

Complete the following sentences by translating the words given in the parentheses.
Make sure parallel structure is maintained.

> **Example:**
>
> Localities including Beijing, Sichuan, and Jiangxi have rolled out supportive measures
> increasing leave for couples, such as offering parental leave, <u>extending</u> (延长) maternity and
> marriage leave, and <u>increasing</u> (增加) paternity leave.

1. Through a sense of responsibility to human civilization, China is making every effort to fight

   climate change, _____ (构建) a community of harmony between humanity and nature, and

   _____ (促进) a new relationship where humanity and nature can both live and prosper in

   harmony.

2. Gaming platforms must assume primary responsibility to _____ (建立) anti-addiction

   systems and _____ (完善) real-name registration technology.

3. Qinghai Lake has seen its largest water area as a result of _____ (降雨增多) and

   _____ (生态改善).

Review how to achieve parallel structure at different levels and translate the following
sentences into English. Make sure every sentence adheres to parallelism.

1. 中国正以前所未有的（unprecedented）广度、深度和力度参与全球治理体制（global governance
   system）的改革与优化。

   _____

2. 各国一起发展才是真发展，各国共同繁荣才是真繁荣。

   _____

3. 中华传统文化是中国的根与魂，代表着最深厚的文化软实力，蕴含着丰富的治国理政智慧。

   _____

Use periodic and loose sentences for desired effects

As student writers, we are always told to vary our sentence types to keep readers interested. But what sentence types are available to us? How can we use them effectively?

Learning outcomes

At the end of this clinic, you will be able to

- identify the two sentence types: loose sentences and periodic sentences;
- analyze the different effects these two types of sentences can produce;
- use them effectively to achieve desired writing purposes.

Core knowledge input

Micro-lecture Loose Sentences vs Periodic Sentences

Loose Sentences vs Periodic Sentences

What are they?

You'll love *Casablanca* if you're the kind of person who likes to cry at movies.

If you're the kind of person who likes to cry at the movies, you'll love *Casablanca*.

Can you see the difference between these two sentences? In the first one, the main statement is placed at the beginning, followed by one or more modifying clauses or phrases. This type of sentence is called a **loose sentence**. In contrast, the second one is a **periodic sentence**, in which the main clause, or main point, occurs at the end of the sentence, preceded by one or more modifying clauses or phrases.

Their different effects in writing

A loose sentence presents readers with a natural speech order, which can be easily and directly understood. They usually have relatively simple structures and plain meanings. Therefore, they are more commonly used, especially in daily communication. Loose sentences are useful when you want to provide both an immediate understanding of the main idea and a great deal of supporting detail. However, readers may refuse to read the supplementary part.

Periodic sentences are on the opposite of the loose sentence. Since the main point is presented at the end in such sentences, they can impress readers by creating suspense. However, periodic sentences tend to be long, unnatural, and hard to understand. Readers may forget the long supplementary part at the beginning when they finally reach the end of a sentence. As a result, periodic sentences are commonly used in formal writing, and thus enjoy a lower frequency of use.

	Loose sentences	Periodic sentences
Effect	easily understood; natural; direct	suspenseful; dramatic; literary
Frequency	high	low
Purpose	• creating a straightforward expression • emphasizing the idea in the main clause	• creating suspense • forcing the reader to read the complementary details
Risk	• dull if repeatedly used • readers refusing to read the supplementary details	• difficult to understand • pompous

Practice LC4-1

Decide if the following sentences are loose (L) or periodic (P) ones. Write the corresponding letter in the parentheses.

1. He now came to London, a literary adventurer, with many projects in his head, and very little money in his pocket. (   )

2. A man, doubtful of his dinner, or trembling at a creditor, is not much disposed to abstracted meditation or remote inquiries. (   )

3. Given that the level of neutralizing antibodies produced by seniors after vaccination is lower than that of young people, and all age groups see a decline in the level as time passes, the elderly are encouraged to get a vaccine booster as soon as possible. (   )

4. Pan absorbed himself in gaining professional knowledge, learning English, and undergoing physical training for nearly three years, working even harder than he did in college. (   )

5. A native of Shandong province and mother of a 5-year-old girl, Wang Yaping joined the People's Liberation Army Air Force in August 1997 and the second group of astronauts at the PLA Astronaut Division in May 2010. (   )

6. China's literature and philosophy are admired and studied around the world, containing the seeds of wisdom that have been cherished by all of humanity. (   )

Practice LC4-2

Decide if each of the following sentences is a loose (L) or periodic (P) one. Write the corresponding letter in the parentheses. Then convert the sentence into the other type.

1. Students cannot make great progress in their study without good study habits. (   )

   _____

2. Although the boy is only nine years old, he has defeated many experienced adults at chess. (   )

   _____

3. Driven by free trade mechanisms such as the upgraded China-ASEAN Free Trade Agreement and the Regional Comprehensive Economic Partnership, the trade volume between China and ASEAN has grown rapidly. (   )

   _____

   _____

4. The central government has reviewed and revised over 2,300 pieces of laws and regulations, and local governments over 190,000 pieces, which all helped unleash market and social vitality. (   )

   _____

   _____

Writing effects and sentence types

Study the model sentences and notice the analysis of their writing effects.

Model Sentence 1

<u>Maggie will be nervous</u> [until after her sister goes]: <u>She will stand</u> [hopelessly in concern,
main clause first   [an adverbial clause added]   another main clause   [another series of adverbials]

homely and ashamed of the burn scars down her arms and legs, eying her sister with a

mixture of envy and awe.]

Analysis: It is a loose sentence. It creates a direct understanding of Maggie's feeling and
reaction before providing rich details to help readers imagine the scene.

Model Sentence 2

<u>China has become an active promoter and important contributor to reforming the system of</u>

<u>global economic governance</u>, [while its international influence, strength of appeal, and power
main clause first   [an adverbial clause added]

to shape the environment have also been further enhanced].

Analysis: It is a loose sentence. It states directly China's general role in global economic
governance before offering the specific aspects.

Model Sentence 3

[If these measures are combined with shifting dietary patterns], <u>it is estimated that greenhouse</u>
[an adverbial clause first]   main clause

<u>emissions from agrifood systems can be reduced by almost 50 percent in 2060</u>.

Analysis: It is a periodic sentence. It forces readers to notice the measures to be taken before
revealing the estimated result of reductions in greenhouse emissions from agrifood
systems.

Model Sentence 4

[Through Chinese innovation and manufacturing expertise as well as the diligence, sacrifice,

and perseverance of its workers], <u>companies like ZTE and others have provided low-cost,</u>
[an adverbial]   the main clause

reliable, and technologically superior service and products to the world.

Analysis: It is a periodic sentence. It forces readers to notice the reasons why Chinses companies can serve the world.

Practice LC4-3

Choose the proper writing effects for the following sentences.

1. Instead of an awkward silence, broken by attempts at wit or dull commonplaces, my journey is that undisturbed silence of the heart which alone is perfect eloquence.

   A. direct and natural　　　　　　　　B. suspenseful or literary

2. China's whole-process democracy ensures that its people can widely exercise their right to vote, undertake extensive deliberations, take part in carrying out the decisions they have reached, and manage their own affairs.

   A. direct and natural　　　　　　　　B. suspenseful or literary

3. In the face of the pandemic and changes unseen in a century, standing at the crossroads of history, it was further proposed to build a China-Africa community with a shared future in the new era.

   A. direct and natural　　　　　　　　B. suspenseful or literary

4. Transition from demographic dividend to talent dividend is a major issue that needs to be addressed for China's further economic development.

   A. direct and natural　　　　　　　　B. suspenseful or literary

Practice LC4-4

Translate the following sentences into either a loose sentence or a periodic one to create the desired writing effect specified in the parentheses.

Example:

本月早些时候，神舟 12 号飞船上的三名宇航员与天河号对接（dock with），中国又迎来了一个重要里程碑。（**desired writing effect:** a direct emphasis on the significance of this event）

China reached another important milestone earlier this month when three taikonauts aboard the Shenzhou-12 spacecraft docked with the Tianhe.

1. 从中国西南部云南省昆明市到老挝首都万象，长达 1000 多公里的电气化客货铁路（electrified passenger and cargo railway）将于 12 月初通车。（**desired writing effect:** forcing the reader to notice the start and the end of the railway before telling about the event）

_____

_____

_____

2. 中国加入世贸组织是顺应经济全球化趋势的正确选择，此举掀起了国内发展新风潮，也为世界经济注入新动力（injecting fresh impetus into）。（**desired writing effect:** directly stating the conclusion that it is the right choice）

_____

_____

_____

3. 北大、清华和南开三所大学为了抵抗日军占领，选择迁往中国内地（China's interior），以便在战争中能继续提供高等教育。（**desired writing effect:** suspensefully emphasizing the purpose of the move before revealing the event）

_____

_____

_____

Core knowledge input

Avoid a Succession of Loose Sentences

Over-using complex and periodic sentences is never a good idea; an occasional loose sentence prevents the style from becoming too formal and gives readers a moment of relief. But the reverse is equally dangerous. Too many loose sentences in one paragraph, especially those consisting of two clauses connected by a conjunction such as *and*, *or*, *but*, will make the writing unskillful and mechanical. Compare the following two paragraphs.

The second gathering of the reading club took place last evening, and most of the club members were in attendance. Dr. Jeff White was the guiding instructor, and one of his Ph.D. students assisted him. Mr. White showed himself to be an outstanding scholar, while the Ph.D. candidate proved himself a promising young scholar. The audience was interested in their beautiful reading and insightful ideas, and Dr. White felt so gratified that he decided to plan another reading session on a similar topic next month.

People's relationship with work is complex. For all the complaining about the tedium and bureaucracy, the power-crazed bosses, and recalcitrant colleagues, individuals need the security of a job. A century of research has shown that unemployment is bad for mental health, leading to depression, anxiety, and reduced self-esteem. But how much work do you need to do? A recent paper by the Centre for Business Research at Cambridge University took the opportunity of the pandemic to examine the impact of reduced working hours on well-being.

The first paragraph is boring because of its monotonous sentence type — "Clause A, and Clause B" repeatedly. The author of the second paragraph breaks up such monotony by using simple sentences, periodic sentences, and complex sentences — whichever best expresses the intended meaning.

Practice LC4-5

Translate the following passages into English. Use proper sentence types to achieve the desired effect specified in the parentheses.

1. 第九届乌镇戏剧节（Wuzhen Theater Festival）将于 11 月 25 日至 12 月 4 日在浙江省乌镇举行。本届主题为"丰"。戏剧节组委会在 6 月 28 日公布了本届竞演的命题——"酒瓶、空白、遥控器"。戏剧艺术家们可于 9 月 10 日之前，在官方网站上注册参加比赛。（**desired effect:** providing clear information and emphasising important dates）

_____

_____

_____

_____

2. 袁隆平一生最大的梦想是培育更多的杂交水稻（hybrid rice）品种，并用它来解决世界许多地方不断发生的饥荒问题。袁和他的团队在过去的 40 年里，不断举办研讨会，开设课程，向来自近 80 个国家的约 14 000 名学生传授他的方法。这位农学家（agronomist）即使在晚年仍远赴非洲帮助提高收成（boost harvests）。（**desired effect:** emphasizing Yuan Longping's dedication to his dream）

_____

_____

_____

_____

Use correct capitalization and punctuation

Capital letters and punctuations are useful signals for readers. They help to make our message meaningful and clear, and they tell readers how to read our sentences. Wrongly used punctuation and capitalization can confuse readers, or make our writing sound unpolished. But what are the correct ways to use them? How do we preserve capitalization and punctuation conventions?

Learning outcomes

At the end of this clinic, you will be able to

- understand the basic rules for using capitalization;
- produce proper capitalizations in essay writing;
- apply six commonly used punctuation marks correctly.

Core knowledge input

Micro-lecture Capitalization

Capitalization

What is it?

Capitalization is the process of capitalizing words — making their first letter a capital letter (an uppercase letter) and the remaining letters in lowercase, in a writing system with a case distinction. The full rules of capitalization for English are complicated, but several rules are frequently used in essay writing.

Capitalization rules

1. The first word of a complete sentence or quotation:

   Mom asked, "Where are you going?"

2. Only the first word of salutations and closings in letters unless a proper noun is used:

   - Salutations: **D**ear Mr. Mooney
   - Closings: **S**incerely, **A**ll the best

3. The first person pronoun *I*:

   Susie and **I** are very good classmates.

4. All proper nouns including:

   1) Names of specific persons, pet animals, and things:

      Mary has a little dog called **P**udding.

   2) Names of nationalities, languages, races, etc.:

      Americans typically speak **E**nglish.

   3) Names of buildings, monuments, bridges, tunnels, streets, roads, etc.:

      The **E**mpire **S**tate **B**uilding is located on the west side of **F**ifth **A**venue in **M**anhattan.

   4) Names of institutions, organizations, companies, trademarks, government departments, political groups, etc.:

      The **W**orld **T**rade **O**rganization deals with the global rules of trade between nations.

   5) Names of planets (except the sun and the moon), mountains, mountain ranges, hills, water bodies, volcanoes, etc.:

      Jupiter has the distinction of being the largest planet.

   6) Names of days, months, special occasions, but not seasons except when they are parts of proper nouns:

      Edward's son was born on a **M**onday in the summer month of **A**ugust.

   7) Names of historical events, eras, documents, etc.:

      The **R**enaissance marks the transition from the **M**iddle **A**ges to the **M**odern **E**ra.

5. Adjectives derived from proper nouns:

   I love to read **S**hakespearean sonnets and **C**hinese novels.

6. People's titles:

   - Will you check my blood pressure, **D**octor?
   - Yesterday, I met **P**rofessor **A**lex in the classroom.

7. Family relationship words:

   I discussed the matter with **M**om and **D**ad.

8. Educational degrees, specific course titles, and names of languages used as academic subjects but not the names of general academic subjects:

   - He was granted the **B**achelor of **A**rts.
   - I took *Art 101* and *Biology 111* last semester. However, my favorite subjects are history & social science.

9. Initials and acronyms:

   - Dr. Brown works on an **HIV** project for the **WHO**.
   - The author **C.S.** Lewis is better known by his initials than by his full name, Clive Staples Lewis.

Practice LC5-1

Determine if each of the following sentences has proper use of capitalization. If yes, check the box in front. If not, cross the box and correct it.

1. ☐　My friend is from sweden.

_____

2. ☐　I work in the library every Monday morning.

_____

3. ☐　Peru is located in south America.

_____

4. ☐　The novel, regarded as one of China's four great classical novels, was written in the middle of the 18th century.

_____

5. ☐　*Records of the Grand Historian* was written by Sima qian, a famous historian, writer, and thinker of the western Han dynasty.

_____

6. ☐　Most of the relief supplies to Tsunami-hit Tonga have been raised by the Chinese embassy in fiji.

_____

7. ☐　Cambridge university is one of the oldest universities in the world.

_____

8. ☐　In his visit to Kenya last Weekend, China's foreign minister emphasized China's support for economic progress in Africa.

_____

Practice LC5-2

Find and fix the capitalization errors in the following paragraphs.

1. Elijah was born before the civil war ended. His mother and father were ex-slaves. they escaped to canada on the underground railroad. later, they returned to the united states. their son, elijah,

went to britain to study Engineering. When he returned, no one would hire an african american engineer. in spite of that, Elijah became a famous inventor.

2. One of my favorite parts of the summer camp was to see the statue of liberty. My teacher told me it was a gift to the united states from the French a hundred years ago. On another day, we met the Mayor, his name was mayor Bloomberg. My dad suggested, "next year we're going to las vegas."

Core knowledge input

Capitalization in Titles

The capitalization rules for titles of books, movies, and other works vary a lot according to different writing styles. However, some general rules apply.

- Capitalize the first word and last word, all nouns, all verbs (even short ones, like is), all adjectives, and all proper nouns.
- Use lowercase for articles, conjunctions, and prepositions for most occasions. If located in the first or last position in a title, they should nevertheless be in their uppercase letters.

Model LC5-1

Capitalization in titles

- *Writing a Good Business Letter* was published yesterday.
- *Sense and Sensibility* is better than *Pride and Prejudice*.
- *Gone with the Wind* is a great novel.
- *On Protracted War* is a work comprising a series of speeches by Mao Zedong given at the Yan'an Association for the Study of the War of Resistance Against Japan.
- *The Analects of Confucius* is an anthology of brief passages that present the words of Confucius and his disciples.

Practice LC5-3

Underline the title in each of the following sentences. Decide if it is written correctly. If yes, check the box in front. If not, cross the box and correct it.

1. ☐ The popular classic Chinese TV series a Dream of Red Mansions is now being dubbed in the Lao language for broadcast on Lao National Television.

_____

2. ☐ The Chinese TV adaptation of Liu Cixin's Hugo Award-winning sci-fi novel the Three-body Problem is coming soon.

_____

3. ☐ The film my People, my Country was released on October 1, 2019 to mark the 70th anniversary of the founding of the People's Republic of China.

_____

4. ☐ This episode of "China In The Classics" explores Songs of Chu, the first anthology of romantic poetry in the history of Chinese literature.

_____

Practice LC5-4

Rewrite the following titles with correct capitalization. Then translate them into Chinese.

1. outlaws of the marsh

_____

2. a journey to the west

_____

3. romance of the three kingdoms

_____

4. the story of the western wing

_____

5. six chapters from a floating life

_____

6. a moment in peking

_____

Micro-lecture Common Punctuation Marks

Common Punctuation Marks

Punctuation marks are essential in our writing. They show readers where sentences start and finish. If they are used properly, they make our writing easy to understand. Study the following practical guidance on how to use full stops, commas, colons, and semicolons.

Full stop (.)

The full stop is the British English term for this punctuation mark; it is known as a period in American English. Full stops are used in the following situations.

1. To mark the end of a sentence that is a complete statement
   - My name is Bella and I am 18 this year.
   - After leaving school, Judy went to an insurance company to take a part-time job.
2. In some abbreviations
   etc.   p.m.
3. In website and E-mail addresses
   www.   .com   .net
4. If an abbreviation with a full stop comes at the end of a sentence, we don't need to add another full stop.
   In the final exam, bring your own pencils, erasers, rulers, etc.

Comma (,)

A comma marks a slight break between different parts of a sentence. Used properly, commas make the meaning of sentences clear by grouping and separating words, phrases, and clauses. Commas are used in the following ways.

1. In lists
   - Saturday morning started with a hearty breakfast of scrambled eggs, bacon, sausage, and French toast.
   - The school has a vegetable garden in which the children grow cabbages, onions, potatoes, and carrots.

2. In direct speeches
   - Bloomberg replied, "No problem."
   - "Thinking positively," she added, "I didn't even expect to win."

3. To separate clauses
   - I first saw her in Britain, where I lived in the early 1990s.
   - Since the sun won't shine today, we will not go to the beach.

4. To mark off parts of the sentence
   - Gunpowder is not, of course, a chemical compound.
   - A good deal of discretion, however, is left in the hands of area managers.

5. To separate a coordinating conjunction

   My dad likes this restaurant, but I don't like it at all.

Note:

When we are listing three or more items, the final comma — the one that comes before "and" — is optional, as illustrated in the examples below. Whether or not we use the comma is a style choice. Many newspapers do not use it. Many trade books do use it. In our own writing,we can decide for ourselves whether to use it or not — just be consistent.

Saturday morning started with a hearty breakfast of scrambled eggs, bacon, sausage, and French toast.

Saturday morning started with a hearty breakfast of scrambled eggs, bacon, sausage and French toast.

Colon (:)

Colons are punctuation marks used to direct attention to matter (as a list, explanation, quotation, or amplification) that follows. They are used after complete sentences.

1. Between two main clauses in cases where the second clause explains or follows from the first
   - That is the secret of my life: Always do the unexpected.
   - It wasn't easy: To begin with, I had to find the right house.
2. To introduce a list

   The job calls for skills in the following areas: proofing, editing, and computing.

Semicolon (;)

     The main task of the semicolon is to mark a break that is stronger than a comma but not as final as a full stop. It appears in the following situations.

1. To connect the two complete thoughts in a sentence

   The road runs through a beautiful wooded valley; the railway line follows it.
2. As a stronger division in a sentence that already contains commas

   The study showed the following: 76% of surveyed firms monitor employee Web-surfing activities, with 65% blocking access to unauthorized Internet locations; over 33% of the firms monitor employee computer keystrokes; half reported storing and reviewing employee e-mails; 57% monitor employee telephone behavior, including the inappropriate use of voicemail.
3. Before a transitional word and a comma to join two complete thoughts

   It is the hottest day in this summer; however, Nancy still works on her project with all her classmates.

Practice LC5-5

Choose the sentence with the appropriate use of punctuation in each of the groups. Correct the wrong ones.

1. A. Earth is old; it was formed 4.5 billion years ago.

   B. Xinjiang is beautiful; it is an autonomous region in the westernmost part of China.

   C. I laughed; loudly.

   D. I swear I saw a rabbit; bear; or mouse downstairs.

2. A. She had doctorates in two areas; philosophy and physics.

   B. Home to cities such as: Urumqi, Kashgar, and Altay Prefecture, there's no shortage of things to do and see in Xinjiang.

   C. I have to get surgery on my arm, I fell out of a tree.

   D. I knew exactly what I wanted: pizza.

3. A. The store had mangoes, apples, kiwis, etc..

    B. The store had mangoes, apples, kiwis, etc.

    C. The store had, mangoes, apples, kiwis, etc.

    D. The store had: mangoes, apples, kiwis, etc.

Core knowledge input

Micro-lecture Apostrophes and Quotation Marks

Apostrophes and Quotation Marks

Apostrophes and quotation marks are used especially when writing direct speeches, abbreviations, and to show possession.

Apostrophe (')

There are two main cases when apostrophes are needed: to show possession and to show omission. When an apostrophe is used to show omission, the letters have been omitted. Study the examples below.

I'm — I am

he'll — he will

she'd — she had or she would

it's hot — it is hot

didn't — did not

But when it comes to apostrophes for possession, the rules are more complex.

1. With a singular noun or most personal names, add an apostrophe plus *s*.
    * We met at Ben's party.
    * Yesterday's weather was dreadful.

2. With a plural noun that already ends in *s, add* an apostrophe after the *s*.
    * The mansion was converted into a girls' school.
    * The work is due to start in two weeks' time.

3. With a plural noun that doesn't end in *s, add* an apostrophe plus *s*.
    * The children's father came round to see me.
    * He employs 14 people at his men's clothing store.

> **Quotation marks (" ")**
>
> In essay writing, a writer often wants to tell readers what someone has said as evidence to support their argument. In such circumstances, the speaker's words can be quoted directly with the help of quotation marks, as in the example below. Note that there should be a comma, full stop, question mark, or exclamation mark at the end of a piece of speech and it is placed inside the closing quotation marks.
>
> "They think it's a more respectable job," said Jo.
>
> Quotation marks are also used for the titles of shorter pieces of work: poems, articles, book chapters, songs, T.V. episodes, etc. See the examples below. (For your information, the titles of long works, like books, movies, or record albums are italicized.)
>
> Read the article "I Am Writing Blindly" by Roger Rosenblatt.
>
> My favorite song is "Free to Be You and Me."

Practice LC5-6

Examine the punctuation uses in the following sentences. Correct those with errors.

1. "We need two copies of each document", the office manager explained.

   _____

2. Sammie clearly lacked confidence about the decision because she used "maybe" and "if" with every expressed thought.

   _____

3. Jeremy yelled; "We're over here!"

   _____

4. John said that, "I should take the afternoon off because business was slow."

   _____

5. Joannie enthusiastically inquired, "How many gifts under the tree are for me"?

   _____

Practice LC5-7

Add proper punctuation in the blanks in the following sentences.

1. Several countries participated in the airlift__Italy_Belgium__France__and Luxembourg__

2. __There_s no room for error__said the engineer__so we have to double-check every calculation_

3. In last week_s *New Yorker*__one of my favorite magazines__I enjoyed reading Leland_s article__How Not to Go Camping__

4. __Yes__Jim said__I_ll be home by ten__

5. Montaigne wrote the following__A wise man never loses anything__if he has himself__

6. The following are the primary colors__red__blue__and yellow__

7. Arriving on the 8:10 plane were Liz Brooks__ my old roommate__her husband__and Tim__their son__

8. The automobile dealer handled three makes of cars__Volkswagens__Porsche__and Mercedes Benz__

9. He used the phrase__you know__so often that I finally said__No__I don__t know__

10. __Who ever thought__said Helen__that Jack would be elected class president__

Practice LC5-8

Use capitalized letters and punctuation marks where necessary in the following texts.

1. arent you going to have any asparagus said i no i never eat asparagus i know there are people who dont like them the fact is that you ruin your palate by all the meat you eat she said

2. the teacher said to the girl do you think that honesty is the best policy yes sir think so said the girl then learn to be honest from your childhood thank you sir said the girl

3. would you please tell me one reason for air pollution yes the smoke from our household activities vehicles factories etc is causing air pollution

4. do not worry about a few mistakes said the teacher you can learn a lot through your mistakes do we learn from our mistakes asked the boy

Avoid pitfalls of word choice

Diction, or the choice of words, plays a key role in deciding the clarity and formality of writing. In the previous language clinics, we have learned some practical strategies to improve our word choice. Besides those what-to-do tips, it is also important to pay attention to the common pitfalls of diction that may spoil our writing.

Learning outcomes

At the end of this clinic, you will be able to

- identify common pitfalls of word choice;
- evaluate good and bad examples of word choice;
- avoid the pitfalls and use proper words in writing.

Core knowledge input

Micro-lecture Common Pitfalls of Word Choice

Common Pitfalls of Word Choice

Colloquial expressions

The term "colloquial" refers to a style of writing that is conversational (how we talk on a daily basis). Colloquial expressions include contractions (i.e., *can't, don't, doesn't, couldn't, shouldn't, wanna, gonna*), filler words (i.e., *really, very, quite, a lot, pretty*), and slang (i.e., *dude, ain't, kid, bail, cram, awesome, fire,* and *how come*).

We tend to hear colloquial words "out in the streets" more often than we see them in newspapers or books. In most forms of English writing, colloquialism is considered unprofessional. Unless there is a purpose for using them, remove colloquial expressions from our writing, especially if our readers are academics or professionals.

Jargon

Jargon is the unnecessarily complicated language used to impress, rather than to inform, readers. Avoiding jargon does not mean to exclude technical terms from writing, but means to discard unnecessary technical language.

For example, there may not be another correct way to refer to a "brinulator valve control ring." But that does not prevent you from saying "Tighten the brinulator valve control ring securely." instead of "Apply sufficient torque to the brinulator valve control ring to ensure that the control ring assembly is securely attached to the terminal such that loosening cannot occur under normal conditions." The first is a necessary use of a technical term. The second is jargon.

When you have no way to express an idea except to use technical language, make sure to define your terms.

Clichés

Clichés are words and phrases that have been used so often that they are no longer very interesting or effective. They may have started out as colorful, inventive phrases, like "as far as I'm concerned," but they have been used so widely and indiscriminately that they have lost their impact and become stale.

When we write on a more formal level, we should try to avoid using clichés. They create an impression of laziness or a lack of careful thought. Some people just tune out when they hear a cliché, and so they may miss the point that we are trying to make.

Noun strings

Noun strings are groups of nouns "sandwiched" together, such as "a hospital employee relations improvement program." Readability suffers when three words that are ordinarily separate nouns follow in succession. Once you get past three, the string becomes unbearable. Technically, clustering nouns turns all but the last noun into adjectives. However, many users will think they have found the noun when they are still reading adjectives, and will become confused.

To revise such expressions, bring these constructions under control by eliminating descriptive words that are not essential. If you cannot do that, open up the construction by using more prepositions and articles to clarify the relationships among the words. So the example above could be revised as "a program to improve relations among employees."

Avoiding colloquial expressions

Don't say	Say
The **kid nicked** a hundred **bucks**.	The **child stole** a hundred **dollars**.
The man was **nailed** for stealing the car.	The man was **convicted** for stealing the car.
I can't handle **cramming for** tests.	I cannot handle **studying for** tests **at the last minute**.
It was a significant challenge, but they **got through it**.	It was a significant challenge, but they **persevered**.
He has **a lot of** reasons for justifying his actions.	He has **several** reasons for justifying his actions.
When pouring the solution, **just** be certain not to spill its contents.	When pouring the solution, be certain not to spill its contents.

Practice LC6-1

Underline the colloquial expressions in the following sentences, and convert them into formal writing.

1. This ain't working.

   _____

2. The students didn't get the teacher.

   _____

3. This is a pretty good investment that your company should consider.

   _____

4. I had no butterflies in my stomach after I prepared my lessons carefully.

   _____

5. The writer did a great job in the book because it talks so much about her life as an actress.

   _____

6. I hope you break a leg in your performance tonight!

   _____

7. I don't mean to burst your bubble, but you're not the only one who got an award.

_____

8. She's the only applicant for the job, so she's bound to get it — it's a slam dunk.

_____

Model LC6-2

Avoiding jargon

Don't say	Say
riverine avifauna	river birds
involuntarily undomiciled	homeless
The patient is being given positive-pressure ventilatory support.	The patient is on a respirator.
The heat transforms the yolk's properties. The yolks change from liquid to solid. The newly-transformed yolks are now edible scrambled eggs.	Heat cooks the yolks, transforming them into scrambled eggs.

Practice LC6-2

Underline the jargon in the following sentences, and convert them into formal writing.

1. You probably know the basics of human immunodeficiency virus, which causes acquired immunodeficiency syndrome.

_____

2. The beverage dissemination officer beamed a warm smile at her.

_____

3. The company decided to have a brain dump at the beginning of the new project.

_____

4. This discovery will bring about a paradigm shift in our understanding of evolution.

_____

5. Members of Generation Z have been exposed to electronic products since they were born.

6. Studies show that delayed gratification is one of the most effective personal traits of successful people.

Avoiding clichés

Don't say	Say
In this day and age, websites are one of the most significant public faces of any organization.	**Today**, websites are one of the most significant public faces of any organization.
The long-term prospects for the service are looking fairly bleak **at this moment in time**.	The long-term prospects for the service are **currently** looking fairly bleak.
At the end of the day, it is the boss himself who has to make the decision.	**Ultimately**, it is the boss himself who has to make the decision.
Every coin has two sides.	This issue is complex and can be approached from various angles.
As far as I'm concerned, the discussion is inspiring.	The discussion is inspiring.
It goes without saying that to be an entrepreneur you have to take risks.	To be an entrepreneur **intrinsically requires** the willingness to take risks.
There's no denying that 2020 was an incredibly difficult year for the world.	**Obviously,** 2020 was an incredibly difficult year for the world.

Practice LC6-3

Underline the clichés in the following sentences, and convert them into formal writing.

1. Recent years have witnessed the development of machine translation.

2. With the development of science and technology, our daily life is becoming more colorful and more convenient.

_____

3. People's views on the effect of digital learning vary from person to person.

_____

4. It is well acknowledged that lexicon accumulation is a key factor for smooth communication.

_____

5. Nothing is more important than the fact that you met a great teacher.

_____

Model LC6-4

Avoid noun strings

Don't say	Say
International Space Station astronaut living-quarters module development project	Developing the module that will provide living quarters for the astronauts aboard the International Space Station
National Highway Traffic Safety Administration's automobile seat belt interlock rule	The National Highway Traffic Safety Administration's interlock rule applying to automotive seat belts
Underground mine worker safety protection procedures development	Developing procedures to protect the safety of workers in underground mines
Draft laboratory animal rights protection regulations	Draft regulations to protect the rights of laboratory animals

Practice LC6-4

Underline the noun strings in the following sentences, and convert them into formal writing.

1. The investigator described the energy shortfall makeup technology.

_____

2. WBTech is initiating an employee charity giving encouragement program.

_____

3. The newly developed computer system can be configured to meet a wide range of user data communication requirements.

_____

4. His job involves fault analysis systems troubleshooting handbook preparation.

_____

5. Government planning agencies and commissions have initiated the project of the water-oriented greenway.

_____

Language Clinic 7

Avoid redundancy

Vigorous writing is concise. A sentence should contain no unnecessary words and a paragraph no unnecessary sentences, for the same reason that a drawing should have no unnecessary lines and a machine no unnecessary parts. This does not mean that we should make all sentences short, avoid all details, or present ideas only in outline, but it does mean that we should avoid redundancy and make every word count.

Learning outcomes

At the end of this clinic, you will be able to

- identify four types of redundancies in writing;
- eliminate redundancy in writing with proper strategies;
- understand the significance of concise writing.

Core knowledge input

Micro-lecture Ways to Eliminate Redundancy

Ways to Eliminate Redundancy

What is redundancy?

Redundancy in writing is the unnecessary repetition or duplication of words, phrases, sentences, ideas, information, etc. — anything that could be omitted without loss of significance or meaning. They distract and confuse readers by adding unnecessary length to the writing while contributing nothing to its quality.

Types of redundancies and ways to eliminate them

- **Empty words and phrases**

They are words or phrases that contain little information. Shortening them to their essential meaning, or cutting them entirely will make writing move faster.

Examples of empty expressions	Solutions
	Cut the empty phrases entirely.
all things considered	~~all things considered~~
as far as I'm concerned	~~as far as I'm concerned~~
for all intents and purposes	~~for all intents and purposes~~
for the most part	~~for the most part~~
in a manner of speaking	~~in a manner of speaking~~
due to the fact that	~~in my opinion~~
last but not least	~~last but not least~~
more or less	~~more or less~~
	Reduce them to a single word.
at all times	→ always
at the present time	→ now
for the purpose of	→ for
in order to	→ to
for the reason that	→ because
in the event that	→ if
by means of	→ by

- **Unnecessary repetition**

     The words in the following phrases imply each other. Saying the same thing twice is not emphatic but useless and tedious.

Examples of unnecessary repetition	Solutions
	Keep the main word, and eliminate *the redundant word(s)*.
unexpected surprise	surprise
hopeful optimism	optimism
large *in size*	large
few *in number*	few
extreme *in degree*	extreme
the future *to come*	the future
circle *around*	circle
repeat *again*	repeat
biography *of his life*	biography

- **Wordy modifiers**

     Wordy modifiers are subordinate clauses, phrases, or single words that can be reduced without loss of emphasis or clarity. To reduce wordiness, it is good to remember the following advice: Do not use a dependent clause if a phrase will do; do not use a phrase if a word will do.

Examples of wordy modifiers	Solutions
The Channel Tunnel, *which runs between Britain and France*, has been in operation since 1944.	**Reduce clauses to phrases.** The Channel Tunnel *between Britain and France* has been in operation since 1944.
The Channel Tunnel bores through *a bed of solid chalk that is twenty-three miles across.*	**Reduce phrases to words.** The Channel Tunnel bores *through twenty-three miles of solid chalk.*

- **Unnecessary passive voice**

   Passive voice can make a sentence wordy unless it is necessary. In this case, use active voice. Review Language Clinic 1 for more.

Model LC7-1

Eliminating redundancy

Compare the original and revised sentences. Notice the analysis of the redundancy types and ways to eliminate them.

1. **Original:** <u>As far as I am concerned</u>, the development of artificial intelligence
   empty phrase

   <u>continues to exist</u> <u>in the field of technology</u> <u>for all intents and purposes</u>.
   unnecessary repetition   empty phrase   empty phrase

   Revised: Development of artificial intelligence continues in technology.

2. **Original:** <u>At this point in time</u>, the software is expensive <u>due to the fact that</u> it has no
                 empty phrase   empty phrase

   competition.

   Revised: The software is expensive now because it has no competition.

3. **Original:** In London, many unskilled workers <u>without training in a particular job</u> are
                                                    unnecessary repetition

   unemployed <u>and do not have any work</u>.
              unnecessary repetition

   Revised: In London, many unskilled workers are unemployed.

4. **Original:** Because <u>the circumstances</u> leading to the cancellation of classes were

   <u>murky and unclear</u>, the editor of the student newspaper assigned
   unnecessary repetition.

   <u>a staff reporter</u> to investigate and file a report on <u>the circumstances</u>.
   unnecessary repetition   unnecessary repetition.

   Revised: Because the circumstances leading to the cancellation of classes were unclear, the editor of the student newspaper assigned someone to investigate and report the story.

5. **Original:** The weight-loss industry faces new competition from lipolysis, <u>which is</u> a
   wordy modifier

   cosmetic procedure <u>that is</u> relatively non-invasive.
   wordy modifier

   Revised: The weight-loss industry faces new competition from lipolysis, a relatively non-invasive cosmetic procedure.

6. **Original:** The possibility of cold fusion <u>has been</u> examined by physicists for many years.
   unnecessary passive voice

   Revised: Physicists have examined the possibility of cold fusion for many years.

Practice LC7-1

Underline the redundancies in the following sentences. Revise the sentences into concise ones. Avoid unnecessary passive voice, empty expressions, unnecessary repetitions, and wordy modifiers.

1. In my opinion, the council's proposal to improve the city center is adequate, all things considered.

   _____

   _____

2. In order to completely finish their job, they collaborated together and presented the new innovation.

   _____

   _____

3. A total of fifty students in the Department of Education reviewed important essentials of the course.

_____

_____

4. It is very unusual to find someone who has never told a deliberate lie on purpose.

_____

_____

5. He dropped out of school on account of the fact that it was necessary for him to help support his family.

_____

_____

6. The subjects that are considered most important by students are those that have been shown to be useful to them after graduation.

_____

_____

7. China's aim, which is to build a global community that shares the same future, has its basis on restoring harmony between nature and humanity.

_____

_____

8. Some key elements of societal stability are actually indicated by China's approach to strategic planning that aims at long-term development.

_____

_____

9. Despite the widely-spread global energy crisis, official data from the government shows China's foreign trade moved up another notch in 2022.

_____

_____

10. All the crew on board the China Space Station are working in an effort to get ready for their second spacewalk since they arrived in October.

_____

_____

Revise the following passage and eliminate redundancy.

The highly pressured nature of critical-care nursing is due to the fact that the patients have life-threatening illnesses. Critical-care nurses must possess steady nerves to care for patients who are critically ill and very sick. The nurses must also possess interpersonal skills. They must also have medical skills. It is considered by most healthcare professionals that these nurses are essential if there is to be improvement of patients who are now in critical care from that status to the status of intermediate care.

_____

_____

_____

_____

_____

Avoid run-ons

A run-on sentence is one of the most common grammar mistakes in English writing. But what is a run-on? How do we correct run-on sentences?

Learning outcomes

At the end of this clinic, you will be able to

- identify two types of run-on sentences;
- correct run-on sentences in four ways.

Core knowledge input

 Micro-lecture What Are Run-Ons

What Are Run-Ons?

What is a run-on sentence?

A **run-on** consists of two or more complete thoughts or independent clauses run together without adequate punctuation to signal the break between them. It is missing proper punctuation, such as commas, semicolons, or conjunctions to clearly separate the ideas. Run-on sentences may occur when the writer is unable to recognize where one complete thought ends and another thought begins; when the writer is not sure of the standard ways of connecting ideas; or when two or more independent clauses are connected incorrectly.

Despite the name, run-on sentences have nothing to do with length. They can be short or long. A long sentence isn't necessarily a run-on sentence. The only thing that determines a run-on sentence is when more than one independent clause exists without the proper means to combine them.

What are the common types of run-on errors?

- **Fused sentences:** two independent clauses joined together without any punctuation
- **Comma splices:** two or more independent clauses joined with a comma but without a coordinating or subordinating conjunction

How to identify run-ons?

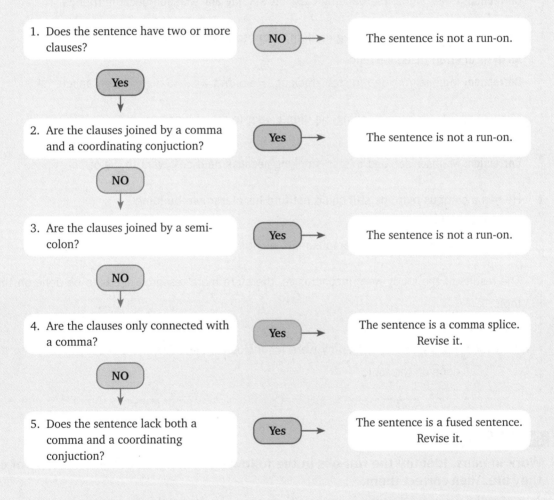

1. Does the sentence have two or more clauses? — NO → The sentence is not a run-on.

Yes

2. Are the clauses joined by a comma and a coordinating conjuction? — Yes → The sentence is not a run-on.

NO

3. Are the clauses joined by a semi-colon? — Yes → The sentence is not a run-on.

NO

4. Are the clauses only connected with a comma? — Yes → The sentence is a comma splice. Revise it.

NO

5. Does the sentence lack both a comma and a coordinating conjuction? — Yes → The sentence is a fused sentence. Revise it.

Model LC8-1

Examples of different types of run-ons

Read the following run-on sentences and notice the analysis and correction.

I met Linda in a dancing class on Sunday we soon became friends.

Analysis of error: fused sentence

Correction: I met Linda in a dancing class on Sunday **and** we soon became friends.

Michael decided to stop smoking he didn't want to die of lung cancer.

Analysis of error: fused sentence

Correction: Michael decided to stop smoking. He didn't want to die of lung cancer.

Michael decided to stop smoking, he didn't want to die of lung cancer.

Analysis of error: comma splice

Correction: Michael decided to stop smoking **because** he didn't want to die of lung cancer.

He had a campus map, he still could not find his classroom building.

Analysis of error: comma splice

Correction: Although he had a campus map, he still could not find his classroom building.

The results of the study were inconclusive, therefore more research needs to be done on the topic.

Analysis of error: comma splice

Correction: The results of the study were inconclusive; **therefore,** more research needs to be done on the topic.

Practice LC8-1

Work in pairs. Identify the run-ons in the following sentences. State what type of error they are. Then correct them.

1. Susan likes strawberry muffins, she eats them every day for breakfast.

_____

2. We are going to leave at 9, then we stop for lunch at 11.

_____

3. Harry had all the best tackle, however, he failed to catch a single fish.

_____

4. Remarkably, the crime rates in our neighborhood have decreased auto thefts and burglaries are on the decline.

_____

5. To evaluate a charity, you should start by examining its goals, then you should investigate its management practices.

_____

6. China's small home appliance industry added more than 190,000 companies this year, it is an increase of 11.5 percent year-on-year.

_____

7. The lawsuit cost the company several million dollars, the company went out of business a short time later.

_____

8. Among them is the family education law lawmakers will review its third draft.

_____

Core knowledge input

Micro-lecture How to Correct Run-Ons

How to Correct Run-Ons

When you correct a run-on sentence, the first thing to do is to identify those two clauses. Then you can focus on the two main problems that cause run-ons: missing commas and conjunctions (fused sentences), or misusing commas when there should be a semicolon (comma splices).

Here are four common methods of correcting run-ons.

Method 1: Use a period and a capital letter.

The easiest way to fix a run-on is to split the sentence into smaller sentences. Correct the run-on by putting a period at the end of the first thought and a capital letter at the start of the second thought. This revision works especially well with longer sentences. Use this method especially if the thoughts are not closely related or if another method would make the sentence too long.

Method 2: Use a comma plus a coordinating conjunction.

Use a comma plus a coordinating conjunction to connect the two complete thoughts. These coordinating conjunctions indicate how the two clauses are related. Seven coordinating conjunctions are often used.

Conjunction	Meaning
and	to add an idea
nor	to add an idea when both clauses are in the negative
but	to contrast two opposing ideas
yet	to emphasize the contrast between two opposing ideas
for	to introduce a reason
or	to show a choice
so	to introduce a result

Method 3: Use a semicolon.

A third method of correcting a run-on is to use a semicolon (sometimes with a transition) to mark the break between two thoughts. The semicolon signals more of a pause than a comma alone but not quite the full pause of a period. You might choose the semicolon if the grammatical structure of each independent clause is similar or if the ideas in each independent clause are very closely related. The table below shows some common transitional words that can be used after a semicolon in this case.

Common transitional words		
however	moreover	therefore
on the other hand	in addition	as a result
nevertheless	also	consequently
instead	furthermore	otherwise

Method 4: Use a subordination.

Subordination is a way of showing that one thought in a sentence is not as important as another thought. You can revise a run-on sentence by adding a subordinating conjunction (such as *because* or *although*) to one of the independent clauses, thereby making it a dependent clause. Below are some frequently used subordinating conjunctions.

Frequently used subordinating conjunctions	
Time	after, before, when, whenever, while, as soon as, until, till, since
Place	where, wherever
Cause & effect	because, since, as, so, so that
Condition	if, unless, provided, assuming that
Concession	though, although, even though
Comparison	than, as...as...
Manner	as if, as though

Model LC8-2

Correcting run-ons

1. **Use a period and a capital letter:** Independent clause 1. Independent clause 2.

   Run-on: A résumé should be directed to a specific audience it should emphasize the applicant's potential value to the company. (fused sentence)

   A résumé should be directed to a specific audience. It should emphasize the applicant's potential value to the company.

2. **Use a comma plus a coordinating conjunction:** Independent clause 1, + coordinating conjunction + independent clause 2.

   Run-on: The two detectives carefully checked the scene for fingerprints they could not find one clear print. (fused sentence)

   Correction: The two detectives carefully checked the scene for fingerprints, but they could not find one clear print. (contrast)

   Run-on: More than 95,000 smart medical-related companies were established this year, the number of medical robot-related companies grew by 45 percent year-on-year. (comma splice)

Correction: More than 95,000 smart medical-related companies were established this year, and the number of medical robot-related companies grew by 45 percent year-on-year. (addition)

3. **Use a semicolon:** Independent clause 1; independent clause 2.

Run-on: Linda was watching *Monday Night Football*, she was doing her homework as well. (comma splice)

Correction: Linda was watching *Monday Night Football*; she was doing her homework as well.

Run-on: Duty is what one expects from others, it is not what one does oneself. (comma splice)

Correction: Duty is what one expects from others; it is not what one does oneself.

Run-on: It was raining harder than ever, however, Bobby was determined to go to see a doctor. (comma splice)

Correction: It was raining harder than ever; however, Bobby was determined to go to see a doctor.

Run-on: Sharon didn't understand the instructor's point, therefore, she asked him to repeat it. (comma splice)

Correction: Sharon didn't understand the instructor's point; therefore, she asked him to repeat it.

4. **Use a subordination:** Subordinating conjunction + dependent clause + independent clause
Or Independent clause + subordinating conjunction + dependent clause.

Run-on: The students had been misbehaving, therefore the principal canceled the school play. (comma splice)

Correction: The students had been misbehaving, so the principal canceled the school play.

Or: Because the students had been misbehaving, the principal canceled the school play.

Model LC8-3

Correcting run-ons in a passage

In conversation, when we retell events that have occurred, we often link our thoughts together in one long narrative. Here is what one person involved in a car accident reported to a police officer at the scene:

I was driving along on Route 50 and my son asked my wife to change the radio station and my wife told my son to do it himself so my son unhooked his seatbelt and reached over from the back seat to change the station but then his sister tickled him and he lost his balance and fell on the gear shift and that moved the gear into neutral so the car instantly lost power and that's when we were hit by the van behind us.

Correction:

I was driving along on Route 50 **when** my son asked my wife to change the radio station. **My** wife told my son to do it himself, so my son unhooked his seatbelt and reached over from the back seat to change the station. **However**, just then his sister tickled him; he lost his balance and fell on the gear shift. **The** gear shift was pushed into neutral, **causing** the car to lose power instantly. **That's** when we were hit by the van behind us.

Analysis:

The original version is a super-long run-on sentence though it contains a couple of complete thoughts. It can be separated into five single sentences. Based on the relation between the two complete thoughts in the first line, a subordinating conjunction *when* replaces *and* (Method 4). Then, a period is used to separate it from the following ideas (Method 1). In the second sentence, a comma is added between *himself* and *so* to clarify the cause-effect relation (Method 2). A period plus *however* marks the beginning of the third sentence, where a semicolon is used to connect the two closely related ideas (Method 3). In the fourth sentence, the present participle *causing* turns the originally independent clause into an adverbial. Finally, *and* is cut off and a period is placed before the last sentence to close the whole passage (Method 1).

Practice LC8-2

Correct the following run-on sentences by using the strategies you have learned.

1. In recent years, many celebrities have shared their health situations with the public, this has had a beneficial effect.

_____

_____

2. One of the key challenges to planting trees on common land is the maintenance of the plantation, young trees can be eaten by browsing animals.

_____

_____

3. Weight loss programs encourage proper nutrition, these programs also encourage consistent exercise.

_____

_____

4. An ever-improving business environment will likely draw more international investors, they attach importance to not only social and political stability but also good returns when making investment decisions.

_____

_____

5. Already this year, more than ten prominent universities and institutions have set up carbon-neutrality-research institutes, the Chinese Academy of Sciences launched a center last month.

_____

_____

6. Restoring a painting is, indeed, delicate work too much enthusiasm can be dangerous.

_____

_____

7. Ted cut a few hours from his work schedule, he would have had very little time for studying.

_____

_____

8. All Chinese people need to work together to make the "cake" bigger and better, efforts should be made to divide the "cake" well through proper institutional arrangements.

_____

_____

Answer Keys